FDI and Economic Development in India

FDI and Economic Development in India

Darshana Gopa Minz

KALPAZ

ISBN: 978-93-5324-951-9 (HB)

First Published, 2023

Published by

Kalpaz Publications
C-30, Satyawati Nagar,
Delhi – 110052
Ph.: 011-47034999, 9811692060
www.kalpazpublications.com
E-mail: kalpaz@hotmail.com

Printed at: Gyan Press, Delhi.

DEDICATION

Late Kamala Minz
(Died 15.01.2018)
(Venerable Grandmother)

Whose life began in Icha in Gumla district, Jharkhand and after her schooling she married Sri Goinda Minz (I.A.S.). She travelled the world and her house was a souvenir of not just mementos but collected plants from around the globe which she kept flourishing until she was alive.

She bought me with her when I was 2 and a half years old and took responsibility of my upbringing till secondary schooling education. I was bought up by her as a single child although I had siblings. She facilitated me to peruse my higher education in England though I was slightly sceptical with options.

She was a prodigious community leader, an idealist, a woman of principles and values, strong headed yet a compassionate social worker who led her children and her grandchildren to quality education and etiquettes. She was a strong, independent women who carved her own path, built and expanded her houses after her husband's demise 26 years before her, and managed limited finances smartly and productively. She always came out victorious in the toughest of adversities and I had the privilege to witness it.

As my friends who met her joked, she was 10 generations ahead of her time and too modern for our ages.

Gone but never forgotten and always cherished and loved. She will always be an inspiration to live big, fulfilling life in her own terms.

This work and many more to come will be her inspiration and I dedicate this book to her.

Contents

Preface

In present Global competitive economic circumstances, no country in the world is self-sufficient and self-reliant. Most of them largely depend on other nations in some way. Advance economy with surplus reserves want to integrate other nations who have minerals reserves and skilled labours. Emerging economy in hope to become self-sufficient requires fund for their economical promotion and consolidation, undeveloped economies require funds for their survival. Thus, financial integration through FDI plays paramount role to accelerate the respective economies. With growing globalisation most of the Asian nations have welcomed the FDI and witness surge in its inflow. India with conservative approach to globalisation has been found late comer to the FDI. Its overall market potential, cheap skilled workforce with mineral reserves and safe marine routes along with liberalised policy regime, sustained its attraction as a most preferred destination for foreign investors.

Due to liberalisation, globalisation, deregulation, competitive disintermediation and economic intensification competition has grown as every country wants to become self-reliant and self-sufficient, thus demand for financial resources has grown to many folds. To cater the economic demand, socio-political competition, economic complexities, increasing population, unpredictable challenges and to capitalise the macroeconomic environmental opportunities at optimal level, Government of India (GOI) adopted cataclysmic structural and continuous reforms in Indian macroeconomic system. It started playing a parental role by stoking the engine of economic growth through garnering the internal and external resources in money supply and introduced policy of tectonic economic liberalisation, globalisation, digitalisation and deregulation with metamorphic liberalised policy in financial sector, which in result brought drastic change and ultimate revolution in Indian financial sector and transformed conservative financial sector into global at par, and led to the emergence for new financial windows, non-debt financial capital FDI, new banks, new instruments, new financial institutions and motivated foreign investors to invest in diversified industrial and manufacturing sector.

FDI in India has a significant role in the economic growth and development of India. FDI in India to various sectors can attain sustained economic growth and development through creation of jobs, expansion of existing manufacturing industries. The inflow of FDI in service sectors, construction sectors and development sectors attained substantial sustained economic growth and development through creation of jobs in India. Computer, Software, Hardware, Drugs & Pharmaceuticals sector were the other sectors to which attention was shown by Foreign Direct Investors (FDI). The other sectors in Indian economy the Foreign Direct Investors interest was, in fact has been quite poor.

FDI has helped to raise the output, productivity and employment in some sectors especially in service sector. Indian service sector is generating the proper employment options for skilled worker with high perks. On the other side, banking and insurance sectors help in providing the strength to the Indian economic condition and develop the foreign exchange system in the country. FDI helps to create employment in the country and also support the small-scale industries and helps country to put an impression on the world wide level through liberalisation and globalisation.

Looking at the challenges, it is evident that the Government of India has to be on its foot always to take and overview of the resources, man-power, technology, and outsourcing which can affect the FDI inflows and outflows; hence the policy-makers need to be flexible enough to modify the existing rules and make it more stringent if required or more flexible depending on the situation.

India has many opportunities for FDI in the development and management of infrastructure. Since infrastructure projects may not be financially viable on their own, public private partnership (PPP) is sought here to bring in private resources and techno managerial capabilities through FDI. The Government is providing 'viability gap funding' in the form of capital grants, operation and management support and interest subsidies etc. for projects related to roads, railways, sea ports, airports, water supply, sewerage and solid waste disposal etc. Moreover, ten years tax holiday is given for road, highways and ports projects. Recent Government initiatives like extending the existing network of roads, developing the highways under National Highway Development Programme (NHDP) through Golden Quadrilateral and North-South East-West (NSEW) Corridor necessitate vast pool of foreign investment.

Acknowledgement

On the completion of this book, I, first of all, extend my deepest gratitude to Almighty God for blessing me with sound health, intellect, knowledge and support from wise and cultivated individuals, which starts from my own family to the perspicacious associates who have inspired me on my academic journey.

Deep gratitude to my mother Dr. Delo Mai Hansda, a Professor of Economics for her astute guidance, keen interest and precious advice in every step of this work. Her stimulating discussion, constructive criticism and personal interest enabled the present piece of work to materialise. She gave me the privilege to peep into the realms of this study and made me increase my knowledge in this particular field.

I am grateful to M. Shyam for his academic support extended during the study.

I consecrate this study to my father Dr. Diwakar Minz, who has been Dean and Proctor of Ranchi University, and HOD of Department of History, for his unconditional support and blessings, without which I would have never been able to conduct this study.

Last but not the least, I feel indebted to all those who proved instrumental for the completion of this journey and hence would like to thank them all for making my endeavour worthwhile.

Dr. Darshana Gopa Minz

Asst. Professor

(MBA, Liverpool, United Kingdom)

CHAPTER – 1

Introduction

1.1 Introduction

Foreign Direct Investment (FDI) in India has played an important role in the development of the Indian economy. It has in lot of ways facilitated India to achieve a certain degree of financial stability, growth and development. It is the objective of the Government of India to attract and promote foreign direct investment in order to supplement domestic capital, technology and skills, for accelerated economic growth. Foreign Direct Investment (FDI) and trade are often seen as important catalysts for economic growth in the developing countries. FDI is an important vehicle of technology transfer from developed countries to developing countries. FDI is one example of international factor movement. An investment abroad, usually where the company being invested in is controlled by the foreign corporation. The simplest explanation of FDI would be a direct investment by a corporation in a commercial venture in another country. A key to separating this action from involvement in other venture in foreign country is that the business enterprise operates completely outside the economy of the corporation's home country.[1] The rapid expansion in FDI by multinational enterprises since the mid-eighties may be attributed to significant changes in technologies, greater liberalisation of trade and investment regimes, and deregulation and privatisation of markets in many countries including developing countries like India. FDI is not permitted in the arms, nuclear, railway, coal or mining industries. The objective behind allowing FDI is to harmonize and complement domestic investment, for achieving a higher level of economic development and providing more opportunities for upgradation of technologies as well as to have an access to global managerial skills and practices.

FDI is as an engine of capital, technology, managerial skills, technological progress and capacity, access to foreign markets and in maintaining economic growth and development for developing countries, whereas for developed countries it is considered as a tool for accessing the market of emerging economies.[2] Foreign investors showed keen interest in Indian economy because of liberalised regime pursued and followed by Indian economy. This may be due to the low flow of FDI into India both at the macro level as well as at the sartorial level. It implies that the spirit in which the economy has been liberalised and exposed to the world economy at the late eighties and early nineties has not been achieved after so many years. This calls for

1. Khan, A.Q., Strategy for Foreign Investment Management in 21st century, Kitab Mahal Publication, New Delhi, 2018, p. 5.
2. Khan, A.Q., Strategy for Foreign Investment Management in 21st century, *op.cit,* p. 5.

a judicious policy decision towards FDI at the sartorial level. A large number of changes that were introduced in the country`s regulatory economic policies heralded the liberalisation era of the FDI policy regime in India and brought about a structural breakthrough in the volume of the FDI inflows into the economy maintained a fluctuating and unsteady trend during the study period. It might be interesting to note that more than 50 percent of the total FDI inflows received in India come from Mauritius, Singapore and the USA. The main reason for higher levels of investment from Mauritius was the fact that India entered into a Double Taxation Avoidance Agreement (DTAA) with Mauritius were protected from taxation in India. Among the different sectors, the service sector had received the larger proportion followed by computer software and hardware sector and then telecommunication sector. The process of economic reforms which was initiated in July 1991 to liberalise and globalise the economy had gradually opened up many sectors of its economy for the foreign investors.[1]

1.2 Conceptual Framework of Foreign Direct Investment (FDI)

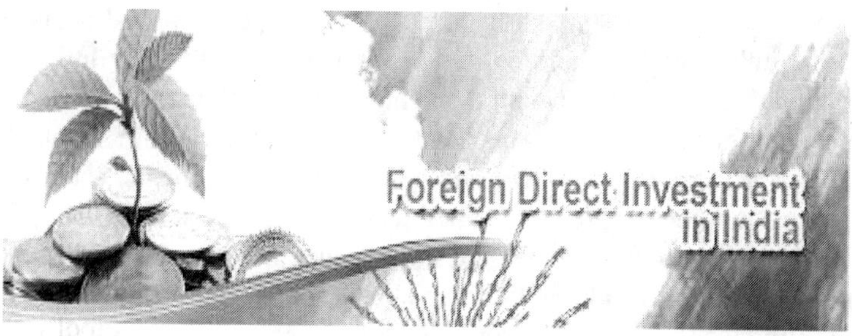

Foreign Direct Investment (FDI) is a type of investment in to an enterprise in a country by another enterprises located in another country by buying a company in the target country or by expanding operations of an existing business in that country. In the era of globalisation FDI takes vital part in the development of both developing and developed countries. FDI has been associated with improved economic growth and development in the host countries which has led to the emergence of global competition to attract FDI.

1. Khan, A.Q., Strategy for Foreign Investment Management in 21st century, *op.cit.*

- Foreign direct investments (FDI) are investments made by one company into another located in another country.
- FDIs are actively utilised in open markets rather than closed markets for investors.
- Horizontal, vertical, and conglomerate are types of FDIs. Horizontal is establishing the same type of business in another country, while vertical is related but different, and conglomerate is an unrelated business venture.
- The Bureau of Economic Analysis continuously tracks FDIs into the US.
- Apple's investment in China is an example of an FDI.

Foreign Direct Investment (FDI) is considered as an engine of economic growth. Before the Economic reforms the flow of foreign direct investment to India has been comparatively limited because of the type of industrial development strategy and the various foreign investment policy followed by the nation. Not only India but much heralded FDI boom worldwide constitutes a major element of economic globalisation. Foreign investment was normally permitted only in high technology industries in priority areas and in export-oriented areas. So, the inflow of FDI before 1990's was very low. To fully utilise the country's immense economic potential, the government launched Economic reforms in 1991. The new Government policies are simple, transparent and promotes domestic and foreign investments. India's abundant and diversified natural resources, its sound economic policy, good market condition and high skilled human resources make it a proper destination for FDI.[1] After long years of journey FDI was also introduced in various sectors and states in India. The Investment of FDI in various states and sectors leads to rapid growth of Indian economy. Foreign Direct Investment in India is allowed through four basic routes namely, financial collaborations, technical collaborations and joint ventures, capital markets via Euro issues, and private placement or preferential allotments. India has opened up its economy and allowed MNEs in core sectors such as Power & Fuels, Electrical Equipment's, Transport, Chemicals, Food Processing, Drugs &

1. Shandilya, T.K., Thakur, A.K., Foreign Direct Investment in India: Problems and Prospects, Deep and Deep Publication, New Delhi, 2018, p. 21.

Pharmaceuticals, Textiles, Industrial Machinery, insurance as well as telecommunication.

Foreign direct investment refers to the investment in a business from another country for which the foreign investor has control over the company purchased. According to Organisation of Economic Cooperation and Development (OECD) for an FDI, control should be 10 percent or more of business. A parent business enterprise and its foreign affiliates are the two sides of the FDI relationship. Together they comprise an MNC or MNEs. The parent enterprise through its foreign direct investment effort seeks to exercise substantial control over the foreign affiliate company. Control as defined by UN is ownership of greater than or equal to 10 percent of the ordinary shares or access to voting rights in an incorporated firm. Ownership share amounting to less than that stated above is termed as portfolio investment and is not categorised as FDI.[1]

The historical background of FDI in India can be traced back with the establishment of East India Company of Britain. British capital came to India during the colonial era of Britain in India. The industrial policy of 1965, allowed MNCs to venture through technical collaboration in India. Therefore, the government adopted a liberal attitude by allowing more frequent equity.[2]

---

1. *Ibid.*
2. Narayanana, M. R., Inflow of Foreign Direct Investment in India-Patterns, Performance, Implications, Foreign Trade Review, Vol. XXXIV, 2019, p. 3.

In the critical face of Indian economy, the government of India with the help of World Bank and IMF introduced the macro-economic stabilisation and structural adjustment programme. As a result of these reforms India opened its door to FDI inflows and adopted a more liberal foreign policy in order to restore the confidence of foreign investors. Further, under the new foreign investment policy, Government of India constituted FIPB (Foreign Investment Promotion Board) whose main function was to invite and facilitate foreign investment. Starting from a baseline of less than USD 1 billion in 1990, a recent UNCTAD survey projected India as the second most important FDI destination (after China) for transnational corporations. As per the data, the sectors which attracted higher inflows were services, telecommunication, construction activities and computer software and hardware. Mauritius, Singapore, the US and the UK were among the leading sources of FDI to the country.

India attracted FDI worth US$ 22.42 billion. Tourism, pharmaceuticals, services, chemicals and construction were among the biggest beneficiaries. For Indian economy which has tremendous potential, FDI has had a positive impact. FDI inflow supplements domestic capital, as well as technology and skills of existing companies. It also helps to establish new companies. All of these contribute to economic growth of the Indian Economy.[1] India's Foreign Direct Investment (FDI) policy has been gradually liberalised to make the market more investor friendly. The results have been encouraging. These days, the country is consistently ranked among the top three

1. Kumar, Nagesh, Globalisation and the Quality of FDI, Oxford University Press, New Delhi, 2019, p. 42.

global investment destinations by all international bodies, including the World Bank.

1.3 Definitions of FDI

According to the Balance of Payment Manual by the International Monetary Fund, "FDI refers to an investment made to acquire lasting interest in enterprises operating outside of the economy of the investor."[1]

The **International Monetary Fund (IMF)** tries to put some quantitative elements to the definition of foreign investment as "direct" when an investor holds 10 percent or more on the equity of an enterprise abroad – usually enough to give the investor some power in the management of the entity.

The encyclopaedia of Public International Law defines "foreign investment is transfer of funds or materials from one country (called the capital exporting country) to another country (called the host country) in return for a direct or indirect participation in the earnings of the enterprise".[2]

According to **Sornarajah, M,** "Foreign Investment involves the transfer of tangible or intangible assets from one country into another for the purpose of use in that country to generate wealth under the total or partial control of the owner of the assets".[3]

The United Nations Conference on Trade and Development, defines FDI as "an investment involving a long term relationship and reflecting a lasting interest and control by a resident entity in

1. International Monetary, Balance of Payment Manual, New York.
2. Encyclopaedia, Volume 8, 1980, p. 246.
3. Sornarajah, M (1994), The International Law on Foreign Investment, Cambridge University Press, 1994, p. 4.

one economy (foreign investor or parent enterprise) in an enterprise resident in an economy other than that of the foreign direct investor (FDI enterprise or foreign affiliate)". Another definition by the United Nations sees FDI as "investment made to acquire a lasting interest in or effective control over an enterprise operating outside the economy of the investors."[1]

Wallace, D.C., Direct Foreign Investment broadly defined as "the establishment or acquisition of substantial ownership in a commercial enterprise in a foreign country, or an increase in the amount of an already existing investment abroad to achieve substantial ownership."[2] In other terms, Direct Foreign Investment involves the acquisition of physical items, such as, Machineries, Plants, Factories, Buildings, etc for use in production processes, which unavoidably involves the involvement of the foreign investor.

In another definition, **Morrison Janet**, defines FDI as "an investment by an organisation in a business in another country, with the view to establishing production in the host country."[3]

Moosa Imad A., Foreign Direct Investment (FDI) is "the process whereby residents of one country (the source country) acquire ownership of assets for the purpose of controlling the production, distribution and other activities of a firm in another country (the host country). It involves the transfer of financial capital, technology and other skills such as managerial, marketing, accounting, etc."[4]

Frankel and Romer, stated that "FDI is often seen as one of the important catalysts for economic growth in the developing countries."[5]

The term Foreign Institutional Investor is defined by SEBI as "Means an institution established or incorporated outside India which proposes to make investment in India in securities. Provided that a

1. UNCTAD, World Investment Report, 2008.
2. Wallace, D.C., Foreign Investment: A New Climate in the Third World, Amsterdam: Martinus Nijhoff Publishers, 1990.
3. Morrison Janet (2009), International Business, Macmillan, St. Martin's Press, New York.
4. Moosa, Imad. A (2002), Foreign Direct Investment-Theory, Evidence and Practice, Palgrave Publishers Ltd, New York, USA.
5. Frankel, J.A and Romer, D, Does trade cause growth? American Economic Review, Issue 89, 2018.

domestic asset management company or domestic portfolio manager who manages funds raised or collected or brought from outside India for investment in India on behalf of a sub-account, shall be deemed to be a Foreign Institutional Investor."

Entities covered by the term Foreign Institutional Investor include "Overseas pension funds, mutual funds, investment trust, asset management company, nominee company, bank, institutional portfolio manager, university funds, endowments, foundations, charitable trusts, charitable societies, a trustee or power of attorney holders incorporated or established outside India proposing to make proprietary investment or investment on behalf of a broad-based funds.

1.4 Advantages of FDI

Foreign Direct Investment (FDI) is made into a business or a sector by an individual or a company from another country. It is different from portfolio investment, which is made more indirectly into another country's economy by using financial instruments, such as bonds and stocks. There are various levels and forms of Foreign Direct Investment, depending on the type of companies involved and the reasons for investment. A foreign direct investor might purchase a company in the target country by means of a merger or acquisition, setting up a new venture or expanding the operations of an existing one. Other forms of FDI include the acquisition of shares in an associated enterprise, the incorporation of a wholly owned company or subsidiary and participation in an equity joint venture across international boundaries.[1]

1. ibid.

- Foreign Direct Investment can stimulate the target country's economic development, creating a more conducive environment for the investor and benefits for the local industry.
- Commonly, a country has its own import tariff, and this is one of the reasons why trading with it is quite difficult. Also, there are industries that usually require their presence in the international markets to ensure their sales and goals will be completely met. With FDI, all these will be made easier.
- Foreign Direct Investment creates new jobs, as investors build new companies in the target country, create new opportunities. This leads to an increase in income and more buying power to the people, which in turn leads to an economic boost.

- One big advantage brought about by FDI is the development of human capital resources, which is also often understated as it is not immediately apparent. Human capital is the competence and knowledge of those able to perform labour, more known to us as the workforce. The attributes gained by training and sharing experience would increase the education and overall human capital of a country. Its resource is not a tangible asset that is owned by companies, but instead something that is on loan. With this in mind, a country with FDI can benefit greatly by developing its human resources while maintaining ownership.
- Parent enterprises would also provide foreign direct investment to get additional expertise, technology and products. As a foreign investor, one can receive tax incentives that will be highly useful in their selected field of business.

- Foreign direct investment will allow resource transfer and other exchanges of knowledge, where various countries are given access to new technologies and skills.
- Foreign direct investment can reduce the disparity between revenues and costs. With such, countries will be able to make sure that production costs will be the same and can be sold easily.
- The facilities and equipment provided by foreign investors can increase a workforce's productivity in the target country.
- Another big advantage of foreign direct investment is the increase of the target country's income. With more jobs and higher wages, the national income normally increases. As a result, economic growth is spurred. Take note that larger corporations would usually offer higher salary levels than what you would normally find in the target country, which can lead to increment in income.

1.5 Objectives of Foreign Direct Investment[1]

Sustaining a High Level of Investment

Since the underdeveloped countries want to industrialise themselves within a short period of time, it becomes necessary to raise the level of investment largely. This requires, in turn, a high level of savings.

Technological Gap

The under developed countries have very low level of technology as compared to the advanced countries. Developed countries have

1. Khan, A.Q., Strategy for Foreign Investment Management in 21st century, Kitab Mahal Publication, New Delhi, 2018, p. 12.

necessity for importing technology from advanced countries. Such technology usually comes with foreign capital when it assumes the form of private foreign investment or foreign collaboration. In the Indian case technical assistance received from abroad has helped in filling the technological gap through the following three ways,

(i) Provision for expert services
(ii) Training of Indian personnel
(iii) Education research and training institution in the country

Utilisation of Natural Resources

A number of underdeveloped countries possess huge mineral resources, which await utilisation. These countries themselves do not have the required technical skill and expertise to achieve this task. As a consequence, they have to depend upon foreign capital to undertake the utilisation of their mineral wealth.

Undertaking the Initial Risk

Many under developed countries suffer from acute private entrepreneurs. This creates barriers in the programmes of industrialisation. An argument advanced in favour of the foreign capital is that it undertakes the risk of investment in host countries and thus provides the much-needed impetus to the process of industrialisation. Once the programmes of industrialisation get started with the initiative of foreign capital, domestic industrial activity starts picking up as more and more of the host country enter the industrial field.

Development of basic Economic Infrastructure

It has been observed that the domestic capital of the underdeveloped countries is often too inadequate to build up the economic infrastructure of its own. Thus, these countries require the assistance of foreign capital to undertake this task. In the latter half of the 20th century, especially during the last 3 and 4 decades, international financial institutions and many governments of advanced countries have made substantial capital available to the underdeveloped countries to develop their system of Transport and Communications, Generation and Distribution of Electricity, Development of Irrigation Facilities, etc.

Improvement in Balance of Payments Position

In the initial phase of the Economic Development, the under-developed countries need much larger imports (such as Machinery, Capital Goods, Industrial Raw Materials, Spares and Components) then they can possibly export. As a result, the balance of payments generally turns adverse. This creates a gap between the earnings and foreign exchanges.

1.6 Historical background of FDI in India

The history of FDI in India dates back to the years of East India Company. The volume of British capital imported into India during the regime of the company, however, was very small because export of British capital during early 1800s was only in a restricted sense. Residents of Britain acquired a number of business concerns in India through Rupee capital owned by British servants working in India. The investments constituted British capital only in the sense of increasing Indian liabilities to British residents. But the nineteenth century witnessed the growth of vast network of British enterprise on Indian soil. The East India Company's monopoly over trade ended in

1830s. It was then that the management contracts between the British Companies and 'Anglo-Indian merchants' as resident British traders were then called, first came to be known. Due to the management contracts between the parent companies of Britain and the agencies in India, by 1850s, India began to attract a flood of British Capital. This marked the evolution of foreign direct investment to India. Starting from that time, till now the history of FDI in India can be divided into six periods on the basis of certain milestones like period of world war and independence of the country etc.[1]

1.6.1 Pre-First World War Period (1854-1914)

India being ruled by Britain during this period had its economic policy totally geared to the purpose of preserving the British order. The top priority was attached to the investment which could help raise the repatriation to Britain. So, during this period almost total FDI came from Britain and British companies. Rough estimates shows that 14 percent share of total British investments came to India alone, during the period 1865-1914. The estimates of foreign capital relating to this early period are scanty and all the estimates differ considerably from one another. However, many individual researchers have made some studies for this period. Leland Hamilton Jenks, a famous economist, gave a rough figure of about £ million 150 (Rs 225 crores) as volume of British capital was invested in India during the period 1854-69. According to him, British capital inflows to India took place at the rate of about £ million 5 per annum during 1870s. The inflows reached its climax immediately after the mutiny of 1857. A more exhaustive estimate of foreign capital was made in 1896 by Edgar Crammond.

1. Pant, Manoj Kumar, FDI in India: History, Policy and the Asian Perspective, Orient Blackswan Private Limited, New Delhi, 2019, p. 34.

Another important feature of the foreign investment in India during this period was that it was managed through managing agencies which were very large in size and managed a large number of businesses. Many of these agents held as many as 15-20 different types of companies engaged in jute, tea, sugar and indigo plantations. Other areas of their interest were timber, paper, coal, shipping and insurance. There were nearly 204 British Managing agents and a few manufacturing companies from U.K., Switzerland, Netherlands, Germany, USA and Japan engaged in trading and manufacturing during this period.[1]

Most of the companies like Unilever, ITC, Glaxo, ICI, GEC, Britania etc. just traded their goods in India by importing from parent companies but some American companies like Ludlow Jute and Japanese companies like Denso held their operations in India. It can be said broadly that there were less manufacturing and more of trading activities by the foreign companies during this period.

Because of lack of political unification in India during this period, there was no specific industrial policy and FDI policy in the country. As such there were no restrictions to foreign investments. Not only India but the whole global environment was open as far as trade and investment were concerned. India ranked eighth as a host to foreign investment in 1914.

1.6.2 Pre-Independence Period (1914-1947)

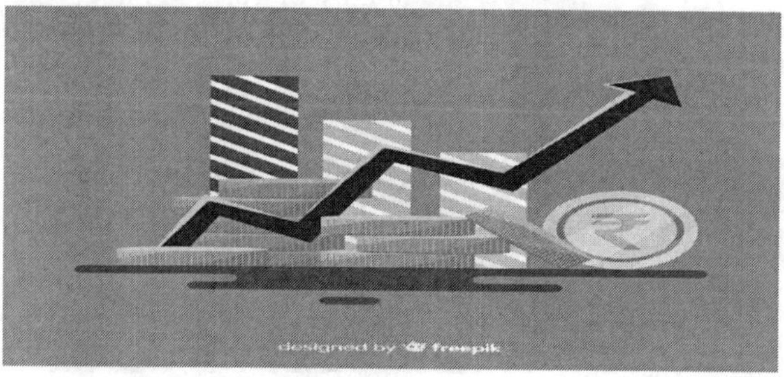

After the First World War, radical changes took place in our trade relations with Great Britain and in the economic policy pursued by the

1. Pant, Manoj Kumar, FDI in India: History, Policy and the Asian Perspective, *op.cit.*

government of India. Although Indian interests still remained subject to the imperial interests but the links between the Indian economy and the imperial economy were weakened. United States of America and Japan emerged as major competitors with Britain in the field of foreign capital to India particularly in industries like cotton textiles.[1]

The policy of encouraging British Private Capital to railways was deliberately initiated by Lord Dalhousie. Consequently, large amounts of capital were invested by British companies in Indian railways. It was done under a system of government guarantee of interest; guarantee was given for 5 percent interest on capital invested. Land was given free. As regards profits, that part of the profit which was over and above the 5 percent interest guaranteed was to be divided between the private companies and the government. Thus, British investments remained large in India during this period. The leading companies like Burmah Oil Company, Glaxo, ICI, Dunlop, Godfrey Philips and Metal Box were having their large operations in India. Between 1930 and 1945, as many as 28 new manufacturing British subsidiaries started their operations in India. Many trading British Companies, started with the manufacturing operations. For example, the company named Unilever started the manufacturing of soaps and toiletries under the name of Hindustan Lever. After that, Lever Brothers entered the manufacturing of vegetable oil (vanaspati ghee); Dunlop invested in manufacturing of tyres in 1936. Alkali and Chemical Corporation of India, Acme Thread company, J and P Coats, began their manufacturing activities during this period only. That is why the number of registered manufacturing companies grew from 111 in the year 1923 to 365 by the year 1940.

1.6.3 Early Post-Independence Period (1947-1961)

IndoClassified

1. Pant, Manoj Kumar, FDI in India: History, Policy and the Asian Perspective, *op.cit*, 36.

During this period Indian government's attitude towards FDI was mainly reflected in the industrial policy resolution of 1956 and various high-level pronouncements made from time to time. The industrial policy statement of 1948 and the statements on foreign capital of 1949 set the early pattern of private foreign investment in India. (In these statements it was said that foreign industrial know how should be sought, but effective control of new enterprises should be in Indian hands, except in unusual cases, calculated to serve the national interest.) At the same time the Nehru Resolution (Industrial Policy 1956) continued to serve as the Magna Carta on private foreign capital and guided its entry, proliferation and repatriation right through this period. Since the economic and industrial development of India was one of the major objectives, the government of India nationalised many companies in some industries which were considered strategic like power, oil, petroleum, mining, banking and airlines etc. Government itself sought the financial and technical support of Russia, Germany and the United Kingdom to setup large industrial projects. It followed a dual policy of State as well as private involvement in industry. Severe global competition necessitated the upgradations of technology which gave birth to the need of foreign technology and foreign capital. Moreover, there was severe foreign exchange problem. Due to all these factors, despite opposition from local industrialists and important lobbies in the government and the parliament, private foreign investment came thereafter with a comparatively easier run. After independence FDI inflow was enhanced and encouraged due to liberal policy guidelines of Government of India. Companies from Britain and America entered in large number. There were also qualitative changes in the nature of FDI. A large number of foreign enterprises which were earlier serving Indian market through exports started establishing manufacturing affiliates in the country. This was the period when western multinational enterprises started showing real interest in India.

1.6.4 Pre-Liberalisation Period (1978-1990)

At the time of independence in 1947, India was a host of significant stock of FDI and it was mostly owed to her regal master: the UK. Soon after independence, India embarked on a strategy of industrialisation with dynamic governmental involvement. Domestic enterprises accumulated considerable capabilities in the process of industrialisation which influenced the pattern of FDI flows to the economy in the subsequent periods. The changes in the government policies had also an important bearing on the FDI position of India. The Indian government's attitude towards foreign investment evolved over the post-independence period in four distinct phases. The period from independence up to the late 1960s was marked by gradual liberalisation attitude. The period from the late 1960s through to the 1970s was characterised by a more selective stance. The 1980s were marked by a certain liberalisation policy. In 1991, India liberalised its policy regime with respect to FDI as a part of the reform process.[1]

The Reserve Bank of India's (RBI) survey on international assets and liabilities in India shows that foreign investment in the country was only Rs 2.56 billion in the mid-1948. The bulk of the FDI stock was of natural resource seeking and of trading type, which had concentrated on raw materials, extractive or service sectors. It can be

1. Shandilya, T.K., Thakur, A.K., Foreign Direct Investment in India: Problems and Prospects, *op.cit,* p. 40.

observed that tea plantation and Jute accounted for a higher share of FDI as compared to manufacturing and service sectors in mid-1948. It is important to note that the locational advantages encouraged the market seeking FDI in spite of more protections accorded to local manufacture as evidenced from the FDI policy in India. In fact, most of the foreign enterprises served in the Indian market through exports started establishing manufacturing affiliates in the country during that period. In the later stage, the western multinational enterprises started showing real interest in India especially in late 1950s and early 1960s. In fact, their response was not enthusiastic except in the case of one-shot investment in oil refineries in early 1950s. Most of the foreign drug companies exporting to India also set up their manufacturing subsidiaries in India during this period. As a result, the FDI stock in the country increased more than two times. It accounted for nearly Rs 565.5 Crores in 1964 as compared to Rs 256 Crores in 1948. Though there was increase in the total FDI stock in 1964, the sector-wise composition changed during the period. It shows that the manufacturing and petroleum sectors gained with FDI stock, which accounted for nearly 40.5 and 14.7 percent respectively.

The absolute difference of total FDI inflows between 1964 and 1974 were around Rs 35 Crores. The composition of sector-wise FDI inflows indicates that manufacturing sector attracted more FDI during the period. It accounted for nearly Rs 628.6 Crores with a share of around 68 percent. It may be due to the liquidation of FDI stock in non-manufacturing sector, which was largely through taking over certain government activities such as general insurance companies in 1971 and of petroleum sector between 1974 and 1976. Within the manufacturing sector, new inflows were directed to technology intensive sectors such as electrical goods, machinery/machine tools and chemical/allied products. These three sub-sectors of manufacturing accounted for nearly 58 percent of total FDI in 1980 as against 41 percent in 1964. It is also important to note that the rise in technology intensive products in the FDI stock has been at the expense of traditional consumer goods industries such as food/beverages, textile products and other chemical products.[1]

1. Kumar, Nagesh, Globalisation and the Quality of FDI, Oxford University Press, New Delhi, 2015, p. 54.

The restrictions put on FDI during 1970s had virtually neutralised the internalisation incentives for potential foreign investors in the country. As a result, FDI inflows into India did not gain significantly. The total FDI inflow into India accounted for only Rs 933.2 Crores in 1980 as compared to Rs 916 Crores in 1974. The share of manufacturing sector continued to rise during the period, which accounted for nearly 87 percent of the total FDI inflows of the country. The liberalisation of industrial, trade and foreign collaboration policies in 1980s improved the investment climate and helped the country attract more inflows of FDI (RBI, 1985). The liberalisation also eased the near total restriction of FDI flows to technology intensive manufacturing sector, which resulted in a three time increase of total FDI inflows in 1990.

To sum up, there was an absolute increase in the FDI stock during the pre-liberalisation period. The sector-wise distribution of FDI stock shows that manufacturing sector gained more attention by foreign investors as compared to other sectors (such as plantation, mining, petroleum and service). This might be due to an import substituting policy of the government during this period, as much of the imports were manufacturing products. Thus, the liberalisation in the manufacturing sector helped to attract more FDI into it. However, the overall picture of FDI flows into India was not encouraging before 1991 with the exception of manufacturing sector.

1.6.5 Post-Liberalisation Period (1991-2010)

Broadly speaking, the new policy was initiated to increase the stake of foreign investors in Indian companies, provided a bigger room for their entry, axed the procedural formalities, provided additive incentive for the import of technology and to the NRIs. Thus, the main objective of the new FDI policy was to create a friendly environment for FDI inflows in India by Diluting the provisions of the Foreign

Exchange Regulation Act (FERA), the new policy removes the 40 percent ceiling for foreign equity participation that existed during the pre-reform period.[1]

Moreover, it provided for automatic approval of foreign collaborations in many cases. In case of nine categories of industries, viz., Mining Services, Basic Metal/Alloys, Electric Generation/ Transmission, Non-Conventional Energy Generation/ Distribution Constructions, Land/Water Transport, Storage/ Warehousing Services and some manufactures like industrial/scientific instruments, the RBI granted automatic approval of foreign collaboration even if foreign participation in equity goes up to 74 percent. In case of infrastructural projects of this group, automatic approval would be availed even with 100 percent foreign equity participation. In case of three categories of industries, such as mining of iron ore, metal ore and non-metallic minerals, foreign equity participation was not to exceed 50 percent if automatic approval was expected. In addition to this, in 1999-2000, the list of automatic approvals was widened covering important industrial and services sectors (Secretariat of Industrial Assistance, SIA Newsletter, 2001).

However, if a foreign investor wished to have greater participation in equity than that mentioned document had to be routed through the Foreign Investment Promotion Board (FIPB), which was under the

1. Kumar, Nagesh, Globalisation and the Quality of FDI, *op.cit*, p. 55.

Industry Ministry of the Government of India. The FIPB sanctions even 100 percent equity participation in cases where Indian companies were unable to raise funds or in cases where at least one-half of output is meant for export. It was also done in cases where foreign investors were to bring in proprietary technology.[1]

The new policy extended FDI to trading, hotels/tourism related companies, units of export processing zones, banking/non-banking financial services, of course, with varying degree of foreign equity participation. The non-banking financial services now included credit card and money changing businesses. The multilateral financial institutions were allowed to contribute equity to the extent of shortfall in the holdings of NRIs within the overall permissible limit of 40 percent in the public sector banks. FDI was also allowed in those areas where the big industrial houses were not previously allowed to invest. The new policy permits for opening of branch/liaison offices of foreign companies, revoking the prohibition of 1973. The branch office could be set up for conducting research and development, undertake export/import activities and for making available desired technology. An offshore venture capital company might contribute to an entire equity base of a domestic venture capital fund and might also set up a domestic asset management company (Indian Investment Centre, 1997).

FDI does not always involve investment in cash. A purely technical collaboration involves permission to use patents or trademark and transfer of technology for which the Indian Company pays royalty, technical service fees. In case of technology import, the new policy also provides for automatic approval if the collaboration agreement involves royalty payment up to $ 2 million (net of taxes) to be made in a lump sum amount or up to 5 percent of domestic sale and 8 percent of export over a ten years period from the date of agreement or seven years from the date of commencement of business. In hiring of foreign technicians, there is no bar if the RBI guidelines are followed. There is also no bar on the use of foreign brand name.[2]

The policy cut the procedural delays significantly. Abolition of industrial licencing almost in all cases (except public sector

1. Bhasin, Niti, Foreign Direct Investment (FDI) in India, New Century Publications, New Delhi, 2018, p. 34.
2. Bhasin, Niti, Foreign Direct Investment (FDI) in India, *op.cit*, p. 35.

units and those units producing hazardous items) is another example. The Foreign Investment Promotion Council was set up in 1996 to identify projects within the country that required foreign investment and to target specific countries from where FDI could be brought in (IIC, 1997). To promote speedy approvals, the FIPB had been asked to give its decision within a period of 30 days, for speedy implementation of the approved investment, the government set up the Foreign Investment Implementation Authority that convened its first meeting in the last week of September1999 (SIA Newsletter, 2000).

The NRIs making FDI got special treatment. They made direct investments either on repatriable terms or on non-repatriable terms. In case of repatriable investments, their share can go up to 100 percent of the equity if the project concerns high priority industry, housing and real estate development, air taxi operations, sick unit, 100 percent export-oriented units or a unit in export processing zone and a trading house. On non-repatriable terms, NRIs participation could go up to 100 percent of bonus issues in an Indian company if the company is not engaged in agriculture or plantation and real estate. Non-repatriable investment could also flow into proprietary/partnership concerns engaged in industrial, trading and commercial activities.

The Indian government became quite liberal regarding dividend repatriation abroad. There was no bar if taxes were paid. However, in a limited number of consumer goods, such outflow had to be balanced with export earnings for a period of seven years. Disinvestments 100 percent could be made subject to a few RBI formalities. Foreign Direct Investment proposals under the policy are approved under two routes, viz., automatic route and foreign investment promotion board (FIPB) route. Apart from the Foreign Investment Implementation

Authority (FIIA), Foreign Investment Promotion Council (FIPC) and the Secretariat of Industrial Assistance (SIA) also helped to facilitate the promotion of FDI in India.

1.7 Need for Foreign Investment

The need for larger FDI exists because India is at a stage where it needs not only US investments, but also technology, and management policies to sustain and enhance its economic growth.

This was not a very encouraging figure in view of the goal of increasing the GDP. Therefore, there is a need for larger FDI.[1]

- India still requires an FDI component equal to 4 percent of the GDP. The US needs to invest more in various sectors of the Indian economy. There is a potential to attract more FDIs in areas like infrastructure, IT hardware, automobiles, leather, textiles, gems, jewellery, and the financial sector. As such, India is rated as the 2nd best economy to invest in, after China. Surprisingly, the US is rated 3rd in this domain.
- Focus is on the insurance and banking sector, in context with Foreign Direct Investments. Only 10 percent of the insurance sector has been tapped for foreign investment. Foreign companies need to persuade the parliament for increasing Foreign Direct Investment capital.
- The banking sector is in the process of liberalisation which will continue. The insurance sector is looking forward to increase in the capital as more and more FDIs happen. So the insurance sector is also planning on liberalisation, taking a cue from the banking sector.

The need for larger FDI calls for major issues and areas to be taken into consideration, such as:

- Market potential and accessibility
- Political stability
- Market infrastructure
- Easy currency conversion

1. Kumar, Nagesh, Globalisation and the Quality of FDI, Oxford University Press, New Delhi, 2015, p. 42.

India is the ideal country to make Foreign Direct investments in because of its features like:

- Developing economy
- Low salaried employees
- Low wage workers
- Abundant human resources
- Big private economy
- India is looking forward to a high growth rate of almost 16 percent double that of the current 8 percent. Hence, there is a distinct need for larger FDI.
- Further, FDI prospects are expected to be bright if liberalisation is initiated in the telecom sector as well. Already, brands like Hutchison, Vodafone, and Singtel are in the Indian market and thanks to these investors, the FDI capital in this sector has been raised to 74 percent.
- There are others necessities which a larger FDI will cater to viz., employment generation, income generation, technology transfer, and economic stability. Hence, the need for larger FDI is a pressing situation these days in India. Foreign countries are well aware of this, and many of them arc taking extra initiative to invest in the Indian economy.[1]

1.8 Routes of FDI Inflow[2]

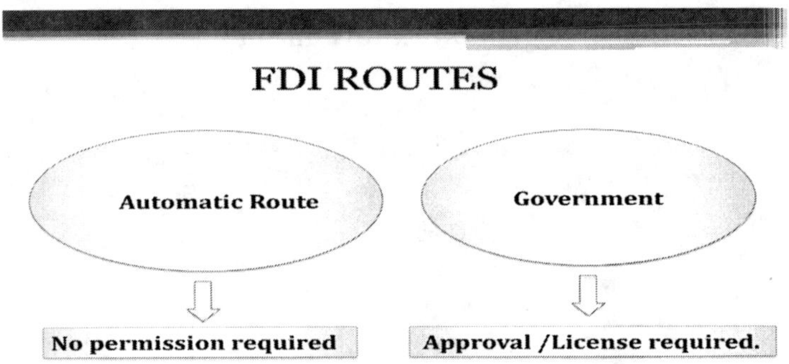

1. Grubaugh, S.J., Determinants of Direct Foreign Investment, Review of Economics & Statistics, November, 2018, p. 147.
2. *ibid.*

An Indian company may receive Foreign Direct Investment under the two routes as given under:

Automatic Route: FDI in sectors /activities to the extent permitted under the automatic route does not require any prior approval either of the Government or the Reserve Bank of India.

Government Route: Prior approval by government is needed via this route. The application needs to be made through Foreign Investment Facilitation Portal, which will facilitate single window clearance of FDI application under Approval Route. The application will be forwarded to the respective ministries which will act on the application as per the standard operating procedure. Foreign Investment Promotion Board (FIPB) which was the responsible agency to oversee this route was abolished on May 24, 2017. It held its last meeting on 17th April, which was the 245th meeting of the Board. On 24 May 2017, Foreign Investment Promotion Board was scrapped by the Union Government. Henceforth, the work relating to processing of applications for FDI and approval of the Government thereon under the extant FDI Policy and FEMA, shall now be handled by the concerned Ministries/Departments in consultation with the Department for Promotion of Industry and Internal Trade (DPIIT), Ministry of Commerce, which will also issue the Standard Operating Procedure (SOP) for processing of applications and decision of the Government under the extant FDI policy.

1.9 Theories of Foreign Direct Investment

FDI theories were at first developed in the early 1960s in an attempt to explain how the determinants of FDI influence the flow of capital from one country to another country. Theories of FDI can be split into two groups: micro - level determinants of FDI and macro-level determinants of FDI. The micro level theories of determinants of FDI try to give answers to the questions why multinational companies prefer opening subsidiaries in foreign countries before exporting or licencing their products, how MNCs prefer their investment locations. The macro level determinants deal with the host countries situations that determine the inflow of FDI. Some of the FDI theories that have been developed are discussed briefly below:

Micro Level Theories of FDI

Neoclassical Trade Theory

Early FDI theory was based on the neoclassical trade theory that observed FDI as international capital that would be invested in countries where firms would expect to earn higher incomes. The main reason for the differentiation in capital returns in different countries is due to different factor endowments that result in an international factor pricing differential. This is supported by the market disequilibrium hypothesis. In some instances, disequilibrium in labour factor prices can result in FDI to flow from countries with high labour costs to countries with low labour costs until equilibrium is achieved in the labour markets. In this case low labour costs become an important determinant of FDI. For example, in South Africa, inward FDI in the clothing and textile industry by Chinese firms could be a lot influenced by the attraction of a cheap labour market compared to other countries.[1]

Imperfect Markets Theory

A firm's decision to invest abroad is influenced by the potential to make profit due to specific advantages it has over domestic firms. The imperfect market theory was developed in 1960 by Hymer and developed further by Kindleberger in 1969 in response to the neoclassical trade theory which was criticized as being insufficient to explain the flow of FDI due to its assumption of perfect competition. According to the imperfect market theory, FDI is influenced by ownership advantages. These could include superior technology,

1. DIPP, Consolidated FDI Policy, Ministry of Commerce and Industry, Government of India, April 2014, p. 39.

management expertise and product differentiation. These ownership advantages give foreign firms an advantage when competing with firms in the domestic economy. This is consistent with reiter and argument that imperfect markets are the main reason for MNCs undertakes FDI. Toyota of Japan's entry into the North American market could have been influenced by the company's perceived advantage of management knowledge over North America car manufacturing companies. The aptitude to transfer skills and superior technology is critical to a MNCs decision to undertake FDI as this gives it a competitive edge over local companies.[1]

The Internalisation Theory

The internalisation theory, developed by Buckley and Casson in 1976, is based on the premise that because markets are imperfect MNCs can be more efficient by internalising their operations. MNCs are exposed to imperfect intermediate markets, factors of production, services, technology and marketing techniques which, in turn, makes the cost of transferring information, bargaining and enforcement significantly high.

This drives MNCs to replace imperfect market transactions with internal transactions. Due to having more efficient processes of transferring information, it is more economical for an MNC to get bigger into another country and produce in that market than to exports or imports. Being efficient in transferring complicated information as a result of experience, knowledge and expertise enables MNCs to have a competitive advantage over domestic firms.

1. Rusike, T.G., Trends and Determinants of Inward Foreign Direct Investment to South Africa, Rhodes University, 2007.

The Eclectic Theory or OLI Paradigm

The eclectic theory builds on the internationalisation theory by adding two independent variables in explaining FDI by MNCs and these are firm specific advantages and location advantages. According to Dunning (2000), this theory was first developed in 1977 and proposes that FDI by MNCs can be explained by the interface of these three independent variables that provide a framework for explaining the determinants of FDI by MNCs. The internalisation theory variable explains how MNCs choose to enter other markets. The more efficient internal processes, the more likely firms will expand internally across borders where localisation factors are attractive through FDI.

The ownership advantages variable explains how firm specific strengths like management expertise or superior technology provide MNCs with a competitive advantage over domestic firms which influences their decision to undertake FDI. Dunning opines that the higher the ownership advantages of MNCs, the higher the likelihood of them undertaking FDI. The location characteristics of different host countries influence the level of FDI they receive. Location factors, such as wealthy natural resources and the size of the local market, are important determinants of FDI.

According to Dunning (2000), the more such factors can be combined with ownership advantages of the investing MNC, the more likely the MNC will consider investing in the foreign country. For example, inward FDI in South Africa's mining sector by Chinese firms could be influenced by location factors in terms large quantity of minerals in the country joint with ownership advantages in terms superior technology in mining techniques and internalisation factors such as tariffs.

Product Life Cycle Hypothesis

Rusike (2007) recognize the product life cycle hypothesis developed by Vernon in 1966. This theory declares that MNCs involved in the production of innovative products will engage in FDI at the maturity stage of the product life cycle in order to take advantage of production and cost advantages in foreign markets.

In the beginning stages of the new product life cycle, production takes place in the domestic country due to nearness of customers and the need to continue efficient communication processes between market and firm. In the maturity stage of the product life cycle, competition increases, the market becomes saturated which leads to a decrease in demand. At this stage, a firm will start exporting to other countries in search of new markets.[1]

According to Moosa (2002), improved equality of production processes and rising demand from other countries will result in the firm setting up production amenities in foreign countries. The propensity of western firms like General Electric to place production facilities in developing countries like Mexico provides an obvious example of the product life cycle hypothesis.

The Oligopolistic Reactions Hypothesis

In an oligopolistic industry environment, there is powerful competition and a move by one firm is habitually met with a oppose move by other firms in the same industry. In 1973, Knickerbocker applied this concept in the case of FDI. A shift by a firm in an

1. Faeth, I, Determinants of Foreign Direct Investment - A Tale of Nine Theoretical Models, Journal of Economic Survey, Volume 23, 2009.

oligopolistic environment to engage in FDI would be met by a similar move by other firms in order to shelter market share cites the example of General Motors. A move by General Motors to set up production facilities for its engines in Mexico resulted in other major foreign car manufacturers follow suit.

Macro Economic Theory

Kojima's theory could be measured a highlight in the theory of FDI. The theories were mostly structured for US firms investing abroad, differentiating them from the Japanese FDI. The latter are mainly trade oriented and respond to the dictates of the principle of relative advantage. In contrast, US activity was mainly within an oligopolistic market structure. There was less emphasis on trade and activity was focused on firm specific profit orientation. Kojima's approach predicted that export oriented FDI occurred in countries with a comparative advantage for the host country. Thus, when exports grow FDI is characterised as welfare improving and trade creating. Due to Kojima's liking for Japanese style management, his approach could be viewed as biased. Dunning and John H, pointed out Kojima's neoclassical framework was incapable to capture the role of firm specific advantages in determining FDI flows. He further declared that Kojima's theory failed to explain much modern trade; it could not, for example, provide sufficient rationale for trade flows, which are based less on the allocation of factor donations and more on the need to exploit the economies of scale, product segregation and other appearance of market failure.

1.10 Characteristics of FDI

The following are the positive characteristics of Foreign Direct Investment (FDI):[1]

(i) Foreign investment can fill the gap between desired investment and locally mobilised savings. Local capital markets are often not well developed. Thus, they cannot meet the capital requirements for large investment projects. Besides, access to the hard currency, needed to purchase investment goods not available locally, can be difficult. FDI solves both these problems at once, as it is a direct source of external capital. It can fill desired foreign exchange requirements and those derived from net export earnings.

(ii) Foreign investment can supply a package of needed resources such as management, experience, entrepreneurial organisational and technological skills. Foreign investment brings with it technological knowledge, while transferring machinery and equipment to developing countries. Production units in developing countries use outdated equipment and techniques that can reduce the productivity of workers and lead to the production of goods of a lower standard. The ability of domestic producers to compete abroad for export markets are reduced which, in turn, contributes to the difficulties of the developing countries to earn hard currencies. FDI can solve this problem because investment goods generally embody advanced technology.

(iii) Foreign investment can create employment in the modern sectors of developing countries.

(iv) It can benefit consumers in Low-Developed Countries (LDCs) through lower prices / improved quality of goods and new products.

(v) Foreign investment can stimulate domestic investment through forward and backward linkages. For example, output of a foreign firm can be an input of domestic industries. Similarly, output of the domestic industries can be inputs for

1. Bhasin, Nitin, FDI in India: Policies, Conditions & Procedures, New Century Publications, New Delhi, 2016, p. 34.

the foreign firms. If this is so, foreign firms create demand for industries producing goods needed by them.

Some of the negative characteristics are[1]

(i) Foreign investment contributed to under development of India by concentrating on the production and export of raw materials and foodstuffs.

(ii) It went into sectors, which catered to foreign markets and not Indians home market.

(iii) The multiplier effects in terms of income, employment, capital; technical knowledge and growth of external economies of these investments were largely exported back to developed countries.

1.11 Who can invest in India

(i) According to FDI policy, Govt. of India gives permission to a non-resident entity to invest in India, provided they are not citizens of Pakistan and Bangladesh. An entity incorporated in Pakistan or Bangladesh can only invest subject to prior approval of FIPB.

(ii) NRIs citizens and residents in Nepal and Bhutan have the necessary permission by Government of India to invest in the capital of Indian companies on repatriation basis.

(iii) Overseas Corporate Bodies (OCBs) which are integrated outside India and are not under the adverse notice of RBI are allowed to invest in India as per FDI Policy with formal permission from Government of India and RBI as required.

1.12 Factors affecting Foreign Direct Investment

Foreign Direct Investment (FDI) means companies purchase capital and invest in a foreign country. For example, if a US multinational, such as Nike built a factory for making trainers in Pakistan; this would count as foreign direct investment.[2]

---

1. Grubaugh, S.J., Determinants of Direct Foreign Investment, Review of Economics & Statistics, November, 2015, pp. 149-152.
2. Shandilya, T.K., Thakur, A.K., Foreign Direct Investment in India: Problems and Prospects, Deep and Deep Publication, New Delhi, 2018, p. 48.

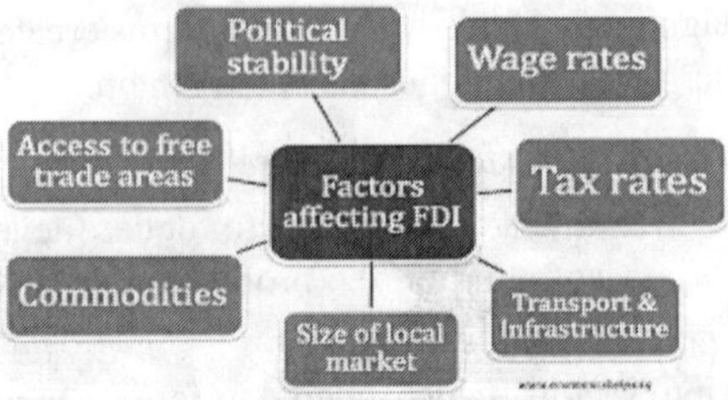

In summary, the main factors that affect foreign direct investment are:

(i) Infrastructure and access to raw materials

(ii) Communication and transport links

(iii) Skills and wage costs of labour

1. Wage Rates

A major incentive for a multinational to invest abroad is to outsource labour-intensive production to countries with lower wages. If average wages in the US are \$15 an hour, but \$1 an hour in the Indian sub-continent, costs can be reduced by outsourcing production. This is why many Western firms have invested in clothing factories in the Indian sub-continent.

However, wage rates alone do not determine FDI, countries with high wage rates can still attract higher tech investment. A firm may be reluctant to invest in Sub-Saharan Africa because low wages are outweighed by other drawbacks, such as lack of infrastructure and transport links.

2. Labour Skills

Some industries require higher skilled labourers, for example, pharmaceuticals and electronics. Therefore, multinationals will invest in those countries with a combination of low wages, but high labour productivity and skills. For example, India has attracted significant investment in call centers, because a high percentage of the population speaks English, but wages are low. This makes it an attractive place for outsourcing and therefore attracts investment.

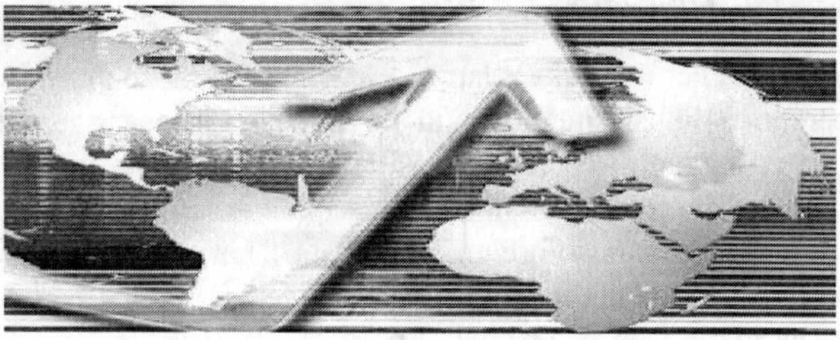

3. Tax Rates

Large multinationals, such as Apple, Google and Microsoft have sought to invest in countries with lower corporation tax rates. For example, Ireland has been successful in attracting investment from Google and Microsoft. In fact, it has been controversial because Google has tried to funnel all profits through Ireland, despite having operations in all European countries.

4. Transport and Infrastructure

A key factor in the desirability of investment is the transport costs and levels of infrastructure. A country may have low labour costs, but if there is a high transport cost to get the goods onto the world market, this is a drawback. Countries with access to the sea are at an advantage to landlocked countries, who will have higher costs to ship goods.

5. Size of the Economy / Potential for Growth

Foreign Direct Investment is often targeted to selling goods directly to the country involved in attracting the investment. Therefore, the size of the population and scope for economic growth will be important for attracting investment. For example, Eastern European countries, with a large population, e.g. Poland offers scope for new markets. This may attract foreign car firms, e.g. Volkswagen, Fiat to invest and build factories in Poland to sell to the growing consumer class. Small countries may be at a disadvantage because it is not worth investing for a small population. China will be a target for foreign investment as the newly emerging Chinese middle class could have a very strong demand for the goods and services of multinationals.

6. Political Stability / Property Rights

Foreign Direct Investment has an element of risk. Countries with an uncertain political situation will be a major disincentive. Also, economic crisis can discourage investment. For example, the recent Russian economic crisis, combined with economic sanctions, will be a major factor to discourage foreign investment. This is one reason why former Communist countries in the East are keen to join the European Union. The EU is seen as a signal of political and economic stability, which encourages foreign investment.

Related to political stability is the level of corruption and trust in institutions, especially judiciary and the extent of law and order.

7. Commodities

One reason for foreign investment is the existence of commodities. This has been a major reason for the growth in FDI within Africa – often by Chinese firms looking for a secure supply of commodities.

8. Exchange Rate

A weak exchange rate in the host country can attract more FDI because it will be cheaper for the multinational to purchase assets. However, exchange rate volatility could discourage investment.

9. Clustering Effects

Foreign firms often are attracted to invest in similar areas to existing FDI. The reason is that they can benefit from external economies of scale – growth of service industries and transport links.

Also, there will be greater confidence to invest in areas with a good track record. Therefore, some countries can create a virtuous cycle of attracting investment and then these initial investments attracting more. It is also sometimes known as an agglomeration effect.

10. Access to Free Trade Areas

A significant factor for firms investing in Europe is access to EU Single Market, which is a free trade area but also has very low non-tariff barriers because of harmonisation of rules, regulations and free movement of people. For example, UK post-Brexit is likely to be less attractive to FDI, if it is outside the Single Market.

There are many different factors that determine foreign direct investment (FDI) and it is hard to isolate individual factors, given there are many different variables. It also depends on the type of industry. For example, with manufacturing FDI, low wage costs tend to be the most important, as they are a labour-intensive industry. For the service sector, FDI, macro-economic stability and political openness tend to be more important.

1.13 Is Foreign Direct Investment (FDI) Necessary for India?

An integral part of a country's economic development, foreign direct investment has a direct positive impact on domestic capital, productivity, and employment. This is the reason why FDI has become an indispensable tool for initiating economic growth for countries.

In order to facilitate economic development, the government of India had decided to liberalise norms and policies for overseas investments in 1991. FDI in India has effectively contributed to the overall growth of the economy. Apart from being a critical driver of economic growth, foreign direct investment equity inflows also are responsible for an inflow of new technology, innovative and fresh ideas, improved infrastructure, and business innovation. All this has led to a highly competitive business environment.

India only opened up its economy to foreign investments in 1991. India can grow without foreign direct investment and it is logical to not solely rely on funds from overseas. However, external help in the form of investment will certainly affect the level and pace of growth.

Take India for example. The growth trends and patterns without foreign investments before 1980's is completely different from that of 1990's, after India introduced economic liberalisation.

Developing countries like India require significant foreign inflows to accelerate economic growth and development. In order to make its way up to the top ranks, the country needs an influx of investments, both domestic and international. **FDI in India** helps in fastening economic activity and also brings with it technological expertise, managerial knowledge and experience and improved infrastructure.

Apart from bringing in investment, foreign direct investment helps in revenue generation, employment generation, getting the latest technology. It also facilitates cultural exchange across borders and helps in improving existing infrastructure.

1.14 FDI in Capital Formation

FDI has a role in India's Capital Formation. The positive impact of foreign direct investments (FDI) on transition economies has been widely acknowledged. FDI is an important source of financing for transition economies as it helps to cover the current account deficit, fiscal deficit (in case of privatisation-related FDI), and supplements inadequate domestic resources to finance both ownership change and capital formation. When compared with other financing options FDI also facilitates transfer of technology, know-how and skills, and helps local enterprises to expand into foreign markets. Having seen the importance of capital, here a brief look into the process of capital formation may be observed. Capital formation has three stages, firstly, increased real savings so that resources may be withdrawn from consumption and diverted to investment in capital production goods. Second is financial credit mechanism so that resources may be claimed by the investor i.e. process of converting savings into investment by the financial intermediaries and finally, the act of investment so that resources may be utilised for the production of capital goods i.e. investing by the producer among the various opportunities into most gainful projects.[1]

1. Shandilya, T.K., Thakur, A.K., Foreign Direct Investment in India: Problems and Prospects, *op.cit*, p. 68.

1.15 Forms of Foreign Direct Investment

Foreign Direct Investment is an investment that is made to acquire a lasting interest in an enterprise. In addition to it, foreign direct investment refers to long term participation by a country into another. It usually involves participation in management, joint venture, transfer of technology and knowhow. Foreign direct investment takes one of the following forms: Greenfield Investment, Brownfield Investment, Mergers and Acquisitions and Joint venture.

1.15.1 Greenfield Investment

A Greenfield Investment is the investment in a manufacturing, office, or other physical company-related structure or group of structures in an area where no previous facilities exist. Greenfield Investing is often mentioned in the context of Foreign Direct Investment. Greenfield investments occur when multinational corporations enter into developing countries to build new factories/stores. Greenfield investment is the primary objective of the host nations as it creates new production capacity and jobs, transfer technology and knowhow, and can lead to linkage to the global market place.[1] Developing countries often offer prospective companies tax-breaks, subsidies and other types of incentives to set up greenfield investments.

1.15.1.1 Advantages of a Greenfield Investment

There are numerous advantages of a Greenfield Investment, including:

- High level of control over business operations
- High-quality control over the manufacturing and sale of products and/or services
- High control over brand image and staffing

- **Economies of scale** and **economies of scope** can be achieved in terms of marketing, research, development, and production
- Bypassing trade restrictions
- Creating jobs for the economy where the Greenfield investment is taking place.

1.15.1.2 Disadvantages of a Greenfield Investment

There are numerous disadvantages of a Greenfield Investment, including:

- An extremely high-risk investment – a Greenfield investment is the riskiest form of foreign direct investments
- Potentially high market entry cost (barriers to entry)
- Government regulations that may prevent foreign direct investments
- High fixed costs involved in establishing a Greenfield location.

1.15.2 Brownfield Investment

Brownfield Investment is formally on acquisition but acquiring firms completely replaces the plant and equipment, labour and product line. This is completely opposite to Greenfield investment. This is also a strategy used in foreign direct investment. The main disadvantage of Brownfield investment is the design and operation efficiency which is often compromised to suit existing constraint and higher risk of cost blowout.[1]

1. Khan, A.Q., Strategy for Foreign Investment Management in 21st century, Kitab Mahal Publication, New Delhi, 2015, p. 43.

Advantages of a Brownfield Investment

A Brownfield Investment offers the following advantages, including:

- The ability to gain access to a new foreign market swiftly
- Lower **fixed costs** due to already established facilities, infrastructure, and network
- Lower staffing and training costs due to already employed workers at the facility
- May include existing approvals and licences from the government or regulators
- Depending if the facility is made to fit, whether modifications exist, or if the facility can be utilised without major alterations and upgrades, a Brownfield investment can be a cost-effective option.

Disadvantages of a Brownfield Investment

A Brownfield Investment offers the following disadvantages, including:

- The facility or infrastructure may require major upgrades, which would increase the foreign investment cost
- The facility may be old and may require high maintenance and upkeep cost
- There may be operational inefficiencies if the facility cannot adapt to new production needs
- There may be **scalability** and expansion issues by using already constructed facilities
- Location constraints
- There may be unforeseen tax and regulatory issues.

1.15.3 Mergers and Acquisitions

M&A is another form of foreign direct investment. In general, a merger is a combination of two companies to form a new company, while an acquisition is the purchase of one company by another in which no new company is formed. In this route foreign firms acquire or merge with an established firm in the host country. M&A made is advantage over Greenfield investment as it is economical in case of acquisition of loss making concern and it also helps in attracting quick access to the market.

Advantages of a Mergers and Acquisitions

- The most common reason for firms to enter into mergers and acquisitions is to merge their power and control over the markets.
- Another advantage is Synergy that is the magic power that allow for increased value efficiencies of the new entity and it takes the shape of returns enrichment and cost savings.
- An economy of scale is formed by sharing the resources and services. Union of 2 firm's leads in overall cost reduction giving a competitive advantage, that is feasible as a result of raised buying power and longer production runs.
- Decrease of risk using innovative techniques of managing financial risk.
- To become competitive, firms have to be compelled to be peak of technological developments and their dealing applications. By M&A of a small business with unique technologies, a large company will retain or grow at competitive edge.
- The biggest advantage is tax benefits. Financial advantages might instigate mergers and corporations will fully build use of tax-shields, increase monetary leverage and utilise alternative tax benefits.

Disadvantages of a Mergers and Acquisitions

- Loss of experienced workers aside from workers in leadership positions. This kind of loss inevitably involves loss of business understand and on the other hand that will be worrying to exchange or will exclusively get replaced at nice value.

- As a result of M&A, employees of the small merging firm may require exhaustive re-skilling.
- Company will face major difficulties thanks to frictions and internal competition that may occur among the staff of the united companies. There is conjointly risk of getting surplus employees in some departments.
- Merging two firms that are doing similar activities may mean duplication and over capability within the company that may need retrenchments.
- Increase in costs might result if the right management of modification and also the implementation of the merger and acquisition dealing are delayed.
- The uncertainty with respect to the approval of the merger by proper assurances.
- In many events, the return of the share of the company that caused buyouts of other company was less than the return of the sector as a whole.

The Mergers and Acquisitions (M&A) reduce flexibility. If a rival makes revolution and may currently market vital resources those are of superior quality, shift is tough. The change expense is the major distinction between the particular merger worth and also the merchandising value of the firm that can be of larger distinction.[1]

1.15.4 Joint Venture

Joint Venture is another popular form of foreign direct investment. An international Joint venture is one of the best modes of entry into new market. A joint venture can take place either with a host country firm or a state institution as well as with any company which is of foreign status host country. In JV, two or more parties agree to pool their resources for the purpose of accomplishing a specific task and each of the participants is responsible for profits, losses and costs associated with it.[2]

1. Khan, A.Q., Strategy for Foreign Investment Management in 21st century, *op.cit,* p. 44.
2. Grubaugh, S.J., Determinants of Direct Foreign Investment, *op.cit,* p. 148.

Advantages of Joint Ventures

The following are the main advantages for a foreign investor choosing a JV structure when entering India:

- Access to the established distribution and marketing channels of the Indian partner;
- Access to the available financial resources of the Indian partners; and
- Access to the established contacts of the Indian partners, which will help ease the process of setting up operations in India.
- A JV also offers the associated parties an opportunity to jointly manage the **risks** associated with new ventures. Through a JV, they can limit their individual exposure by sharing the liabilities.

JV's offer many flexible business diversification opportunities to the partners. A JV may be set up as a prelude to a full merger or only for part of the business.

Certain market sectors remain restricted for foreign investment and a local partner with a certain shareholding in the company is a regulatory necessity for commencing business and making investments.

1.16 The Concept of Globalisation

Globalisation refers to the increasingly global relationships of culture, people and economic activity. Most often, it refers to economics: the global distribution of the production of goods and services, through reduction of barriers to **international trade** such as

tariffs, export fees and **import quotas**. Globalisation accompanied and allegedly contributed to economic growth in developed and developing countries through increased specialisation and the principle of **comparative advantage**. The term can also refer to the transnational circulation of ideas, languages and **popular culture**. Opponents alleged that globalisation's benefits have been overstated and its costs underestimated. Among other points, they argued that it decreased inter-cultural contact while increasing the possibility of international and intra-national conflict.

The term was first employed in a publication entitled Towards New Education in 1930, to denote a holistic view of human experience in education. In the 1960s the term began to be used by economists and other social scientists. The term reached the mainstream press in the latter half of the 1980s. Since its inception, the concept of globalisation has inspired competing definitions and interpretations, with antecedents dating back to the great movements of trade and empire across Asia and the Indian Ocean from the 15th century onwards. Charles Taze Russell coined the related term 'corporate giants' in 1897, to describe the largely national trusts and other large enterprises of the time.[1]

The United Nations Economic and Social Commission for Western Asia (ESCWA) say globalisation is: "a widely-used term that can be defined in a number of different ways. When used in an economic context, it refers to the reduction and removal of barriers between national borders in order to facilitate the flow of goods,

1. Globalisation: Introduction to a Special Issue on Small and Medium-Sized Enterprises in the Global Economy, *Small Business Economics,* 9, pp. 1–6.

capital, services and labour, although considerable barriers remain to the flow of labour. Globalisation is not a new phenomenon. It began towards the end of the nineteenth century, but it slowed down during the period from the start of the First World War until the third quarter of the twentieth century. This slowdown can be attributed to the inward-looking policies pursued by a number of countries in order to protect their respective industries however, the pace of globalisation picked up rapidly during the fourth quarter of the twentieth century."[1]

1.17 FDI in India during Globalisation

Globalisation in India meant shedding its inhibitions about the world market and foreign investments. India had opened its market to select few but with increase in the opportunities in the world market it was forced to open itself to more competition and greater opportunities. It also meant allowing the foreign investors to invest in the infrastructure industries. The infrastructure industries are electricity, coal, finished steel, cement, crude petroleum, refined petroleum products, telecom, oil and gas, roads and bridges, aviation, railways, urban infrastructures, housing, power, ports and shipping's, transportation, railways, water etc., these industries were earlier dominated by the public sectors. To encourage foreign funds flow into the infrastructure in India, the Indian Finance Ministry has allowed Foreign Institutional Investors (FIIs) also to invest in unlisted companies. FIIs now can invest 100 percent of their funds in the Infrastructure in India. In order to make the core sector more attractive for FDI, the Cabinet Committee on Foreign Investment (CCFI) has modified the 49 percent cap on foreign equity in the infrastructure sector to make fund mobilisation easier. This major policy decision which will indirectly raise the foreign equity investment in infrastructure sector to well over 51 percent. Therefore, the paper will try to analyse the foreign direct investment scenario in India after 17 years of globalisation policy. At a time like this when the world is facing the recession and India is also not left out from the global recession effects, the Indian government needs to lure the foreign investors with more flexible policies and foster environment for the FDI investments in the infrastructural sectors which would build India as a leading economy.[2]

1. Summary of the Annual Review of Development in Globalisation and Regional Integration in the Countries of the ESCWA Region.
2. *Ibid.*

Apart from being a critical driver of economic growth, foreign direct investment (FDI) is a major source of non-debt financial resource for the economic development of India. Foreign companies invest in India to take advantage of relatively lower wages, special investment privileges such as tax exemptions, etc. For a country where foreign investments are being made, it also means achieving technical know-how and generating employment. The Indian Government's favourable policy regime and robust business environment have ensured that foreign capital keeps flowing into the country. The government has taken many initiatives in recent years such as relaxing FDI norms across sectors such as defence, PSU oil refineries, telecom, power exchanges, and stock exchanges, among others.[1] According to Department of Industrial Policy and Promotion (DIPP), the total FDI investments India received in FY 2015-16 was US$ 40 billion, indicating that government's effort to improve ease of doing business and relaxation in FDI norms is yielding results.

1.18 Role of FDI in Indian Economy

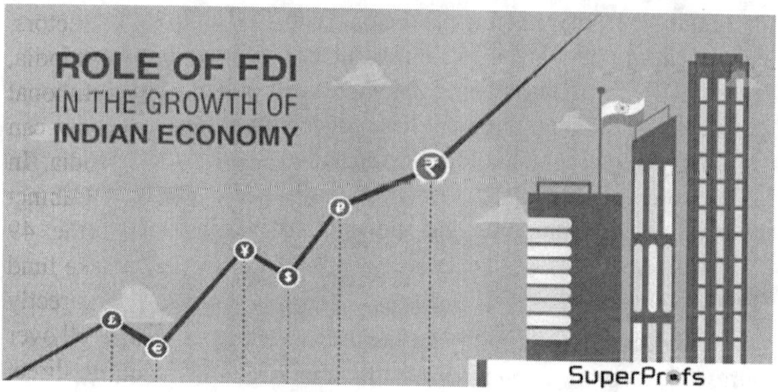

India is the second fastest growing economy in the world with a GDP growth rate of 7.6% in the FY16. In terms of GDP, it is the 10th largest economy in the world and in terms PPP (Purchasing Power Parity) it is the 3rd largest economy in the world. To maintain this growth rate and rank, India requires huge foreign investments. Government of India has taken many initiatives to attract foreign

1. *Ibid.*

investment into India. One of such initiative is "Make in India", programme to make India a 'Manufacturing Hub' of the world.[1]

Accelerated Economic Growth

It has been witnessed that with the increase in FDI inflows in India from $0.13 billion to $30.3 billion in 2010-11, the GDP growth rate of the country has accelerated from 1.43 percent in 1990-91 to 7.6 percent in 2015-16. It shows that India's GDP has increased four times since 1990-91.

Accelerated Economic Development

FDI acts as a catalyst in various sectors mainly in manufacturing and service sectors. With the new government in power, there are many reforms to attract FDI inflows in the country. FDI inflows in 2015-16 are more in the areas of service sectors (18%), construction development (10%), telecommunication (7%), computer software and hardware (6%) etc. While the share of industry in GDP remained stagnant, noteworthy over the period there was structural transformation in manufacturing sector. With FDI inflows there are development in many areas like infrastructure, per capita income and standard of living of the people has increased, poverty has declined in absolute terms, unemployment has reduced by 3 times since 1990-91 to 2013-14, clean technology has installed, roads, dams, bridges, schools, colleges, hospitals have been built with new technology. Thereby, overall development has shown in all over India.

Capital

For the economic growth and development of the country India requires huge capital. To compensate this domestic capital requirement, FDI inflows are one of the important pre-requisites. FDI is helping developing countries in capital formation by bringing fresh capitals.

Technology

Developing countries are lacking technological know-how. With

1. Aggrawal, S., Singla, A., Aggrawal, R., Foreign Direct Investment in India, International Journal of Computational Engineering & Management, 2016, 15 (5), 93-105.

the opening up of their economies for FDI, they will get the access to sophisticated technology from the foreign firms which will enhance their productivity and quality of the products.

Managerial Skills

FDI inflows are not only helping in capital formation but also help in developing managerial skills.

Competitive Environment

FDI inflows have increased the competitive environment for the domestic firms consequently benefitting the consumers by accessing with better quality products at a lesser price.

Reduction in Balance of Payment Deficit

With the transfer of technology and enhancement of production techniques, marketing expertise and modern managerial techniques possibilities of export promotion has also been opened up in new areas. With better quality product at a lower price the demand increased for Indian goods and services abroad consequently there is increase in exports. Therefore, exports have increased from $18 billion to $245 billion.[1] With the enhancement in exports BOP deficits has declined. Government of India has also taken many measures to attract FDI to boost exports.

Employment Generation

With FDI inflows into the country new job opportunities has been created in various sectors. As more employment opportunities are generated mainly in metropolitan cities where FDI inflows are maximum i.e., Delhi and Mumbai. Therefore, more rural-urban migrations are in these cities.

Poverty Alleviation

India is the second largest populated country in the world. With increase in employment opportunities there is reduction in absolute poverty in India. But as the population base is very high in actual

---

1. Aggrawal, S., Singla, A., Aggrawal, R., Foreign Direct Investment in India, International Journal of Computational Engineering & Management, 2016, 15 (5), 93-105.

terms, poverty has increased. So, government has to take measures to attract more FDI and create more employment opportunities to reduce poverty from the country.

Opened up Reserved Area

With the new reforms to boost FDI inflows in India, the PSU's reserved areas i.e. where the state have exclusive rights to produce are opened up for Foreign Direct Investments. Earlier Railways and Defence were reserved for PSU's and now FDI is allowed in these sectors. 100 percent FDI is allowed under automatic routes in most of the areas of Indian Railways such as in bullet train, passenger terminal, railway electrification, mass rapid transport systems and IRCTC. 49 percent FDI is allowed in Defence sector but Atomic energy are still under PSU's reserved areas. To get access to more sophisticated technology in Defence area we have to increase the FDI limit.

Forex Reserves

Forex Reserves has increased from $5.8 billion in 1990-91 to $274 billion in 2010-11. As we witnessed that with increase in FDI inflows into the country foreign exchange reserves has also increased.

In India, the primary sector is in dire needs of foreign investment especially in the areas of agricultural, livestock farming, forestry, fishing etc. FDI inflows into agricultural and allied sectors are still negative despite that 58 percent of Indians are still dependent on agricultural and allied sectors for their livelihood and their contributions to country's GDP has also declined from 56.5 percent in 1950-51 to 16 percent in 2015-16.[1] To attract FDI's into this sector government has to make land reforms and ease in the entry of FDI into this area. Therefore, it has been witnessed that FDI inflows are not even in terms of various sectors and regions.

FDI in India has a significant impact on development of India. FDI in India to various sectors can attain sustained economic growth and development through creation of jobs, expansion of existing manufacturing industries. The inflow of FDI in service sectors and construction and development sector, from April, 2000 to March, 2016

1. Aggrawal, S., Singla, A., Aggrawal, R., Foreign Direct Investment in India, International Journal of Computational Engineering & Management, 2016, 15 (5), 93-105.

attained substantial sustained economic growth and development through creation of jobs in India.

Computer, Software & Hardware and Drugs & Pharmaceuticals sector were the other sectors to which attention was shown by Foreign Direct Investors (FDI).

FDI plays a crucial role in enhancing the economic growth and development of the country. Moreover, FDI as a strategic component of investment is needed by India for achieving the objectives of its second generation of economic reforms and maintaining this pace of growth and development of the economy. Hence FDI is a significant factor which influences the level of economic growth in India. It provides a sound base for economic growth and development by enhancing the financial position of the country. It also contributes to the GDP and foreign exchange reserves of the country.

India attracted FDI worth US$ 22.42 billion. Tourism, pharmaceuticals, services, chemicals and construction were among the biggest beneficiaries. For Indian economy which has tremendous potential, FDI has had a positive impact. FDI inflow supplements domestic capital, as well as technology and skills of existing companies. It also helps to establish new companies. All of these contribute to economic growth of the Indian Economy. India's Foreign Direct Investment (FDI) policy has been gradually liberalised to make the market more investor friendly. The results have been encouraging. These days, the country is consistently ranked among the top three global investment destinations by all international bodies, including the World Bank.[1]

1. Azhar, S., Marimuthu, K.N., An overview of Foreign Direct Investment in India, International Journal of Multidisciplinary Management studies, 2 (1), 2016, pp. 202-214.

Chapter – 2

An Overview of Foreign Direct Investment in India

2.1 Introduction

In present Global competitive economic circumstances, no country in the world is self-sufficient and self-reliant. Most of them largely depend on other nations in some way. Advance economy with surplus reserves want to integrate other nations who have minerals reserves and skilled labours. Emerging economy in hope to become self-sufficient requires fund for their economical promotion and consolidation, undeveloped economies require funds for their survival. Thus, financial integration through FDI played paramount role to accelerate the respective economies. With growing globalisation most of the Asian nations have welcomed the FDI and witness surge in its inflow. India with conservative approach to globalisation has been found latecomer to the FDI. Its overall market potential, cheap skilled workforce with mineral reserves and safe marine routes along with liberalised policy regime sustained its attraction as a most preferred destination for foreign investors.

Nation industrial infra, its growth and development is a backbone of its economy. It reflects nations self-sufficiency's which is herculean task and requires judicious approach to justify factors involved. It imparts the required dynamism to the economy which transforms the socio-psychological environment of its historical, traditional, economic and social structure. The nation's economy and its social growth

depend upon efforts, capital and knowledge. Among these three factors capital has been recognised as a most required and important. Its formation involves multiple activities which are saving, finance and investment. To form capital for economic activities there is a need of stable financial sector and within financial sector banking sector play crucial role. Due to liberalisation, globalisation, deregulation, competitive disintermediation and economic intensification competition has grown and every country wants to become self-reliant and self-sufficient and thus demand for financial resources grown to many folds.[1] To cater the economic demand, socio-political competition, economic complexities, increasing population, unpredictable challenges and to capitalise the macroeconomic environmental opportunities at optimal level, Government of India (GOI) adopted cataclysmic structural and continuous reforms in Indian macroeconomic system. It started playing a parental role by stoking the engine of economic growth through garnering the internal and external resource in money supply and introduced policy of tectonic economic liberalisation, globalisation, digitalisation and deregulation with metamorphic liberalised policy in financial sector, which in result brought drastic change and ultimate revolution in Indian financial sector and transformed conservative financial sector into global at par, and led to the emergence for new financial windows, non-debt financial capital FDI, new banks, new instruments, new financial institutions and motivated foreign investors to invest in diversified industrial and manufacturing sectors.

Government of India visualised corporate vision and mission and articulated core objectives of corporate financial requirement and liberalised the FDI rules and regulations. To provide strength to the

1. Bhasin, Niti, Foreign Direct Investment (FDI) in India, New Century Publications, New Delhi, 2018, p. 27.

tectonic changes in economic reforms and to accelerate the nation's overall economy government of India passes legislations, rules, regulations, ordinance and amendments in Foreign Direct Investment (FDI) law time to time and strategically enabled the domestic industrial and other economic sector to meet the financial requirement through diversified resources including FDI which is non-debt financial capital and is widely preferred by the firms when they became multinational. With following the government policies and under the constant vigilance of regulators like RBI, SEBI and IRDA, Foreign Direct Investment (FDI) gradually occupied the core status in financing the economic activities. With liberalised FDI rules and restructured financial sector domestic industries and Indian corporate collectively explored untapped resources and found it more lucrative and transparent. Now Indian corporate is free to evolve their own system of financing working capital and can freely raise finances through foreign direct investment.[1]

1. Bhasin, Niti, Foreign Direct Investment (FDI) in India, *op.cit*, p. 28.

The financial management in India has changed drastically in scope and complexities due to restructured financial policies. In Indian context, FDI means the investment by non-resident person or entity of India, in the capital of Indian entity or company, either by buying a company or by expanding operation of an existing business in target country. It is not a charity but in fact it is core profit making investment from other nations and multinational companies' savings. It is contrast to portfolio investment which is a passive investment in the securities of another country such as stock and bonds. Entire FDI are investments made by MNCs and other nation's savers with a time period consideration. The modern approach to fund the corporate economic activities is much wider than the traditional approach. In present competitive global economic environment and economic overlapping to dominate raising funds have become crucial and complicated. Financing is an art and service of managing money requires freedom to acquire funds with safety and transparency. Prior to liberalisation and globalisation financing economic activities through Foreign Direct Investment (FDI) was very complicated. It was very much controlled by the government and was tough for corporate to arrange and manage FDI in free economic environment.

Businesses are considered as a socio-economic activity and embrace all sections of society commonly for collective satisfaction. With growing globalisation economic activities and opportunities increases with diversification and opportunistic desire of society influenced the global business tremendously. Economies started crossing the political boundary and gradually become part of global economic structure. To maintain equilibrium between internal and external financing cost, and global standard between demand and supply in present technologically competitive and metamorphic environmental growth within and outside the political boundary, and to cater the global status requirement, and to develop competitive strength business, entities need financial resources which became possible through FDI. Private sector and corporate entities analysing their ability to handle risk and return factors and financial market conditions; took the decision and started generating funds through FDI according to their market value, goodwill, and managerial efficiency. Foreign Direct Investment (FDI) became ready highbred financial option for corporate which can be effectively mobilised and productively utilised.[1]

1. Khan, A.Q., Strategy for Foreign Investment Management in 21st century, Kitab Mahal Publication, New Delhi, 2018, p. 21.

Generally, FDI arrangements require more wider and complicated set of strategic, economic behavioural consideration which usually becomes motivating factor behind foreign direct investment. Its inflow increases the investment level in the host nation which multiplies the nation's economy and generates employment, income and savings. Its benefits are not immediate but can be achieved in future. It adjudicates complementary role by bridging the gap between domestic investment and savings. Its impact on nation's economy largely depends upon nation's regulated policies and the sector in which FDI has been directed and utilised. Returns on FDI depend upon longevity of investment. Many firms have long gestation period and require funds for long period, and return in such firms is possible when they become operational. Foreign direct investment in stock market response immediately but this inflow is for short period of time and do not contribute in nations growth and development accept it appear in nations balance sheet. FDI which stay in nation's economy for some time only contribute in economic growth.

2.2 Foreign Portfolio/Institutional Investors (FPI/FII)

Foreign Portfolio/Institutional Investors (FPI/FII) have been one of the biggest drivers of India's financial markets and have invested around Rs 13.39 trillion (US$ 191.60 billion) in India between FY02-20 (till December 4, 2019). Highly developed primary and secondary markets have attracted FIIs/FPIs to the country. Investments by FIIs/FPIs in India are regulated by the Securities and Exchange Board of India (SEBI), while the ceilings on such investments are maintained by the Reserve Bank of India (RBI). Following are the few types of FIIs investing in India:[1]

- Hedge Funds
- Foreign Mutual Funds
- Sovereign Wealth Funds
- Pension Funds
- Trusts
- Asset Management Companies
- Endowments, University Funds, etc.

The total market capitalisation (M-cap) of all the companies listed on Bombay Stock Exchange (BSE) rose to a record high level of Rs 151.08 trillion (US$ 2.16 trillion) in 2018-19 and reached Rs 154.12 trillion (US$ 2.20 trillion) in 2019-20.

2.2.1 Recent Developments/Investments[2]

Some of the recent significant FII/FPI developments are as follows:

- In 2018-19, India ranked seventh with a market cap of US$ 2.1 trillion.

1. https://www.ibef.org/economy/foreign-institutional-investors.aspx
2. https://www.ibef.org/economy/foreign-institutional-investors.aspx

- From February to June 2019, FIIs invested a net of US$ 11.4 billion in Indian equities.
- Domestic Institutional Investors (DIIs) and foreign portfolio investors (FPI) together invested Rs 1.43 lakh crore (around US$ 20 billion) in 2019.
- Foreign institutional ownership increased to an eight-quarter high of 20.93 percent by the end of September for 414 firms in the BSE 500 index.
- In quarter 2 (up to September 2019), FIIs have sold Indian shares worth US$ 3.17 billion.
- Union Bank of Switzerland (UBS) maintained its Nifty target at 9,500 by March 2019.
- Morgan Stanley has set its Sensex target to 40,000 by June 2020.
- Investments by foreign portfolio investors (FPIs) in Indian capital markets have reached net Rs 10,312 crore (US$ 1.48 billion) investments in June 2019. FPIs invested Rs 1,937.54 crore (US$ 277.23 million) into debt segment during August 1-9- 2019.
- In September 2018, Embassy Office Parks filed the papers for India's first Real Estate Investment Trusts (REIT). In September 2019, Embassy Office Parks announced plans to expand its portfolio in Hyderabad and Chennai and list nation's second REIT in 2020-21.

2.2.2 Government/Regulatory Initiatives

- In May 2019, SEBI proposed reducing the overall time taken for rights issue from 55-58 days to around 31 days. This will make the application and allotment process more efficient.
- In September 2018, SEBI has reduced the time to list shares on stock exchange after initial public offerings to three days from previous six days.
- A report filed by a panel appointed by the Securities and Exchange Board of India (SEBI) on December 04, 2018 has proposed direct overseas listing of Indian companies and other regulatory changes.

- In September 2018, the Securities and Exchange Board of India (SEBI) relaxed the Know-Your-Client (KYC) requirement for Foreign Portfolio Investors (FPIs).
- In September 2018, SEBI allowed Bombay Stock Exchange (BSE) and National Stock Exchange (NSE) to start commodity derivate segments.
- SEBI has also allowed foreign entities to participate in the commodity derivatives segment of Indian stock exchanges, to help them hedge their exposures. It has also proposed to allow Non-Resident Indians (NRIs) to invest through FPI route after meeting specific KYC norms.
- In August 2018, SEBI reduced the timeline for public issue of debt securities from 12 days to six days.
- Foreign Portfolio Investors are also allowed to invest up to 25 percent in Category III Alternative Investment Funds (AIF) in India. Different types of funds such as hedge funds, Private Investment in Public Equity (PIPE) funds, etc. are operating in India as Category III AIFs.
- Investments by FPIs have also been allowed in Real Estate Investment Trusts (REITs) and Infrastructure Investment Trust (InvITs).

2.2.3 Path Ahead

India is being viewed as a potential opportunity by investors, with the economy having the capacity to grow tremendously. Buoyed by strong support from the government, FII investments have been strong and are expected to continue to improve going forward.

Mark Machin, Chief Executive Officer, Canada Pension Plan Investment Board (CPPIB), has expressed confidence in the Indian equity market and stated that the country is one of the best investment destinations based on its demographic growth, increased productivity, and long-term economic growth potential.

2.3 Difference between FDI (Foreign Direct Investment) and FPI (Foreign Portfolio Investment)

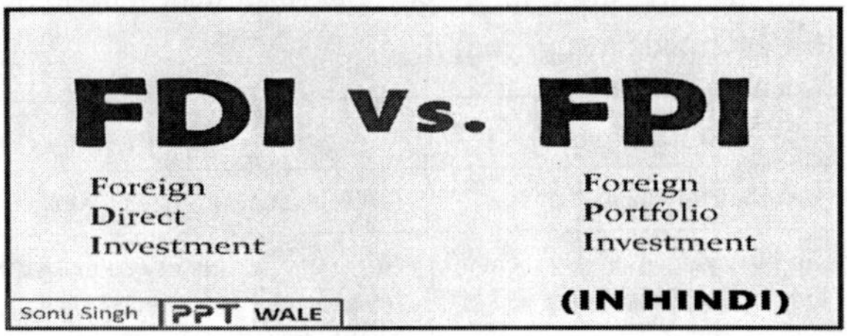

Foreign Direct Investment refers to international investment in which the investor obtains a lasting interest in an enterprise in another country.

Most concretely, it may take the form of buying or constructing a factory in a foreign country or adding improvements to such a facility, in the form of property, plants, or equipment.

FDI is calculated to include all kinds of capital contributions, such as the purchases of stocks, as well as the reinvestment of earnings by a wholly owned company incorporated abroad (subsidiary), and the lending of funds to a foreign subsidiary or branch. The reinvestment of earnings and transfer of assets between a parent company and its subsidiary often constitutes a significant part of FDI calculations.[1]

FDI is more difficult to pull out or sell off. Consequently, direct investors may be more committed to managing their international investments, and less likely to pull out at the first sign of trouble.

On the other hand, FPI (Foreign Portfolio Investment) represents passive holdings of securities such as foreign stocks, bonds, or other financial assets, none of which entails active management or control of the securities' issuer by the investor.

Unlike FDI, it is very easy to sell off the securities and pull out the foreign portfolio investment. Hence, FPI can be much more volatile than FDI. For a country on the rise, FPI can bring about rapid development, helping an emerging economy move quickly to take advantage of economic opportunity, creating many new jobs and

1. Khan, A.Q., Strategy for Foreign Investment Management in 21st century, *op.cit,* p. 28.

significant wealth. However, when a country's economic situation takes a downturn, sometimes just by failing to meet the expectations of international investors, the large flow of money into a country can turn into a stampede away from it.

FDI	FPI
Projects are efficiently managed	Projects are less efficiently managed
Involved in management and ownership control; long-term interest	No active involvement in management. Investment instruments that are more easily traded less permanent and do not represent a controlling stake in an enterprise.
It is more difficult to sell off or pull out.	It is fairly easy to sell securities and pull out because they are liquid.
Tends to be undertaken by Multinational organisations	Comes from more diverse sources e.g. a small company's pension fund or through mutual funds held by individuals; investment via equity instruments (stocks) or debt (bonds) of a foreign enterprise.
Involves the transfer of non-financial assets e.g. technology and intellectual capital, in addition to financial assets.	Only investment of financial assets.
Foreign Direct Investment	Foreign Portfolio Investment
Having smaller in net inflows	Having larger net inflows

2.4 Benefits of FDI in India

Foreign Direct Investment is most striking features of the international economy today. One of the most salient features of today's globalisation drive is conscious support of cross-border investments, especially by transnational companies and firms. Many countries and continents (particularly developing) at the present see attracting FDI as a significant element in their strategy for economic growth. This is most probably since FDI is seen as an amalgamation of capital, technology, marketing and management.

FDI is particularly essential for developing countries since it offers access to resources that would otherwise be unavailable to these countries. Moreover, the advantages of Foreign Direct Investment are very positive for a country or region.

The government must think all possible benefits, both direct and indirect. Some of the most common benefits are the following:[1]

Capital

A new investor will carry in capital with which a new manufacture facility will be constructed, or a local company obtained.

Employment

Though the number of jobs created varies in agreement with the size of the investment and the manufacture process itself, the most familiar benefit associated with FDI is improved or protected employment. Naturally, the new employment creates further income and expenditure power for home residents.

Revenue Benefits

FDI broaden the local tax base and contributes to government revenues. Even if foreign investors are arranged full release from taxes for a short period of time during investment incentives, governments can earn increased revenue from the payment of personal income taxes

1. Bhasin, Niti, Foreign Direct Investment (FDI) in India, *op.cit*, p. 103.

for the motivation from the fresh jobs formed by FDI. Additionally, export-oriented investment creates foreign exchange earnings.

Wage Premium

Foreign owned companies normally give higher wages, which has multiplier effects for the local economy.

Favourable Impact on Local Investment

FDI inflows tend to lead to an increase in domestic investment as companies gain access to distribution channels opened by TNCs (Transnational Corporations), become suppliers to TNCs, or respond to competition from TNCs.

Foreign Exchange

FDI can be a starting place of foreign exchange in countries with low savings or access to capital.

Technology Transfer

FDI can recover a country's access to technology through licencing, joint ventures and local trade. Employees of TNCs may take knowledge they have acquired and set up new companies or join existing local companies. Whatever the form, technology transfer tends to direct recovered productivity growth.

Knowledge Transfer through Research and Development

Research and development relations between MNCs and domestic firms can guide to knowledge transfer to domestic firms. Domestic firms can be trained from the research and development activities of MNCs and thereby develop upon their own research.

Improved Labour Skills

Foreign firms usually carry out more on the work training than do local firms, and TNCs in particular frequently engage in actions that use relatively high levels of experienced workers. These skills are frequently transferred to other sectors and actions when employees search for new jobs or found their own businesses.

Innovation

Foreign Direct Investment can strengthen local market competition, creating the stimulus for innovation.

Improved Exports

Much FDI is export oriented and TNCs frequently account for a significant share of host country exports. Many developing countries have been able to use FDI as a way to increase their export levels and get better foreign exchange earnings. Additionally, the presence of foreign owned exporting firms has been dominant in many countries in encouraging local firms to enter export markets.

Improved International Competitiveness of Local Firms

Foreign firms regularly introduce new products to the local economy and domestic firms are frequently encouraged to contend with these products. Through their interface with a foreign owned company, suppliers, customers and competitors in the host country are continually encouraged to higher levels of investments, productivity and innovation. The result is usually greater economic efficiency and higher quality production by domestic firms. FDI can develop overall economic growth by increasing competition in sectors earlier dominated by only one or two local firms.

Higher Productivity

Foreign investors on an average have high productivity than domestic companies, which raise overall productivity and therefore competitiveness of the local economy. Simultaneously, local companies through working with inward investors are exposed to the newest management practices which can encourage local companies to implement new productivity increasing practices.

2.5 In quest of Foreign Direct Investment

As a result of these benefits of FDI, a lot of developing countries are now energetically seeking foreign investment by taking measures that include economic and political reforms designed to recover their investment environment.

Market

FDI is a significant motive to access to host country markets for processed goods. However, a lot of developing countries have liberalised their import regime after 1980s and this liberalisation policy enabled TNCs to choose between exporting and undertaking FDI. According to Nunnenkamp, there may be a decline in purely market - seeking FDI due to liberalisation policies, but it should also be taken into account that the possible decline of market seeking FDI is basically restricted to FDI in manufacturing industries. The opportunity of service industries to FDI is the reason behind the existence of market - seeking FDI motive today. Some other reasons of market - seeking FDI are transport costs, differences in consumer tastes and total magnitude of the host economy[1].

Efficiency

1. Bhasin, Niti, Foreign Direct Investment (FDI) in India, *op.cit,* p. 132.

TNCs invest in developing countries to increase efficiency beyond the simple reallocation of labour - intensive production. Key factors for efficiency seeking investment include labour costs, skills availability and contact to international markets. Efficiency - seeking FDI is frequently made with the specific objective of accessing low - cost labour, labour - intensive production or taking advantage of relatively abundant supplies of educated and skilled workers. Efficiency - seeking FDI is aggravated by creating new sources of competitiveness for firms and strengthening existing ones whereas market - seeking FDI aims at penetrating the local markets of host countries. Investment related to efficiency seeking may be seen in different forms. One form is that firms in developing countries undertake to supply TNCs with fully manufactured products that will bear the TNCs' brand names. Another form is that foreign enterprises try to offer products adapted to local tastes and quality requirements. The composition of this form of FDI may be either green field investment or M&A. This type of FDI mostly goes to economically advanced developing countries.

Resource

The availability of plentiful or cheap production factors in a developing country is a motivation for transnational corporation presence in that country. Natural resources are a type of production factors that conventionally has attracted most interest among foreign investors. Especially, in the first brandish of globalisation, colonial powers invested in their colonies to take out natural resources and they consequently used them in their home countries.

Natural resource - seeking is still the main FDI motive for TNCs working in sectors such as mining, mineral extraction and operating in large-scale agricultural business. TNCs may seek natural resources for three reasons: to meet the requirements of its own downstream refining or manufacturing activities, to sell the minerals straight in host, home and international markets and to protect the strategic necessities of energy or other minerals for its home country. Human resources-seeking FDI arouses due to the possibility of obtaining economical labour. Human resource - seeking FDI depends on the comparative pricing of labour with a given level of qualifications. Further natural resource seeking, the availability of skilled cheap labour in developing countries is becoming an increasingly important motivation among foreign investors.[1]

1. Prasanna, N., FDI in India: Issues and Challenges, *op-cit,* p. 44.

Strategic Asset

FDI is a means to attain strategic assets such as technology, marketing and management expertise available in a host country. Companies investing abroad with the intention of acquiring strategic assets aim at a competitive boundary, as well a degree of a monopoly just at the beginning. Strategic assets - seeking FDI is popular among medium income and fast-growing industrialising countries as they seek to find a speedy presence in the creative and dynamic markets of the advanced countries.[1]

2.6 The Motivational Factors for FDI in India

FDI represents an important indicator of the increasing interdependence of the economies of countries around the world. FDI in its various forms is considered an artery that maintains continuity in the life of any economy. Therefore, all countries aim to set up programmes and policies to ensure the flow of investment according to the goals and objectives of their respective economic systems. FDI's growing role in global business is extraordinary. It can provide a firm with new markets and marketing channels, cheaper production

1. Bhasin, Niti, Foreign Direct Investment (FDI) in India, *op.cit,* p. 133.

facilities, and access to new technology, products, skills and financing. In recent years, given rapid growth and change in global investment patterns, the definition has been broadened to include the acquisition of a lasting management interest in a company or enterprise outside the investing firm's home country. As such, it may take many forms, such as a direct acquisition of a foreign firm, construction of a facility, or investment in a joint venture or strategic alliance with a local firm with attendant input of technology, licencing of intellectual property.[1] FDI is conducive to the creation of a more competitive environment, or conversely to the worsening of monopolistic and/or oligopolistic elements in the host economy. Foreign direct investment has a significant impact on economic growth which is magnified within a host country. Foreign Direct Investment is an increasing commercial trend in today's commercial world. More and more capital are flowing from developed countries to the developing countries. Awareness among the companies about the potential of the overseas markets especially the developing markets has given boost to the flight of capital from developed world to the developing world. Companies, products and services which were once available or heard in developed world are now readily available in the developing nations. Food products, telecom services, cars, garment brands are now shifting their attention to the emerging markets due to falling revenues in the domestic market and increasing demand in the emerging markets.

Multinational organisations owing to their technological superiority, strong financial base, flexibility, speed, market expertise always seek opportunities to expand their operations in new markets. Foreign direct investment is setting up productive capacity into a foreign land is the most sought modes of entry into new markets. Several well-known organisations like Exxon, Toshiba, BMW, and Starbucks have made their presence felt across the globe by pursuing foreign direct investment mode. These organisations have one common underlining factor that has made their overseas move possible and that is a strong financial base. They have invested huge amount of financial and human resources in order to capitalise on the opportunities offered by the new emerging markets. They have extracted output from their superior competitive position. Along with lucrative prospects in the

1. Sarkar, Tapas, Inflow of Foreign Direct Investment in India- Patterns, Performance, Implications, Foreign Trade Review, 2019, p. 123.

new economies cut throat competition in local markets, rationalising of commercial activity to benefit from economies of scale and increasing raw material prices have prompted firms to move to area rich in natural resources.

Regional and global trade and investment agreements have stimulated the increase in foreign direct investment inflow. Thanks to the increasing trade and investment agreements, wide range of complex issues are considered and resolved in order to make the movement of capital and technology smooth. Foreign investors usually look for nations which are less risky and offer political and economic stability and robust economic growth due to favourable policy measures.

Considering their technological superiority, product differentiation, strong financial base, flexibility, managerial acumen, speed of delivery and market expertise, the multinationals are superior to the local firms. Multinational organisations tend to capitalise on the gap in products and services in the new overseas markets and maximize their profits. Another reason for multinational organisations to move to new markets is to invest in the natural resources and prevent or control their competitor's advantage in critical fields like natural resources, technological acumen etc but the main idea behind investment is increased profitability.[1]

Policy Framework and Policy Coherence

Economic, political and social stability forms the background of a host country's FDI policy. A transparent legal framework and business environment is the first order of importance since it lowers

1. Sarkar, Tapas, Inflow of Foreign Direct Investment in India- Patterns, Performance, Implications, Foreign Trade Review, 2019, p. 124.

the political risk of doing business in an unknown environment. Rules and regulations concerning the entry and operations of foreign firms, and principles of treatment of foreign firms, are particularly applicable in this admiration. The high-quality of corporate governance and fair business practices are equally significant. Also important are policies that impact upon the performance and structure of markets such as policies concerning trade, competition, mergers, acquisitions and privatisation, as well as the policy coherence.

International Trade and International Markets

Openness to international trade and access to international markets are economic reforms and open-door policies and other efforts to promote trade – inter alia by conducting two-sided trade agreements and adopting one-sided actions can attract export-oriented FDI. Attractive and strategic geographic positions adjoin to potential importing countries and providing admission to local and global markets, are also key factors in attracting FDI- mainly FDI flows expected at exports.

Natural and Human Resource Endowments

Natural and human resource endowments are including the productivity and cost of labour. FDI oriented exports seeks to use those proportional advantages related to low labour costs or the profusion of natural resources. Recently attention has shifted from the natural endowments of resources and labour to acquire endowments of resources, such as the availability of intermediate goods and skilled labour, brand names, has also become an important determinant in the location decisions of MNEs.

Physical, Financial and Technological Infrastructure

Physical, Financial and Technological infrastructures influence the FDI location decision not only among contestant countries but also among different regions within a country. FDI is more possible to flow to those areas with good accessibility and accordingly lower transportation costs. Besides highways, railways, ports and airports the level of telecommunication services has gained rising importance with the recent transformations in the information and telecommunications industries of the past decades. High local technological abilities are an essential factor for attracting FDI flows in high value-added activities.

Investment Protection

Proper investment promotion and protection is usually a minimum condition for FDI. Without transparent dispute settlement procedures, or unreasonable interpretation of existing measures, FDI might be deterred. Alternatively, many countries offer investment promotion correspondence to attract FDI. These incentive packages may be part of the location decision of FDI, and can include factors such as tax and more financial incentives that influence net profit rates which seems to be primary concern of the investors.

2.7 Determinants of Foreign Direct Investment in India

Countries of the world, particularly developing economies, are vying with each other to attract foreign capital, particularly Foreign Direct Investment (FDI) to boost their domestic rates of investment as also to acquire new technology and managerial skills. As with many developing nations, encouragement of FDI is an integral part of the on-going economic reforms in India. To formulate a foreign investment policy that is most conducive to attracting FDI, it is imperative to first study the determinants of FDI in a country for the policymakers to ensure that various measures intended to induce FDI are necessary and would lead to incremental investment. In this era of globalisation, foreign direct investment (FDI) flows have been expanding at a faster rate than ever specially so in developing countries and particularly the fastest growing ones. FDI acts as a major stimulus to economic growth in developing countries through creation of wealth and employment in the host country and improvement in the balance of payments via exports.

The Size of Domestic Market

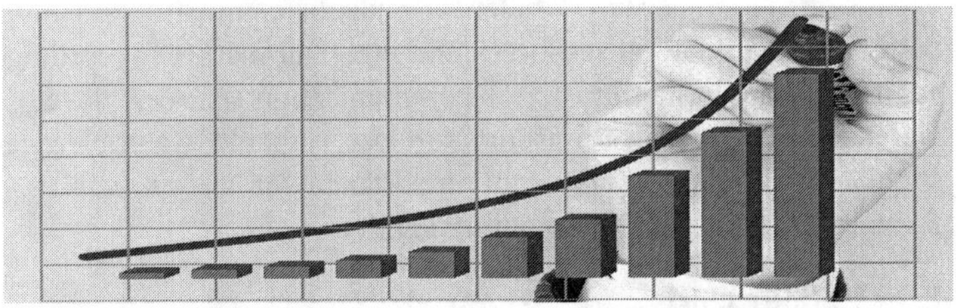

The size of the domestic market is a primary determinant of FDI. The wealth and growth of a country can be used as proxy to measure the size of the domestic market. Most frequently, per capita income (PCI), which is an indicator of effectual demand, is used to determine the size of local market. Additionally, to PCI, the GDP of a country and the population size are also used as an indicator to calculate the size of local market. Though, if a firm is export-oriented and not market seeking, the size of domestic market will not be a significant determinant of FDI. A big market can help firms producing tangible products to attain scale and scope economies. The domestic market growth rate which is measured in terms of population and GDP growth rate also determines the inflow of FDI into a country.[1]

Natural Resources

Natural resources are the most important determinants of FDI. From the 19th century up to the eve of the Second World War about 60 percent of the world stock of FDI was in natural resources. The need to protect economic and reliable sources of mineral and primary products for the industrialising nations of Europe and North America,

1. Prasanna, N., FDI in India: Issues and Challenges, *op.cit,* p. 87.

natural resources were the major reason for the growth of FDI. Countries that have adequate deposit of some minerals can attract foreign investors, mainly those involved in utilisation of natural resources.

Level of Infrastructure

In today's globally competitive business environment, absence and lack of efficient infrastructure means not only high transaction costs for those that are already in business but also a barrier to entry for new firms. Infrastructure development has high importance for the expansion of FDI, because efficient and adequate infrastructure implies better access to natural resources and potential market. According to availability and reliability of telecommunication services, developed and adequate road/air transport services, reliable water/electricity supply facilities have dominant importance for the profitability of foreign companies and in attracting FDI.

Low Labour Cost

As noted by neoclassical economists, labour cost is one of the factors that affect the investment decision of foreign investors and this fact has been proven in many locations. UNCTAD (2004) 38 reported that availability of cheap labour in China is taking jobs from Europe and United States. In addition to cheap labour, the output labour ratio also determines the inflow of FDI.

Inflation

Through its effect on the cost of inputs and the price of outputs, inflation reduces the real return on investment and firms' competitiveness. Hence, countries that follow policies that decrease inflation rate have better chance in attracting FDI. Low and predictable inflation rate is central for the long-term investment of both domestic and foreign companies. Therefore, higher and unpredictable inflation will decrease the inflow of FDI.[1]

Exchange Rate Variability

Regular and erratic changes in exchange rate of the domestic currency affect the inflow of FD. Exchange rate devaluations have a double role in explaining variations in FDI. On one hand, the real value of foreign investors' capital increases when the host country's currency is devalued. Otherwise, frequent and continuous declines in the value of host country's currency would decrease FDI inflow, as it creates high uncertainty.

Foreign Debt

Excessive foreign debt is one source of insecurity in macroeconomic environment of underdeveloped countries. This foreign debt is likely to influence adversely the inflow of FDI. Excessive foreign debt may signal imminent fiscal crises and predict the future economic situation in a country.

Fiscal Deficit

The fiscal deficit of a government, whether it is financed through printing additional bank notes or through taxation, decreases the real return on investment. Furthermore, in many developing countries it is apparent that due to excessive government borrowing the financial resources available for the private sector are limited and the interest rate is high. On the other hand, expansionary fiscal policy may be important for the expansion of public sector investments on infrastructure. In general, the overall impact of fiscal deficit as empirically tested by different studies is ambiguous. However, the theory postulates that there is a negative link among fiscal deficit and FDI inflows.

1. Khan, A.Q., Strategy for Foreign Investment Management in 21st century, *op.cit.*, p. 41.

Geographical Proximity

In the current global economic structure, geographical proximity and cultural and linguistic affinities are becoming one important determinant of foreign direct investment. The IFC (International Finance Corporation) and FIAS (Foreign Investment Advisory Service) study as well confirmed that FDI from developed to developing countries are influenced by geographical proximity. For instance, while Japanese firms tend to open subsidiaries in China and newly industrialised Asian countries, the West European firms tend to open their subsidiary in East Europe.

Political Stability

The economic process of a country and in particular the inflow of FDI into a country can be disrupted by unsettled, implicit or explicit, internal or external political disputes and crises. Without stable political conditions, whatever the economic environment may be, a county's effort to create a more hospitable environment for overseas investors cannot be successful. Political instabilities can delay FDI until the storm weathers away or diverts away for good.

Regulatory Framework

While stable, transparent and reliable legal and regulatory frameworks promote both domestic and foreign investment, an inefficient and ineffective legal system is an obstacle to enforce laws and contacts.

However, UNCTAD indicated that an efficient and transparent legal system and in particular LDCs, does not routinely make a country more attractive for FDI.

Privatisation

Privatisation provides a real vehicle for TNCs to invest in a country. It has generated considerable amounts of FDI in many developing economies. Sound privatisation programmes have three main characteristics: political pledge, business orientation and transparency. Large scale privatisation programmes send a signal to foreign investors that a government is taking steps to create a climate favourable to FDI. Therefore, FDI in privatisation of infrastructure enterprises and industrial enterprises would have huge impact on other FDI flows.

Regional Integration

Regional trade agreements can play an important role in terms of enhancing FDI inflows to member countries, through creating access to regional markets. Thus, strong regional integration through trade agreements can influence the investment decisions of TNCs. Regional integration is a determinant of market seeking FDI. The benefits of regional integration depend on a respective country's domestic market size, level of infrastructure growth and accessibility of skilled and cheap labour force compared to other member countries.

Investment Promotion and Incentive Structure

Investment promotion strategy and incentive structure are FDI policy instruments used to attract foreign investors. These include tax reductions and exemptions, special tax allowances, financial incentives such as low interest loans, subsidies as well as grants. Investment guarantees can also be seen as an incentive to attract TNCs. Bilateral and multilateral investment treaties are also an incentive to increase investment, through creating an unsurprising investment climate, thereby improving direct foreign investor's confidence.

However, investment incentives are not substitutes for other determinants like infrastructure and market size. This clearly indicates that the effectiveness of investment incentives is highly determined by the host country's level of development.

As regards investment promotion, "some economists argue that the countries would only get their investment policies right, investors would search out all worthwhile investment opportunities." In reality, not all prospective investors search for opportunities; as a result, investment promotion is vital particularly in least developed countries (LDCs). Image building, investment generation and investors servicing are the three main elements of flourishing investment promotion. Investment promotion agencies can help the investment process if they identify sectors and clusters of activities where comparative advantages exist and where new ones can be developed.

Human Capital

The existence of workforce populations that are educated and trained to work in modern business organisations has been recognised as a significant determinant of FDI flows. The Republic of Ireland, for instance, has been a main receiver of FDI, partly because of the presence of an educated workforce in the country. In this study, human capital is measured by secondary school enrolment as a percentage of the population in the secondary school age category. This indicator is expected to be positively correlated with FDI flows.[1]

Other Determinants of FDI

In addition to the mentioned determinant of FDI, numerous other factors are mentioned as host country determinants of FDI in the literature. Some of them are: Contract Law, Image of the host country, Availability of Investment Fund, Governance, Human Resource Development, Degree of Openness, Urbanisation, Coherent and Stable Macro and Sectoral Policies, Access to customers, Stable social and political environment, Ease of doing business, Reliability and quality of infrastructure and utilities, Capability to hire technical professionals, Ability to hire management staff, Level of corruption, Cost of labour, Crime and safety, Ability to hire skilled labourers, National taxes, Cost of utilities, Roads, Access to raw materials, Availability and quality of university and technical training, Available land with all services

1. Prasanna, N., FDI in India: Issues and Challenges, *op-cit*, p. 98.

in place, Local taxes, Access to suppliers, Labour relations and unionisation, Air service, etc.

2.8 Policies and Reforms of FDI in India: A Review

The policy of Foreign Direct Investment (FDI) provides a mechanism of investment in an enterprise in one nation by another enterprise in another nation. In the trend of globalisation FDI acts as the bridge to fill in the lacuna between saving and investment of resources and thus, plays one of the most essential roles in the growth of both developed countries as well as developing countries. It aims to increase the efficiency of the rate of input as well as output (which includes existing capacity of production along with the new capacity of production that will be generated). In a way, it also helps in saving the domestic constraint and brings in the superior or ideal technology required for the venture from foreign. This policy proposed by the government has led to benefit of the consumers by introducing more efficient, technologically driven and innovative products in the market. Moreover, the income of a nation is also affected as it produces employment opportunities and introduces new skills which aims to extend the new markets which are developed during the process. Such a policy plays a very crucial part in the countries which are developed because it helps in focusing on the new markets which have the potential of high profits, copious labour, scope for products, etc. However, in our country which is a developing one, the liberalisation of such policies is required to welcome more flow of investment from other countries which have bountiful amount of capital resources. Keeping in view of current requirements and benefits of the nation the government of India comes up with new policies from time to time. Government should design the FDI policy in such a way, where FDI inflows can be utilised as means of enhancing domestic production, savings and exports through the equitable distribution among states by providing much freedom to states, so that they can attract FDI inflows at their own level. FDI plays a significant role in enhancing the level of economic growth of the country. This analysis also helps the future aspirants of research scholars to identify the main determinants of FDI at sectorial level. Finally, the study observes that FDI is a significant factor influencing the economic growth in India. It provides a sound base for economic growth and development by enhancing the financial position of the country.

Government of India after independence adopted mixed economy and it was depended on other countries for industrial goods as well as other products. The first industrial policy regulation was not favourable for foreign capital as the major interest and in ownership and effective control was to be normally in Indian hands. However, the policymaker understood the importance of foreign capitals and gave the relaxation to Indian firms to invite the foreign investors working with collaboration. In 1969, the government introduced Monopolistic and Restrictive Trade Practices Act (MRTPA, 1969) to regulate the entry of large industrial houses including foreign companies other than core industries and requiring heavy investment. Further, the Foreign Exchange Regulation Act, 1973 was introduced to regulate the firms which belonging to FERA and the Indian firms become free for the import of foreign technology. On the other hand, in 1975 the government permitted non-resident Indians to invest in the equity capital up to 20 percent of new issues of capital of new industries. Up to 1980, the government concentrated on the NRIs' investment and gave relaxation for them to set up a new industry, bring the imported machinery and they were required to export more than 60 percent of their output. These measures resulted in creation of balance of payment.[1]

1. http://www.mondaq.com/india/

After second oil crises shocked the Indian policy-makers and they partly liberalised the economy for investment. The government giving more emphasis on the moderation of industry with liberalisation imports of capital goods and technology, exposing the Indian industry to foreign competition by gradually liberalising the trade regime. The Export Processing Zones (EPZ) was set up to attract MNCs to set up export-oriented units. Further, the government has liberalised the facilities of bank deposits and investment in equity, preference share and debenture issued by Indian company. The liberalisation facilities were also extended to the overseas companies, partnership firms, trusts, societies other corporate bodies in which at least 60 percent ownership or benefits interests vested to non-resident individuals on India.

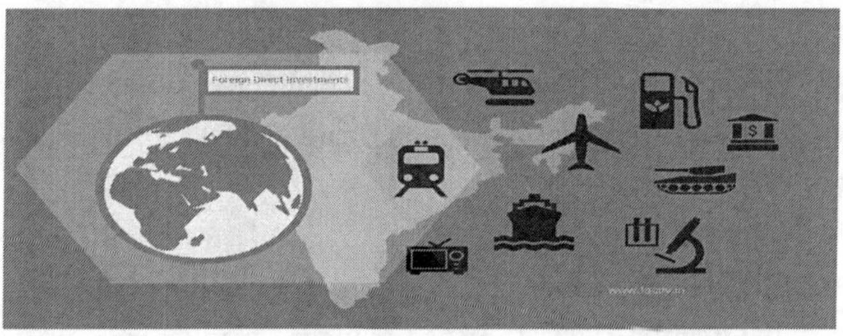

However, the Indian Government adopted the liberalised measures after 1991. The industries reserved for public sectors were reduced and its 51 percent equity reserved for government. The companies engaged with high priority sectors allowed to raise equity capital in abroad. The series of amendment in FERA has been made to attract foreign investment in the country and finally replaced with FEMA in 1999. Further, the foreign investment promotion board established for the purpose of fastest clearances for FDI in some sectors and also automatic route opened for many of the sectors.

2.9 Policy of FDI in India

The policy of Foreign Direct Investment (FDI) provides a mechanism of investment in an enterprise in one nation by another enterprise in another nation.

The consolidated FDI policy which has been in effect from 28th of August 2017 directs towards liberalisation norms and has brought in some key changes which include:[1]

- FDI in LLPs
- Downstream investment intimation
- Cash and carry wholesale form of trading
- FDI in one single brand retailing
- FDI in e-commerce
- Fresh approval for additional FDI
- FDI linked with the performance conditions
- Foreign Investment Promotion Board (FIPB) abolishment
- FDI in start-ups
- Pension sector
- FDI in other financial services
- FDI in infrastructure companies in the securities market
- Liberalisation in:
    - Defence
    - Pharmaceuticals
    - Broadcasting
- Deferred consideration
- Remittance against pre-incorporation expenses.

Under the purview of Make in India, Prime Minister Narendra Modi has introduced the initiative of Start-up India with the ambition to set forth: "Inspiration and strength to the younger generation of India which is talented and intends to do new things for humanity as well as the nation."

This initiative directs towards creating a platform where the promising entrepreneurs achieve the ability to establish themselves

1. Shandilya, T.K., Thakur, A.K., Foreign Direct Investment in India: Problems and Prospects, *op.cit*, p. 46.

smoothly into the market and receive funding support as well as incentives in the fields which deal with law and simplification of the whole business of start-up.

This is for the first time that start-up has been included amongst the policies of FDI. According to the rules, start-up has been given the ability to rise up to complete 100 percent of funds from Foreign Venture Capital Investor (FVCI). Earlier, they could only issue equity or instruments linked to equity or debt instruments to FVCI against the receipt of foreign payment but now, a start-up can issue convertible notes to the foreign investors. By this, the start-up company can issue the corroboration receipt of money which was initially taken as debt as now to an asset which is repayable at the recourse of the holder or allows conversion into equity shares of the start-up company, within the time limit of five years which starts on the date of the issue of the convertible note. So basically, the balance of loan taken can automatically be converted to such number of equity shares at that particular moment which is usually after the valuation of a funding round that takes place later on.[1] This entire task is aimed at providing the investors a friendly environment who is foreign contenders and in turn it is expected to attract more FDI which will consequently provide more job opportunities and boost our economic development. The policy has also intended to simplify the denotation of 'venture capital funds' simply as the funds which are registered under the Securities and Exchange Board of India or SEBI (Venture Capital Funds) Regulations 1996. Earlier the foreign contenders had to maintain a 51 percent stake in the respective company where they invest but now, start-ups have been permitted to take forward losses till the extent where the promoters have the capacity to retain their holding in the venture or company.

2.10 Objective of the Policy

The main aim of the consolidated policy is to ensure more ease at doing business in India and to provide with a friendly atmosphere to the foreign investor in order to pull more FDI in the country. However, the policy specifically mentions two objectives:

---

1. Kumar, Nagesh, Globalisation and the Quality of FDI, Oxford University Press, New Delhi, 2015, p. 76.

Upgrade and attract foreign direct investment so as to supplement domestic capital, skills and technology to direct acceleration towards the wholesome economic growth of the country. The document also states the difference between this from portfolio investment which is dependent upon – lasting interest (in form of a resident) than merely as an investor in the venture.

To issue a regular circular which talks about the consolidated policies of FDI in form of press releases/notes, regulations, clarifications, etc. so as to maintain transparency and predictability and so, it becomes easier for the foreign company to comprehend the rules.[1]

2.11 Review of Policy for Foreign Investment

India has introduced many policy reforms to attract FDI. Restrictive investment regimes have been liberalised. In addition, various types of incentives are being offered to attract foreign direct investment. Greater attention is being paid to make the macro-economic environment more conducive to foreign investors. Provision of infrastructure and other support services are being targeted, financial sector reforms are being undertaken to facilitate financial flows in various forms.

Changes in policy frameworks in India dealing with FDI inflows could be studied in four phases viz.

(i) "Cautions Welcome Policy" from independence to the emergence of crisis in the late sixties (1948-66).

(ii) "Selective and Restrictive Policy" from 1967 till the second oil crises in 1979.

(iii) "Partial Liberalisation Policy" from 1980 to 1990 with progressive attenuation of regulations; and

(iv) "Liberalisation and open door policy" since 1991 onwards signifying liberal investment environment.

Each policy swing in some sense reflects the government's particular type of responses to the foreign exchange crisis in the respective periods, though many factors may have been at work causing the policy swings. The point of emphasis is that, the undercurrent of balance of payments crisis plays important role in shaping the country's attitude and policy towards foreign investments.

1. *ibid.*

To illustrate, the initial caution on foreign investment began to lose its rigidity with the onset of foreign exchange crisis of 1957-58 and the government began to relax its stance towards foreign direct investment. Thus, there was an increase in the number of foreign collaboration approvals.

As the foreign exchange situation assumed drastic proportions in the late sixties and there were increased outflows on account of foreign collaborations, the government began to take a restrictive stance on foreign collaboration. In particular, the enactment of Foreign Exchange Regulation Act (FERA), 1973 became the key to guiding and controlling FDI inflows. Thus, came into being the phase of light regulation and selective policy in the seventies. A highly restrictive and selective policy implemented by an administrative system based on discretionary power prevailed through the seventies.[1]

In the wake of the second oils crisis and India's failure to boost its manufactured exports, the foreign exchange position began to deteriorate by the early eighties. The government adopted a multi-pronged strategy for promotion of exports, including encouraging TNCs to undertake export-oriented manufacturing. The eighties thus, witnessed selective efforts to attract FDI especially, in high technology areas and exports. Many restrictions on large houses and FERA companies were removed signalling a less restrictive policy environment for private investment including foreign investment. The eighties were in a way, the forerunners of the liberalisation policy of the nineties.

As the economy slipped into serious external crisis at the beginning of the nineties, the response of the government was to go in for comprehensive macro-economic and structural adjustment with economic reforms and globalisation as the key elements, since July 1991. This phase in India, foreign collaboration policy is characterised by transparency and openness and is intended to increase foreign direct investment. The degree of openness is seen in terms of the entire policy on (i) sectors open to FDI, (ii) level of foreign equity participation, (iii) transparency in approval procedures.

---

1. Kumar, Nagesh, Globalisation and the Quality of FDI, *op.cit*, p. 77.

2.12 FDI Policy Reform

FDI is a major driver of economic growth and a source of non-debt finance for the economic development of the country. Government has put in place an investor friendly policy on FDI, under which FDI up to 100 percent is permitted on the automatic route in most sectors/ activities. FDI policy provisions have been progressively liberalised across various sectors in recent years to make India an attractive investment destination. Some of the sectors include Defence, Construction Development, Trading, Pharmaceuticals, Power Exchanges, Insurance, Pension, Other Financial Services, Asset reconstruction Companies, Broadcasting and Civil Aviation.

These reforms have contributed to India attracting record FDI inflows in the last 5 years. Total FDI into India from 2014-15 to 2018-19 has been US $ 286 billion as compared to US $ 189 billion in the 5-year period prior to that (2009-10 to 2013-14). In fact, total FDI in 2018-19 i.e. US $ 64.37 billion (provisional figure) is the highest ever FDI received for any financial year.[1]

Global FDI inflows have been facing headwinds for the last few years. As per UNCTAD's World Investment Report 2019, global foreign direct investment (FDI) flows slid by 13 percent in 2018, to US $1.3 trillion from US $1.5 trillion the previous year - the third consecutive annual decline. Despite the dim global picture, India continues to remain a preferred and attractive destination for global FDI flows. However, it is felt that the country has the potential to attract far more foreign investment which can be achieved inter-alia by further liberalising and simplifying the FDI policy regime.

In Union Budget 2019-20, Finance Minister proposed to further consolidate the gains under FDI in order to make India a more

1. https://pib.gov.in

attractive FDI destination. Accordingly, the Government has decided to introduce a number of amendments in the FDI Policy. Details of these changes are given in the following paragraphs.

Coal Mining

As per the present FDI policy, 100 percent FDI under automatic route is allowed for coal and lignite mining for captive consumption by power projects, iron and steel and cement units and other eligible activities permitted under and subject to applicable laws and regulations. Further, 100 percent FDI under automatic route is also permitted for setting up coal processing plants like washeries, subject to the condition that the company shall not do coal mining and shall not sell washed coal or sized coal from its coal processing plants in the open market and shall supply the washed or sized coal to those parties who are supplying raw coal to coal processing plants for washing or sizing.

It has been decided to permit 100 percent FDI under automatic route for sale of coal, for coal mining activities including associated processing infrastructure subject to provisions of Coal Mines (special provisions) Act, 2015 and the Mines and Minerals (development and regulation) Act, 1957 as amended from time to time, and other relevant acts on the subject. "Associated Processing Infrastructure" would include coal washery, crushing, coal handling, and separation (magnetic and non-magnetic).[1]

1. https://pib.gov.in

Contract Manufacturing

- The extant FDI policy provides for 100 percent FDI under automatic route in manufacturing sector. There is no specific provision for Contract Manufacturing in the Policy. In order to provide clarity on contract manufacturing, it has been decided to allow 100 percent FDI under automatic route in contract manufacturing in India as well.
- Subject to the provisions of the FDI policy, foreign investment in 'manufacturing' sector is under automatic route. Manufacturing activities may be conducted either by the investee entity or through contract manufacturing in India under a legally tenable contract, whether on Principal to Principal or Principal to Agent basis.

Single Brand Retail Trading (SBRT)

(i) The extant FDI Policy provides that 30 percent of value of goods has to be procured from India if SBRT entity has FDI more than 51 percent. Further, as regards local sourcing requirement, the same can be met as an average during the first 5 years, and thereafter annually towards its India operations. With a view to provide greater flexibility and ease of operations to SBRT entities, it has been decided that all procurements made from India by the SBRT entity for that single brand shall be counted towards local sourcing, irrespective of whether the goods procured are sold in India or exported. Further, the current cap of considering exports for 5 years only is proposed to be removed, to give an impetus to exports.

(ii) The extant Policy provides that as regards local sourcing requirement, incremental sourcing for global operations by the non-resident entities undertaking single brand retail trading, either directly or through their group companies, will also be counted towards local sourcing requirement for the first 5 years. However, prevalent business models involve not only sourcing from India for global operations by the entity or its group companies, but also through an unrelated third Party, done at the behest of the entity undertaking single brand retail trading or its group companies. In order to cover such business practices, it has been decided that 'sourcing of goods from India for global operations' can be done directly by the entity undertaking SBRT or its group companies (resident or non-resident}, or indirectly by them through a third party under a legally tenable agreement.

(iii) The extant policy provides that only that part of the global sourcing shall be counted towards local sourcing requirement which is over and above the previous year's value. Such requirement of year-on-year incremental increase in exports induces aberrations in the system as companies with lower exports in a base year or any of the subsequent years can meet the current requirements, while a company with consistently high exports gets unduly discriminated against. It has been now decided that entire sourcing from India for global operations shall be considered towards local sourcing requirement. (And no incremental value)

(iv) The present policy requires that SBRT entities have to operate through brick-and-mortar stores before starting retail trading of that brand through e-commerce. This creates an artificial restriction and is out of sync with current market practices. It has therefore been decided that retail trading through online trade can also be undertaken prior to opening of brick-and-mortar stores, subject to the condition that the entity opens brick-and-mortar stores within 2 years from date of start of online retail. Online sales will lead to creation of jobs in logistics, digital payments, customer care, training and product skilling.

Digital Media

The extant FDI policy provides for 49 percent FDI under approval route in Up-linking of 'News & Current Affairs' TV Channels. It has been decided to permit 26 percent FDI under government route for uploading/ streaming of News and Current Affairs through Digital Media, on the lines of print media.[1]

2.13 Major Impact and Benefits from FDI Policy Reform

(i) The changes in FDI policy will result in making India a more

1. https://pib.gov.in

attractive FDI destination, leading to benefits of increased investments, employment and growth.

(ii) In the coal sector, for sale of coal, 100 percent FDI under automatic route for coal mining, activities including associated processing infrastructure will attract international players to create an efficient and competitive coal market.

(iii) Further, manufacturing through contract contributes equally to the objective of Make in India. FDI now being permitted under automatic route in contract manufacturing will be a big boost to Manufacturing sector in India.

(iv) Easing local sourcing norms for FDI in Single Brand Retail Trading (SBRT) was announced in Union Budget Speech of Finance Minister. This will lead to greater flexibility and ease of operations for SBRT entities, besides creating a level playing field for companies with higher exports in a base year. In addition, permitting online sales prior to opening of brick-and-mortar stores brings policy in sync with current market practices. Online sales will also lead to creation of jobs in logistics, digital payments, customer care, training and product skilling.

(v) The above amendments to the FDI Policy are meant to liberalise and simplify the FDI policy to provide ease of doing business in the country, leading to larger FDI inflows and thereby contributing to growth of investment, income and employment.

2.14 Modes of FDI in India

Equity Inflow in FDI

Foreign Direct Investment is a significant source of funding for companies that fail to amass capital that is readily available. FDI is an investment made by an individual or a firm that is placed outside the country where the investment is being made.

As per the Organisation for Economic Corporation and Development (OECD), an investment crossing the threshold of 10 percent is considered as an overseas investment. The Foreign Exchange Management Act, 2000, which is governed by the Reserve Bank of India (RBI), regulates the foreign direct investment policy in India.

Apart from the outlined 11 sectors or activities where Government approval is obligatory, applications in the "grey area" where there is a doubt over which Ministry should the application fall under, the Department of Industrial Policy and Promotion (DIPP) is responsible for identifying who would be the concerned authority.

To eliminate problems and for a smooth functioning of cases, monthly reviews by the responsible Ministries or Authorities and quarterly review meetings that are co-chaired by the Secretary, Department of Economic Affairs and Secretary, DIPP are also proposed to be carried out to discuss pendency of proposals with the Government.

Various categories of overseas investors holding stakes in Indian business entities (company, partnership firms, proprietary concerns, LLPs), are subject to rules and sectoral caps on ownerships. The categories of foreign investors include Foreign Portfolio Investors, Foreign Institutional Investors, Foreign Venture Capital Investor, and Non-Resident Indians.

Foreign Portfolio Investors (FPI's) and Foreign Institutional Investors (FII's) are permitted to invest and trade in equity securities with a maximum total investment of 24 percent of the issued and paid-up capital of a company. This limit can be raised up to the prescribed sectoral cap of that particular industry by passing a special resolution to the effect.

Every non-resident entity is permitted to invest in India under the two approval routes: Automatic route and Government approval route, except in prohibited sectors. However, entities belonging to Bangladesh and Pakistan can only invest via the government route of approval.

Foreign Direct Investment (FDI) equity inflows rose 28 percent in the first quarter of 2019-20 to $16.3 billion from $12.7 billion in the year-ago period, as showed by official data. Singapore continued to be the top source of FDI at $5.3 billion, followed by Mauritius ($4.6 billion).[1]

Among sectors, telecommunications garnered the maximum FDI at $4.2 billion, followed by services sector ($2.8 billion). The services include financial, banking, insurance, non-financial/business, outsourcing, research and development, courier, technology testing and analysis.

India opened its doors further to FDI, diluting the stringent condition of local sourcing for single-brand retail, in continuation of measures aimed at reviving growth. It also allowed 100 percent FDI in commercial coal mining as well as in contract manufacturing through the automatic route, hoping to attract global vendors looking to diversify supply chains as the US and China battle it out in a tariff war.

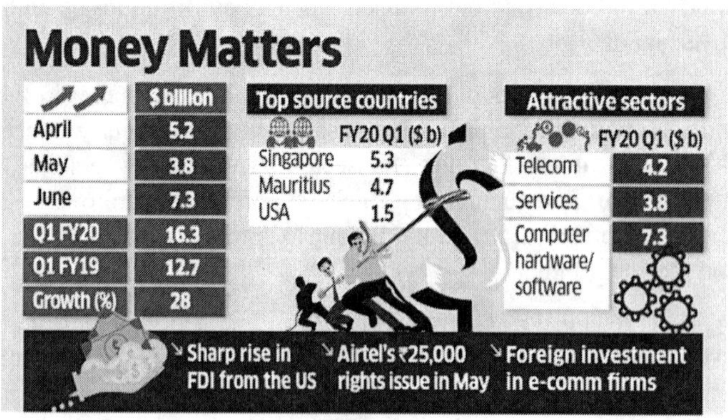

2.15 New India: The Trendsetter

FDI in India has followed a positive trend since the launch of Make in India. FDI inflow from April 2014 to March 2019 ($286 Bn) is 46.94 percent (approx.) of the overall FDI received in the country since April 2000 ($592.08 Bn). For the 1st time, India crossed the $60 Bn mark in FY 2017 - 18 with $55.55 Bn in FDI, due to the investment-friendly policies and opening of FDI allowance in various sectors.

1. https://economictimes.indiatimes.com/

FDI Equity Inflows (US$ Billions)

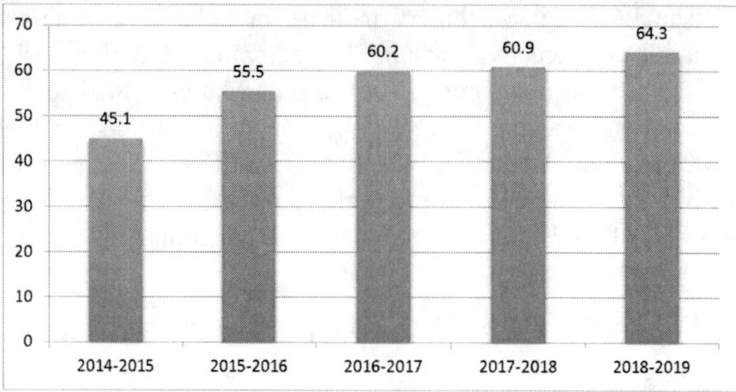

2.16 FDI Equity Inflows- Automobile Industry

The Automobile industry in India witnessed a growth of 25.54 percent during 2017-18 to 2018-19. FDI equity inflows increased substantially to $2.09 Bn during 2017-18. The 2018-19 have seen FDI inflows of $1.598 Bn as against $2.09 Bn in the whole of 2017-18.[1]

FDI Equity Inflows- Automobile Industry

US $ Billion

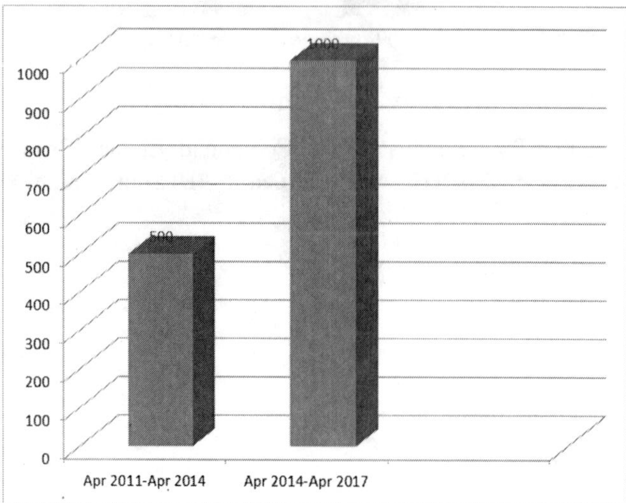

1. https://economictimes.indiatimes.com/

2.17 Electrical Machinery: Sparking a Revolution

The Electrical Machinery industry in India was witness to an incredible 242 percent growth in FDI equity inflows during April 2014 - March 2017 as compared to April 2011 - March 2014. The industry has experienced a growth of 99.81 percent during 2017-18 to 2018-19. The Compound Annual Growth Rate (CAGR) of 15.02 percent was recorded in FDI equity inflows during April 2014 – March 2019. The total FDI of $8.03 Bn attracted the Electrical equipment industry till March 2019.

FDI Equity Inflows- Electrical Equipment Industry[1]

US $ Million

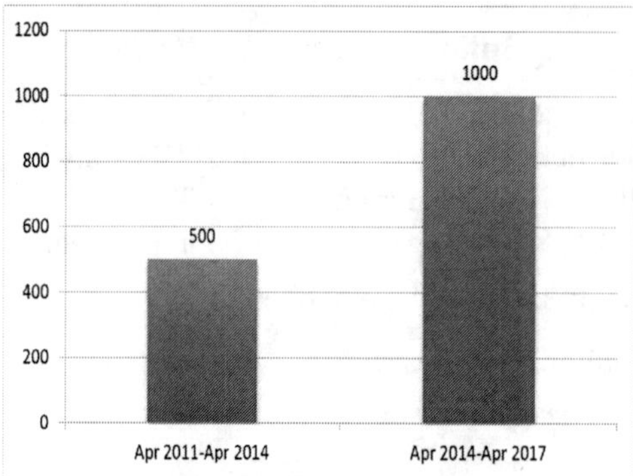

2.18 Textiles: Weaving a New Success Story

In the Textile industry, the Compound Annual Growth Rate (CAGR) of 5.02 percent was recorded in FDI equity inflows during April 2014 – March 2019.

FDI Equity Inflows- Textile Industry

US $ Million

1. *Ibid.*

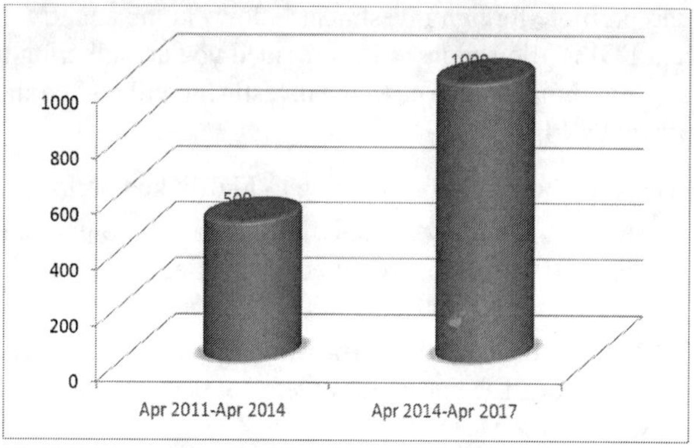

The total FDI in the industry until March 2019 is $3.12 Bn.

2.19 FDI in Partnership Firm/Sole Proprietary Concern

NRIs or Person of Indian Origin (PIO) resident outside India are allowed to contribute to the capital of a partnership firm or sole proprietary concern without prior approval, provided:

1. The contribution is on non-repatriation basis.
2. Investment is done as an inward remittance, or out of NRE/ FCNR (B)/NRO account maintained with AD Category-1 Bank.
3. The Indian firm or proprietary concern should not be engaged in agricultural, print media or real estate business.

In the following cases, investors may apply for prior permission of RBI and Government of India, provided the last two conditions mentioned above are adhered to:

1. Where investment is preferred to be repatriable by NRIs/PIO.
2. For investors other than NRIs/PIO.

The decision for the same will be taken by RBI and Government of India on case-by-case basis.

2.20 FDI in Limited Liability Partnership[1]

FDI in LLPs was liberalised significantly in 2015 with the

1. https://taxguru.in/rbi/foreign-direct-investment-limited-liability-partnerships

objective to promote foreign investment inflows in the country. Up to 100 percent FDI is allowed in LLPs, provided you are adhering to the specific sectoral limits. In that case, the investment will not require any prior approval by FIPB.

1. There are no conditions relating to FDI-linked performance.
2. Foreign companies or individuals can be appointed as Designated Partner as required under Section 7 of Limited Liability Partnership Act, 2008.
3. LLPs can make further downstream investment in another company or LLP. Earlier they were not permitted to make any downstream investments.
4. Repatriation of capital is permissible with adherence of appropriate pricing guidelines and reporting requirements.
5. All investments should comply with relevant provisions of LLP Act, 2008.
6. LLP's can avail External Commercial Borrowings (ECBs).
7. FPIs/FVCI's can contribute to the capital of LLPs in India.
8. In case of companies with FDI, converting into LLP can be done under the automatic route if the investment in sector concerned is within corresponding sectoral limit for automatic investment route.

2.21 FDI in Private Limited Company

A Foreign business entity can enter India via a number of alternatives, subject to general conditions mentioned in FDI Policy:

1. As an Indian Company
   (a) By setting up a wholly owned subsidiary
   (b) Joint Venture with an Indian entity/person
2. Operate as a foreign company and be registered with the Registrar of Companies, MCA.
   (a) Opening up Liaison office - This type of office is only allowed to collect market information and liaison with the foreign company. They are not allowed to earn income from any activities.

(b) Branch Offices - The scope of activities of BOs is much larger as compared to Liaison Offices. BOs are allowed to generate revenue by various alternatives, such as

(i) Providing professional services

(ii) Providing technical support for products imported / assembled / manufactured by the parent/holding company.

(c) Project Offices - Set up to execute specific projects, project offices are allowed in India if:

(i) The foreign entity has secured a contract in India, which will be funded via inward remittance by either a bilateral or multilateral financing agency.

(ii) Loan has been sanctioned by a public financial institution or bank to the Indian company contracting the project. If the above conditions are not met, the foreign investor/entity will have to make an application with RBI via its AD bank.

Partnership firms and sole proprietary concerns set up abroad are not allowed to establish Branch or liaison offices in India. Branch/ Liaison/Project Offices have to open non-interest bearing current accounts in RBI through AD Banks. Application for setting up offices in India has to be made in Form FNC-1 to RBI along with :

1. Certificate of Incorporation or Memorandum & Articles of Association attested by Indian Embassy or Notary Public in their home country.
2. Latest Audited Balance Sheet. This form has to be submitted to the designated AD bank for further submission to the relevant department of Reserve Bank of India (Foreign Investment Division), Mumbai.

NRI's are also allowed to contribute to capital of Indian companies by investing in shares on Recognised Stock Exchanges under Portfolio Investment Route. The investment can be repatriable or non-repatriable, but the maximum limit of investment is 10 percent of paid-up capital of the relevant company. This limit can be raised up to the 24 percent by passing a special resolution to the effect. Investment is done as an inward remittance, or out of NRE/FCNR (B)/

NRO account maintained with AD Category-1 Bank. A report of such investments has to be filed with RBI by AD Bank.[1]

2.22 FDI in Small Scale Industries

Except for the prohibited sectors, foreign investors are allowed to invest in small-scale industrial unit operating in various sectors. The investment is limited to 24 percent of paid-up capital of an SSI unit. To issue more than 24 percent to foreign investors, SSI units have to comply with the following conditions:

1. Give up its status as SSI, i.e. exceeding prescribed limits of investment in plant and machinery according to Micro, Small and Medium Enterprises Development Act, 2006.
2. Not engage in manufacture of reserved items.
3. Comply with relevant sectoral caps.

Approval Process

FDI proposals are processed following a standard operating plan devised by DIPP. The process includes:

1. Submission of proposal and uploading documents (mentioned below) on Foreign Investment Facilitation Portal.
2. Department of Industrial Policy and Promotion (DIPP) assign the case to the concerned Ministry within 2 working days.
   (a) Submission of physical copies to concerned department is not required in case of digitally signed documents.
   (b) For applications not digitally signed, online communication to applicant will be made to submit one

1. https://taxguru.in/rbi/foreign-direct-investment-limited-liability-partnerships

signed physical copy of the proposal to the Competent Authority. Applicants are required to submit required documents within 5 days of such intimation.

3. The proposal is circulated online within 2 days to Reserve Bank of India for review from FEMA perspective. All proposals are shared with Ministry of External Affairs (MEA) and Department of Revenue (DOR) for record. Any advice/ comments from above mentioned departments are directly shared with concerned Administrative Ministry/Department assigned to decide on the proposal.
4. Proposals are scrutinised within 1 week and additional information/ clarifications, if required, are asked for.
5. On getting all required information, the Competent Authority is required to give out its decision in next two weeks. Approval/rejection letters are sent online to the applicant, consulted Ministries/Departments and DIPP. Where total foreign equity inflow is more than Rs 5000 crore, the Competent Authority is required to place the same to Cabinet Committee on Economic Affairs for consideration within timelines.

Following documents are required to be uploaded along with the proposal. Please note, this list is not an exhaustive list - other documents may be required based on specific cases.

1. From both Investee and Investor Companies/Entities:
   (a) Certificate of Incorporation
   (b) Memorandum of Association (MOA)
   (c) Board Resolution
   (d) Audited Financial Statement of Last Financial Year
   (e) Article of Association
2. List of Names, addresses and identification proof of all foreign collaborators of the Investor Company/Entity.
3. Pre- and Post-investment shareholding pattern of the Investee Company.
4. An Affidavit stating that all information provided in hard copy and online is the same and correct.

5. In case of existing ventures, copy of joint venture agreement/ shareholders' agreement/ technology transfer/trademark/ brand assignment agreement (as applicable).
6. Copy of Downstream Intimation.
7. Copy of relevant past FIPB/SIA/RBI approvals, connected with the current proposal.
8. Relevant Foreign Inward Remittance Certificate (FIRC) in case investment has already flowed in.
9. High Court order in case of scheme of arrangement.
10. Valuation certificate as approved by a certified Chartered Accountant.

2.23 Soft Loan in India

With the sole motive of promoting external finance and foreign trade, Foreign Exchange Management Act, 1999 and Foreign Exchange Regulations, 2000 were enforced to control the negative impact of the liberalisation. It prolonged up to outlining the confines of the foreign exchange and clarifying the miscellaneous role of the apex bank of India in it. It also materialised the conception of lending by non-resident Indians or Foreigners to Indian citizens. The global financial markets are a very beneficial source of debt finance, particularly for businesses in India, owing to the Low-interest rates @ *2.75 percent (per annum) fix for the complete tenure* prevailing globally when compared to the Indian financial markets.

Financial markets outside are considered to be as the most lucrative alternative of borrowing/financing attributable to the cheaper interest rates as equated to the Indian financial markets. Reserve Bank of India ("RBI") has been a bit conventional with the assistance of the tools of law that is Foreign Exchange Management Act, 2000 (FEMA) and Foreign Exchange Regulations, 2000. Recently, in regards to the aspect of overseas borrowing, be it commercial or private, rules of the RBI are long debated. The laws have made external borrowings to be wholly legal and are soft loan facilitators but there have been so much of compliances and requirements so as to materialise those transactions.

2.24. Top Five Countries that are making big in India

United States

India and America have had strong business relations over the many years and several American companies are fulfilling the indispensable needs of the Indian market. From searching online through Google to drinking Coca Cola, or using the latest-phones by Apple, the Indian consumer is, by and large, a dedicated follower of American companies. American companies are preparing to set up an alternative to China by investing in India. Some renowned American companies are Amazon, Citibank, Coca-Cola, Ford India, Google, American Express, PepsiCo, Hewlett Packard, IBM, JP Morgan Chase, Adobe Systems Incorporated, Apple Inc., Microsoft Corporation, Cognizant, Oracle.

Japan

Holding the baton in automobiles and electronics sector, Japanese companies were amongst the 1st ones to enter India. An incredible 1,305 Japanese companies are registered in India. Japan and India share strong ties, as India seeks Japanese expertise in sectors such as infrastructure, energy and manufacturing. India-Japan Cooperation Act East Forum, established in 2017 has been a driving force to advance India-Japan cooperation. Japanese companies have a huge opportunity in India and since years Japan is dominating the Indian market through brands like Suzuki, Honda, Sony and Panasonic etc. Japan proposes to triple infrastructure orders to about US$300 bn by 2020. A few big Japanese companies are Hitachi, Mitsubishi, Toshiba, Canon, Toyota, Yamaha, Panasonic, Honda, Sony, Suzuki.

United Arab Emirates

India has strong bilateral ties in the Middle East, especially with the United Arab Emirates. Cumulative foreign direct investment (FDI) equity flows from UAE into India reached US$898 Mn in 2018-2019. In a recent development, Abu Dhabi Investment Authority (ADIA) announced its decision to invest US$ 1 bn in the National Investment & Infrastructure Fund, India's attempt to raise equity funds for the infrastructure sector. The United Arab Emirates (UAE) intends to use India as a food security base and plans to invest in its agriculture sector. More specifically, the UAE plans to increase its imports of Indian food grains and horticulture products. UAE has already launched talks with various state governments for this purpose. Some key companies functioning in India include Emaar, DP World, Abu Dhabi's National Petroleum Construction Company, Abu Dhabi National Energy Company, Drake and Scull International.

Germany

Indo-German trade story dates back to the 16th century when the German companies started manufacturing in India. Some notable names are Krupp AG & Demag, who set-up the Rourkela Steel plant, while, Bosch set-up its 1st unit to make spark plugs in 1953, followed by Siemens, Bayer, Daimler-Benz, etc. India has more than 1,600 German companies and over 600 Indo-German joint ventures in operation which include big names like, BMW, Volkswagen, SAP, Siemens AG, and Merck. FDI from Germany has increased more than 41% from 2013-14 and has reached a cumulative amount of US$ 4.50 bn till 2017-18. Government of India is seeking investments from Germanise companies in areas including smart cities and construction of airports to increase economic cooperation between themselves.[1]

France

The year 2018 has marked the 20th anniversary of the strategic partnership between India and France. The key deliverables are:

- Increase trade in goods to US$ 16.7 Bn by 2022. To encourage SMEs and mid-cap companies, to play a growing role in the economic and commercial exchanges between the two countries.

1. http://www.makeinindia.com/

- Promote Make-in-India initiative for Indian and French defence enterprises to enter into arrangements for co-development and co-production of defence equipment in India. Scorpene submarine; Defence Research and Development Organisation (DRDO) and SAFRAN discussions; Rafale are some prospects being aggressively considered.
- The countries have witnessed exemplary cooperation programme in the Smart Cities of Chandigarh, Nagpur, and Puducherry. The signing of the loan agreement between the Agence Francaise de Developpement (AFD) and the Government of India for US$ 112 Mn in support of the Smart Cities Mission is another achievement.
- France has committed US$ 785 Mn to the International Solar Alliance (ISA), a treaty-based organisation, launched by Indian Prime Minister in 2015, aims to promote solar energy in 121 countries.

2.25 Sectors in which FDI is allowed in India

Government of India has taken various effective steps to simplify the Foreign Direct Investment policy. The Foreign Direct Investment Policy (FDI Policy) of the Government of India prescribes the foreign investment cap in specified industrial sectors. But in the recent times many activities have been transferred to unrestricted sectors in which 100 percent Foreign Direct investment is permitted. Broadly, the industrial sectors are categorised as:

- Restricted
- Prohibited
- Unrestricted Sectors (Up to 100 percent foreign ownership)

All the sectors other than those mentioned below subject to terms and conditions in the FDI policy come under unrestricted sectors for example:

- Mining (except Mining and mineral separation of titanium bearing minerals and ores, its value addition and integrated activities)
- Manufacturing related commercial activities
- Information Technology related activities

- E-commerce (permitted in marketplace model and not the inventory-based model. Also, it applies only to Business- to-Business (B2B) e-commerce and not business to consumer e-commerce).[1]

Sector	FDI Limit	Entry Route & Remarks
Agriculture & Animal Husbandry • Floriculture, Horticulture, Apiculture and Cultivation of Vegetables and Mushrooms under controlled conditions • Development and Production of seeds and planting material • Animal Husbandry (including breeding of dogs), Pisciculture, Aquaculture • Services related to agro and allied sectors	**100%**	**Automatic**
Plantation Sector • Tea sector including tea plantations • Coffee plantations • Rubber plantations • Cardamom plantations • Palm oil tree plantations • Olive oil tree plantations	**100%**	**Automatic**
Mining Mining and Exploration of metal and non-metal ores including diamond, gold, silver and precious ores but excluding titanium bearing minerals and its ores	**100%**	**Automatic**
Mining (Coal & Lignite)	**100%**	**Automatic**
Mining Mining and mineral separation of titanium bearing minerals and ores, its value addition and integrated activities	**100%**	**Government**
Petroleum & Natural Gas Exploration activities of oil and natural gas fields, infrastructure related to marketing of petroleum products and natural gas, marketing of natural gas and petroleum products etc	**100%**	**Automatic**
Petroleum & Natural Gas Petroleum refining by the Public Sector Undertakings (PSU), without any disinvestment or dilution of domestic equity in the existing PSUs.	**49%**	**Automatic**
Defence Manufacturing	**100%**	**Automatic up to 49%** **Above 49% under Government route** in cases resulting in access to modern technology in the country

1. https://factly.in/sectors-fdi-allowed-india/

Sector	FDI Limit	Entry Route & Remarks
Broadcasting • Teleports (setting up of up-linking HUBs/Teleports) • Direct to Home (DTH) • Cable Networks (Multi System operators (MSOs)) operating at National or State or District level and undertaking upgradation of networks towards digitalisation and addressability • Mobile TV • Head end-in-the Sky Broadcasting Service (HITS)	**100%**	**Automatic**
Broadcasting Cable Networks (Other MSOs not undertaking up gradation of networks towards digitalisation and addressability and Local Cable Operators (LCOs))	**100%**	**Automatic**
Broadcasting Content Services • Terrestrial Broadcasting FM (FM Radio) • Up-linking of 'News & Current Affairs' TV Channels	**49%**	**Government**
Up-linking of Non-'News & Current Affairs' TV Channels/ Down-linking of TV Channels	**100%**	**Automatic**
Print Media • Publishing of newspaper and periodicals dealing with news and current affairs • Publication of Indian editions of foreign magazines dealing with news and current affairs	**26%**	**Government**
Publishing/printing of scientific and technical magazines/ specialty journals/ periodicals, subject to compliance with the legal framework as applicable and guidelines issued in this regard from time to time by Ministry of Information and Broadcasting.	**100%**	**Government**
Publication of facsimile edition of foreign newspapers	**100%**	**Government**
Civil Aviation – Airports Green Field Projects & Existing Projects	**100%**	**Automatic**
Civil Aviation – Air Transport Services • Scheduled Air Transport Service/ Domestic Scheduled Passenger Airline • Regional Air Transport Service (Foreign Airlines are barred from Investing in Air India)	**100%**	**Automatic up to 49%** **Above 49% under Government route** **100% Automatic for NRIs**
Civil Aviation • Non-Scheduled Air Transport Service • Helicopter services/seaplane services requiring DGCA approval • Ground Handling Services subject to sectoral regulations and security clearance • Maintenance and Repair organisations; flying training institutes; and technical training institutions	**100%**	**Automatic**
Construction Development: Townships, Housing, Built-up Infrastructure	**100%**	**Automatic**
Industrial Parks (new & existing)	**100%**	**Automatic**

Sector	FDI Limit	Entry Route & Remarks
Satellites-establishment and operation, subject to the sectoral guidelines of Department of Space/ISRO	**100%**	**Government**
Private Security Agencies	**74%**	**Automatic up to 49% Above 49% & up to 74% under Government route**
Telecom Services	**100%**	**Automatic up to 49% Above 49% under Government route**
Cash & Carry Wholesale Trading	**100%**	**Automatic**
E-commerce activities (e-commerce entities would engage only in Business to Business (B2B) e-commerce and not in Business to Consumer (B2C) e-commerce.)	**100%**	**Automatic**
Single Brand retail trading Local sourcing norms will be relaxed up to three years and a relaxed sourcing regime for another five years for entities undertaking Single Brand Retail Trading of products having 'state-of-art' and 'cutting edge' technology.	**100%**	**Automatic up to 49% Above 49% under Government route**
Multi Brand Retail Trading	**51%**	**Government**
Duty Free Shops	**100%**	**Automatic**
Railway Infrastructure Construction, operation and maintenance of the following • Suburban corridor projects through PPP • High speed train projects • Dedicated freight lines • Rolling stock including train sets, and locomotives/ coaches manufacturing and maintenance facilities • Railway Electrification • Signalling systems • Freight terminals • Passenger terminals • Infrastructure in industrial park pertaining to railway line/sidings including electrified railway lines and connectivity to main railway line • Mass Rapid Transport Systems.	**100%**	**Automatic**
Asset Reconstruction Companies	**100%**	**Automatic**
Banking- Private Sector	**74%**	**Automatic up to 49% Above 49% & up to 74% under Government route**
Banking- Public Sector	**20%**	**Government**
Credit Information Companies (CIC)	**100%**	**Automatic**
Infrastructure Company in the Securities Market	**49%**	**Automatic**

Sector	FDI Limit	Entry Route & Remarks
Insurance • Insurance Company • Insurance Brokers • Third Party Administrators • Surveyors and Loss Assessors • Other Insurance Intermediaries	**49%**	**Automatic**
Pension Sector	**49%**	**Automatic**
Power Exchanges	**49%**	**Automatic**
White Label ATM Operations	**100%**	**Automatic**
Financial services activities regulated by RBI, SEBI, IRDA or any other regulator	**100%**	**Automatic**
Pharmaceuticals (Green Field)	**100%**	**Automatic**
Pharmaceuticals (Brown Field)	**100%**	**Automatic up to 74% Above 74% under Government route**
Food products manufactured or produced in India Trading, including through e-commerce, in respect of food products manufactured or produced in India.	**100%**	**Government**

Source: https://factly.in/sectors-fdi-allowed-india/

2.26 Prohibited Sectors: FDI is prohibited in

(i) Lottery Business including Government/private lottery, online lotteries, etc.

(ii) Gambling and Betting including casinos etc.

(iii) Chit funds

(iv) Nidhi company

(v) Trading in Transferable Development Rights (TDRs)

(vi) Real Estate Business or Construction of Farm Houses 'Real estate business' shall not include development of townships, construction of residential /commercial premises, roads or bridges and Real Estate Investment Trusts (REITs) registered and regulated under the SEBI (REITs) Regulations 2014.

(vii) Manufacturing of cigars, cheroots, cigarillos and cigarettes, of tobacco or of tobacco substitutes.

(viii) Activities/sectors not open to private sector investment e.g. (I) Atomic Energy and (II) Railway operations (other than permitted activities.

(ix) Foreign technology collaboration in any form including licensing for franchise, trademark, brand name, management contract is also prohibited for Lottery Business and Gambling and Betting activities.

2.27 Competent Authority for examining FDI proposals from countries of concern

As per the existing procedures, FDI applications involving investments from Countries of Concern, requiring security clearance as per the extant FEMA 20, FDI Policy and security guidelines, amended from time to time, are to be processed by the Ministry of Home Affairs (MHA) for investments falling under automatic route sectors/activities, while cases pertaining to government approval route sectors/ activities requiring security clearance are to be processed by the respective Administrative Ministries/Departments, as the case may be. It has now been decided that for investments in automatic route sectors, requiring approval only on the matter of investment being from country of concern, FDI applications would be processed by Department of Industrial Policy & Promotion (DIPP) for Government approval. Cases under the government approval route, also requiring security clearance with respect to countries of concern, will continue to be processed by concerned Administrative Department/Ministry.

Following are the Competent Authorities for grant of approval for foreign investment for sectors/activities requiring Government approval:

Sl. No.	Activity/ sector	Administrative Ministry/ Department
(i)	Mining	Ministry of Mines
(ii)	Defence	
	(a) Items requiring Industrial Licence under the Industries (Development & Regulation) Act, 1951, and/or Arms Act, 1959 for which the powers have been delegated by Ministry of Home Affairs to DIPP	Department of Defence Production, Ministry of Defence
	(b) Manufacturing of Small Arms and Ammunitions covered under Arms Act 1959	Ministry of Home Affairs

(iii)	Broadcasting	Ministry of Information & Broadcasting
(iv)	Print Media	
(v)	Civil Aviation	Ministry of Civil Aviation
(vi)	Satellites	Department of Space
(vii)	Telecommunication	Department of Telecommunications
(viii)	Private Security Agencies	Ministry of Home Affairs
(ix)	Applications involving investments from *Countries of Concern* which presently include Pakistan and Bangladesh, requiring security clearance as per the extant FEMA 20, FDI Policy and security guidelines, amended from time to time	
(x)	Trading (Single brand, Multi brand and Food Product retail trading)	Department of Industrial Policy & Promotion
(xi)	FDI proposals by Non-Resident Indians (NRIs)/Export Oriented Units requiring approval of the Government	
(xii)	Applications relating to issue of equity shares under the FDI policy under the Government route for import of capital goods/machinery/equipment (excluding second-hand machinery)	
(xiii)	Applications relating to issue of equity shares for pre-operative/pre-incorporation expenses (including payments of rent etc.)	

Source: https://pib.gov.in/

2.28 FDI in Indian State

FDI in different states of India have increased steadily since the early 1990s when the Indian economy was opened up to foreign investments. Maharashtra, Delhi, Karnataka and Tamil Nadu are among the leading states that have attracted maximum FDI.

Sl. No.	RBI's - Regional Office 2	State covered	2016-17	2017-18	2018-19	Cumulative Inflows (April, 00 -March, 19)	%age to total Inflows (in terms of US$)
1.	Mumbai	Maharashtra Dadra & Nagar Haveli, Daman & DIU	131,980 (19,654)	86,244 (13,423)	80,013 (11,383)	713,990 (127,089)	30
2.	New Delhi	Delhi, part of UP and Haryana	39,482 (5,884)	49,366 (7,656)	70,485 (10,142)	484,219 (84,642)	20
3.	Bangalore	Karnataka	14,300 (2,132)	55,334 (8,575)	46,963 (6,721)	225,510 (37,670)	9
4.	Chennai	Tamil Nadu, Pondicherry	14,830 (2,218)	22,354 (3,475)	18,164 (2,613)	173,896 (29,848)	7
5.	Ahmadabad	Gujarat	22,610 (3,367)	13,457 (2,091)	12,618 (1,803)	117,149 (20,545)	5
6.	Hyderabad	Andhra Pradesh	14,767 (2,195)	8,037 (1,246)	23,882 (3,457)	106,242 (18,469)	4
7.	Kolkata	West Bengal, Sikkim, Andaman & Nicobar Islands	332 (50)	1,409 (218)	8,531 (1,229)	31,119 (5,432)	1
8.	Kochi	Kerala, Lakshadweep	3,050 (454)	1,339 (208)	1,807 (257)	12,934 (2,221)	0.5
9.	Chandigarh	Chandigarh, Punjab, Haryana, Himachal Pradesh	39 (6)	697 (108)	4,374 (618)	11,647 (2,090)	0.5
10.	Jaipur	Rajasthan	1,111 (165)	752 (117)	2,553 (363)	11,542 (1,960)	0.5
11.	Bhopal	Madhya Pradesh, Chhattisgarh	515 (76)	181 (28)	224 (32)	7,533 (1,431)	0.3
12.	Panaji	Goa	555 (83)	279 (43)	111 (16)	4,930 (983)	0.2
13.	Kanpur	Uttar Pradesh, Uttaranchal	50 (8)	578 (90)	234 (34)	3,830 (694)	0.2

14.	Bhu-baneswar	Orissa	83 (12)	415 (65)	483 (69)	2,978 (549)	0.1
15.	Guwahati	Assam, Arunachal Pradesh, Manipur, Meghalaya, Mizoram, Nagaland, Tripura	15 (2)	82 (13)	48 (7)	591 (116)	0.03
16.	Patna	Bihar, Jharkhand	69 (10)	64 (10)	0.22 (0.03)	671 (113)	0.03
17.	Jammu	Jammu & Kashmir	2 (0.2)	0 (0)	0.41 (0.06)	39 (6)	0.00
18.	Region not indicated		47,909 (7,162)	48,300 (7,491)	39,377 (5,624)	469,531 (86,164)	21
Sub. Total			291,696 (43,478)	288,889 (44,857)	309,867 (44,366)	2,378,353 (420,021)	
19.	RBI's-NRI schemes (from 2000 to 2002)		0	0	0	533 (121)	-
Grand total			291,696 (43,478)	288,889 (44,857)	309,867 (44,366)	2,378,886 (420,142)	-

Some of the states in India which have witnessed a massive upsurge in FDI Inflows include Maharashtra (30%), Delhi (20%), Karnataka (9%), and Tamil Nadu (7%). Other states which are in the receipt of FDI Inflows in India include Gujarat, Andhra Pradesh, West Bengal and Kerala.

2.29 FDI inflows of the last few years in India[1]

The FDI inflow for financial year (FY) 2009-10 was $37,745 million and over the ensuing decade, the FDI inflows have recorded a steady growth every year. For FY 2018-2019, the inflows were $64,375 million i.e. 70.55 percent higher than the annual inflows in 2009-10.

The FDI inflows decreased compared to the previous year only on two occasions, FY 2010-11 and FY 2012-13 where they fell by 8 percent and a sharp 26 percent respectively. It can be noted that the highest annual increase over the decade was recorded in the year

1. https://factly.in/analysis-the-story-of-fdi-inflows-of-the-last-10-years-which-sectors-are-receiving-a-lions-share/

between these two i.e. FY 2011-12, where the FDI inflows showed an annual increment of 34%. Few Big-ticket deals in the Oil & Gas sectors was said to have contributed for the higher FDI inflow in spite of the lack of FDI reforms during that period.

After a meteoric annual growth during 2014-15 and 2015-16, the FDI inflows only increased by single digit percentage points annually over the last three years (8%, 1% and 6% respectively between 2016-17 and 2018-19).

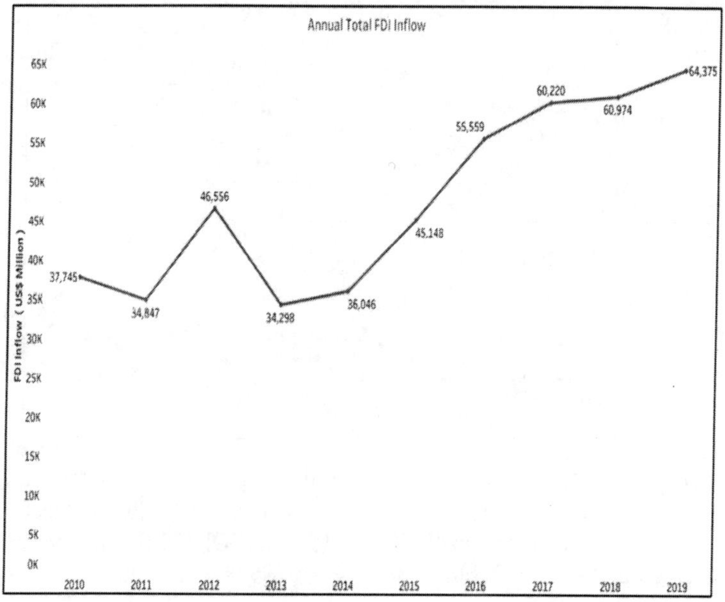

Service Sector, Hardware & Software, Trading and Automobile are the consistent high performing sectors

Service sector has been always had a major share of the FDI inflows every year. Apart from two lean years in 2013-14 and 2014-15, this sector has always recorded a share of minimum 10 percent of the total FDI received annually. Especially during the ensuing four years after the lean period, FDI in Service sector has a share of 14.5 percent, 14.4 percent, 11 percent and 14.2 percent respectively. The FDI in service sector has grown by 181 percent during these four years. i.e., From $3252.97 million in 2014-15 to $9157.54 million in 2018-19. Services under Banking, Insurance, Non-Finance & Business Outsourcing, Finance, R&D, Technology, Testing, Analysis etc. are categorised under service sector.

FDI into Computer (Hardware & Software) sector has increased from $918.66 million in 2009-10 to $6415.21 million in 2018-19. The annual inflow has grown by more than 500 percent in just 5 years between 2014-15 and 2018-19.

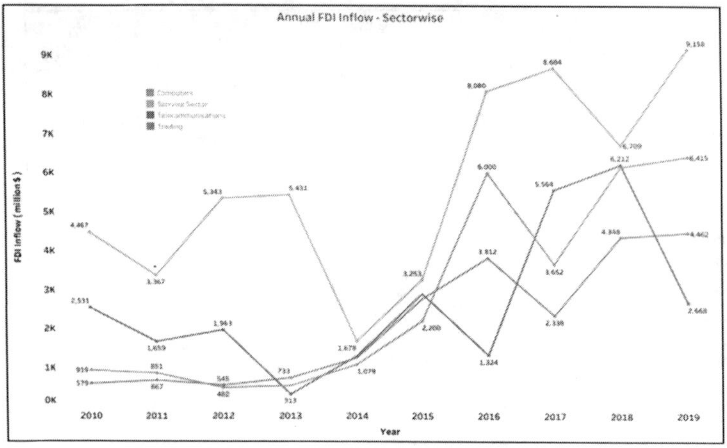

Trading sector includes businesses dealing with trading related to exports, bulk imports, cash and carry wholesale trading, hi-tech goods, medical and diagnostic items etc. The FDI inflows last year were recorded at $4,462 million compared to $578.61 million a decade ago.

Telecommunication sector has also received consistent high volume of FDI annually. Although there was a dip in the FDI received last year (2018-2019), this was after high volume of FDI inflows the previous two year.

In recent years, FDI inflows have increased in Education, Non-Conventional Energy, Hospital and Diagnostic sectors

FDI into Hospitals and Diagnostic centres has shown a gradual and consistent increase all through the decade. In 2009-2010, the inflow was $135.91 million and has shown an incremental increase in the annual inflow every year. Last year, there was the greatest increase in an annual year with 47 percent higher FDI inflows compared to 2017-18.

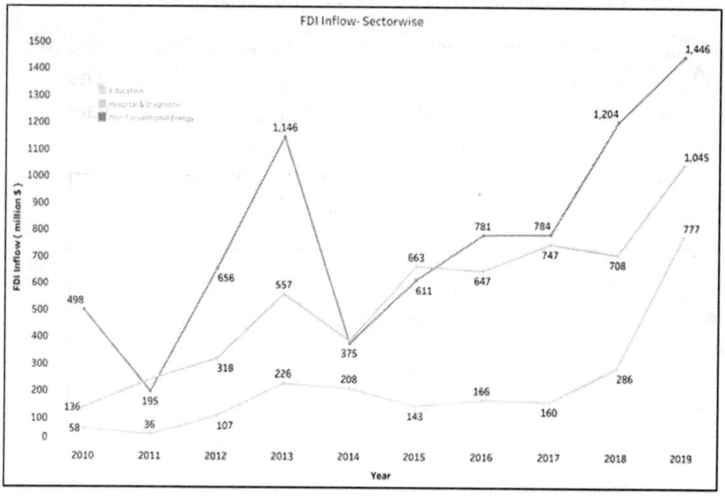

Education Sector has also started receiving higher FDI over the decade, with a dip in the inflows during 2013-15. Last year, has an exponential increase in this sector with FDI inflows at $776.73 million compared to earlier year's $285.75 million. Regulations allow for 100 percent FDI in education. Vocational and Technical education receive most of the foreign investment.

Non-Conventional Energy sector FDI inflows have increased annually since 2014-15, more than doubling up on yearly figures. In the year 2012-13, this sector received FDI to the tune of $1,146 million, which was only surpassed in the last two years i.e. 2017-18 and 2018-19.

Hotel and Tourism, Construction, Drugs and Pharmaceuticals among the sectors receiving inconsistent FDIs annually

The FDI inflows are dependent on various factors apart from the regulation and policies of the government. While positive government initiatives and environment are influencing factors, the actual deals can vary annually. This results in irregular annual FDI inflows in few sectors.

Hotel and Tourism sector received highest FDI over the decade in 2012-13 with $3336.68 million followed by last year 2018-19 ($1310.93 million). It had comparatively lean annual inflows in 2010-11 ($320.73 million) and 2017-18 ($408.75 million).

The categorisation of construction industry has varied the FDI numbers of the government. It's being reported as – Construction Activities, Housing and Real Estate, Construction Development, Construction (Infrastructure) etc. During 2009-10 (15%), 2011-12 (8%) and 2015-16 (8.3%), this sector had major contribution to the FDI inflow albeit with some lean years in between.

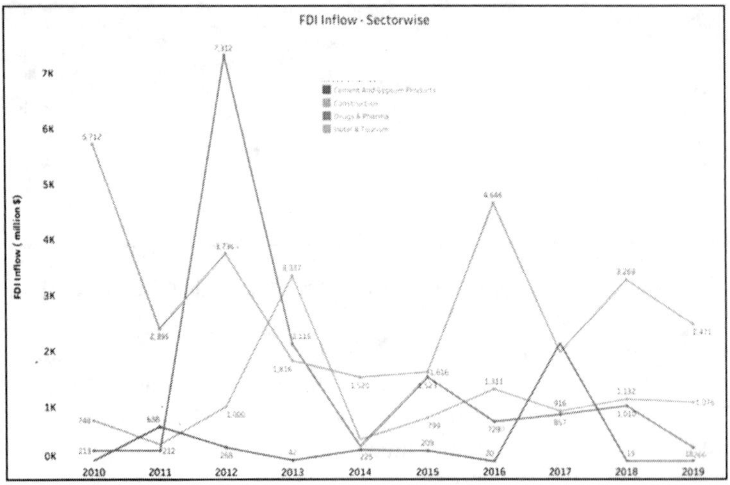

The FDI into Cement and Gypsum sector has been very volatile over the last decade. During 2016-17 it received $2,130 million, encapsulated between years of less FDI- 2015-16 ($19.78 million), 2017-18 ($19.44 million) and 2018-19 ($17.61 million).

Drugs and Pharma sector FDI inflows have also been highly inconsistent over the years. In 2011-12, it received $7,311 million in FDI with the next highest in the immediate next year with $2,115 million.

2.30 Country Wise Break–Up of FDI in India

There is a clear strong worldwide competition for attracting FDI. Generally, FDI means capital inflow or outflow from or to abroad that is invested in productive purpose in the host economy and in usually preferred over other forms of external finance because it is non-debt creating, non-volatile and their return depends on the performance of the project financed by the investors in the host country. Here an attempt has been made to the break-up of FDI in India on the basis of different contributing countries. The break-up of FDI inflow in India on the basis of top ten countries has been given in the table-

Ranks	**Country**	**2017-18 (April – March)**	**2018-19 (April – March)**	**2019-20 (April – June)**	**Cumulative Inflows (April, 00 - June, 19)**	**% age to total Inflows (in terms of US $)**
1.	Mauritius	102,492 (15,941)	57,139 (8,084)	32,484 (4,676)	770,640 (139,145)	32
2.	Singapore	78,542 (12,180)	112,362 (16,228)	37,106 (5,339)	543,052 (88,337)	20
3.	Japan	10,516 (1,633)	20,556 (2,965)	3,284 (472)	176,616 (30,746)	7
4.	Netherlands	18,048 (2,800)	27,036 (3,870)	9,423 (1,356)	171,674 (28,708)	7
5.	U.K.	5,473 (847)	9,352 (1,351)	2,056 (295)	142,425 (27,084)	6
6.	U.S.A.	13,505 (2,095)	22,335 (3,139)	10,119 (1,455)	156,491 (27,011)	6
7.	Germany	7,245 (1,124)	6,187 (886)	1,135 (163)	66,613	3
8.	Cyprus	2,680 (417)	2,134 (296)	406 (58)	51,950 (9,927)	2
9.	France	3,297 (511)	2,890 (406)	854 (123)	37,679 (6,766)	2
10.	UAE	6,767 (1,050)	6,356 (898)	718 (103)	40,027 (6,755)	2

Total FDI Inflows From all Countries		288,889 (44,857)	309,867 (44,366)	113,511 (16,330)	2,492,397 (436,471)	-

Source: Fact sheet on Foreign Direct Investment (FDI) from April, 2000 to March, 2019.

India's foreign direct investment (FDI) equity inflows fell for the first time in six years in 2018-19 with a steep decline in foreign funds in telecom, pharmaceuticals and power.

Data released by the department for promotion of industry and internal trade showed FDI equity inflows into India declined 1 percent to $44.4 billion 2018-19 from $44.8 billion in the previous fiscal.

FDI inflows fell 56 percent in telecommunications to $2.7 billion and 74 percent in pharmaceuticals to $266 million.

2.31 Sectoral Composition of FDI Inflows in India

Several indicators can reflect the quality of FDI inflows into the country, changes in Sectoral composition is one of them. It's very important for a country to analyse the FDI is going to which of its respective sectors. Whether it's going to modern and advanced technology intensive sectors or helping to build productive capabilities thereby crowding out domestic investments. There has been a drastic shift in the composition of FDI inflows since 1991. The FDI's have gradually shifted from manufacturing to services sector. Also, different sectors have been opened up for FDI at different points of time. That partly explains the difference in FDI received in various sectors.[1]

FDI flows in the third quarter of 2018-19 shows that there has been a drastic decline in FDI in six out of the 10 sectors attracting the highest FDI flows. Sectors that have seen a decline in FDI during this period include computer software and hardware, telecommunications, construction, infrastructure, pharmaceuticals and power. In absolute dollar terms, the telecommunications sector took the biggest hit witnessing a decline of almost $3 billion in April-December 2018 as compared to same period last year. In percentage terms, the pharmaceuticals sector took the biggest hit with FDI equity inflows declining by almost 81 percent (or $921 million) during the period.

1. https://dipp.gov.in/sites

Ranks	Sector	**2017-18 (April – March)**	**2018-19 (April – March)**	**2019-20 (April – June)**	**Cumulative Inflows (April, 00 - June, 19)**	**% age to total Inflows (In terms of US$)**
1.	**Services Sector**	43,249 **(6,709)**	63,909 **(9,158)**	19,462 **(2,799)**	435,764 **(76,948)**	**18**
2.	**Computer Software & Hardware**	39,670 **(6,153)**	45,297 **(6,415)**	15,585 **(2,241)**	237,341 **(39,479)**	**9**
3.	**Telecommunications**	39,748 **(6,212)**	18,337 **(2,668)**	29,352 **(4,227)**	217,601 **(37,053)**	**8**
4.	**Construction Development:** Townships, housing, built-up infrastructure and construction-development projects	3,472 **(540)**	1,503 **(213)**	532 **(77)**	120,146 **(25,122)**	**6**
5.	**Trading**	28,078 **(4,348)**	30,963 **(4,462)**	7,921 **(1,138)**	151,520 **(24,160)**	**6**
6.	**Automobile Industry**	13,461 **(2,090)**	18,309 **(2,623)**	6,756 **(972)**	130,745 **(22,359)**	**5**
7.	**Chemicals (Other Than Fertilizers)**	8,425 **(1,308)**	13,685 **(1,981)**	1,008 **(145)**	92,070 **(16,727)**	**4**
8.	**Drugs & Pharmaceuticals**	6,502 **(1,010)**	1,842 **(266)**	1,581 **(227)**	85,746 **(16,210)**	**4**
9.	**Construction (Infrastructure) Activities**	17,571 **(2,730)**	15,927 **(2,258)**	3,698 **(532)**	97,571 **(15,337)**	**4**
10.	**Power**	10,473 **(1,621)**	7,330 **(1,106)**	1,320 **(190)**	79,209 **(14,506)**	**3**

Source: https://dipp.gov.in/sites

Sectors that saw enhanced FDI equity inflows include services, trading, chemicals and automobiles. The chemicals sector was the biggest magnet for foreign investors attracting $6.1 billion in the first nine months of financial year (FY) 2018-19.

This was three times more than FDI equity inflows in the chemical sector in the same period last year. The services sector attracted $5.9 billion–up 28 percent during this period. The automobile sector attracted $1.8 billion–up almost a billion dollars.

2.32 FDI in India: Performance and Overview in FY 2019-20

India is among the world's fastest growing economies and remains a top market for foreign direct investments (FDI) globally. Apart from being a critical driver of economic growth, Foreign Direct Investment (FDI) is a major source of non-debt financial resource for the economic development of India. Foreign companies invest in India to take advantage of relatively lower wages, special investment privileges such as tax exemptions, etc.

The Indian government's favourable policy regime and robust business environment have ensured that foreign capital keeps flowing into the country. The government has taken many initiatives in recent years such as relaxing FDI norms across sectors such as defence, PSU oil refineries, telecom, power exchanges, and stock exchanges, among others.

According to Department for Promotion of Industry and Internal Trade (DPIIT), FDI equity inflows in India in 2018-19 stood at US$ 44.37 billion, indicating that government's effort to improve ease of doing business and relaxation in FDI norms is yielding results.

The net foreign direct investment stood US$ 3.034 billion in May 2019 and US$ 7 billion in June 2019. India invited US$ 7.8 billion of foreign investment in month of June 2019 as compared to US$ 1.6 billion in previous year.

Data for 2018-19 indicates that the services sector attracted the highest FDI equity inflow of US$ 9.16 billion, followed by computer software and hardware – US$ 6.42 billion, trading – US$ 4.46 billion and telecommunications – US$ 2.67 billion. Most recently, the total FDI equity inflows for the month of March 2019 touched US$ 3.60 billion.[1]

During 2018-19, India received the maximum FDI equity inflows from Singapore (US$ 16.23 billion), followed by Mauritius (US$ 8.08

1. https://www.ibef.org/economy/foreign-direct-investment.aspx

billion), Netherlands (US$ 3.87 billion), USA (US$ 3.14 billion), and Japan (US$ 2.97 billion).

Investments/ Developments

India emerged as the top recipient of Greenfield FDI Inflows from the Commonwealth, as per a trade review released by the Commonwealth in 2018.

Some of the recent significant FDI announcements are as follows:

- In August 2019, Reliance Industries (RIL) announced one of India's biggest FDI deals, as Saudi Aramco will buy a 20 percent stake in Reliance's oil-to-chemicals (OTC) business at an enterprise value of US$ 75 billion.
- In October 2018, VMware, a leading software innovating enterprise of US has announced investment of US$ 2 billion in India between by 2023.
- In August 2018, Bharti Airtel received approval of the Government of India for sale of 20 percent stake in its DTH arm to an America based private equity firm, Warburg Pincus, for around $350 million.
- In June 2018, Idea's appeal for 100 percent FDI was approved by Department of Telecommunication (DoT) followed by its Indian merger with Vodafone making Vodafone Idea the largest telecom operator in India.
- In February 2018, Ikea announced its plans to invest up to Rs 4,000 crore (US$ 612 million) in the state of Maharashtra to set up multi-format stores and experience centres.
- Kathmandu based conglomerate, CG Group is looking to invest Rs 1,000 crore (US$ 155.97 million) in India by 2020 in its food and beverage business.
- International Finance Corporation (IFC), the investment arm of the World Bank Group, is planning to invest about US$ 6 billion through 2022 in several sustainable and renewable energy programmes in India.

Government Initiatives

- In Union Budget 2019-2020, the government of India proposed opening of FDI in aviation, media (animation, AVGC) and insurance sectors in consultation with all stakeholders.
- In February 2019, the Government of India released the Draft National e-Commerce Policy which encourages FDI in the marketplace model of e-commerce. Further, it states that the FDI policy for e-commerce sector has been developed to ensure a level playing field for all participants.
- Government of India is planning to consider 100 percent FDI in Insurance intermediaries in India to give a boost to the sector and attracting more funds.
- In December 2018, the Government of India revised FDI rules related to e-commerce. As per the rules 100 percent FDI is allowed in the marketplace based model of e-commerce. Also, sales of any vendor through an e-commerce marketplace entity or its group companies have been limited to 25 percent of the total sales of such vendor.
- In September 2018, the Government of India released the National Digital Communications Policy, 2018 which envisages increasing FDI inflows in the telecommunications sector to US$ 100 billion by 2022.
- In January 2018, Government of India allowed foreign airlines to invest in Air India up to 49 percent with government approval. The investment cannot exceed 49 percent directly or indirectly.
- No government approval will be required for FDI up to an extent of 100 percent in Real Estate Broking Services.
- In September 2017, the Government of India asked the states to focus on strengthening single window clearance system for fast-tracking approval processes, in order to increase Japanese investments in India.
- The Ministry of Commerce and Industry, Government of India has eased the approval mechanism for foreign direct investment (FDI) proposals by doing away with the approval

of Department of Revenue and mandating clearance of all proposals requiring approval within 10 weeks after the receipt of application.

- The Government of India is in talks with stakeholders to further ease foreign direct investment (FDI) in defence under the automatic route to 51 percent from the current 49 percent, in order to give a boost to the Make in India initiative and to generate employment.
- In January 2018, Government of India allowed 100 percent FDI in single brand retail through automatic route.

Road Ahead

- India has become the most attractive emerging market for global partners (GP) investment for the coming years, as per a recent market attractiveness survey conducted by Emerging Market Private Equity Association (EMPEA).
- Annual FDI inflows in the country are expected to rise to US$ 75 billion over the next five years, as per a report by UBS.
- The Government of India is aiming to achieve US$ 100 billion worth of FDI inflows in the next two years.
- The World Bank has stated that private investments in India is continuing to grow by 8.8 percent in FY 2018-19 to overtake private consumption growth of 7.4 percent, and thereby drive the growth in India's gross domestic product (GDP) in FY 2018-19.[1]

1. https://www.ibef.org/economy/foreign-direct-investment.aspx

CHAPTER – 3

Problems and Prospects of FDI in India

3.1 Introduction

Foreign capital inflow in general supplements and compliments domestic capital and stoke the pace of economic growth along with certain benefits like transfer of technology, competitive management practice, employment opportunities and economy of scale in host nation. These benefits from large capital inflows also have certain costs such as appreciation in asset prices, appreciation in exchange rates, balance of payment imbalance, tax holidays, low corporate tax and income tax rates, concessions in other kinds of taxes, special economic zones, preferential tariffs, export processing zone, bonded warehouses, free lands or land subsidies, infrastructure subsidies, relocation and expatriation subsidies, job training and employment subsidies, investment financial subsidies, soft loan or loan guarantees, research and development, derogation from regulations usually for very large projects, declining domestic export competitiveness etc.

The government of India's amendments and policy initiatives have generated positive and encouraging results which accelerated the nation's economic pace. FDI inflow at micro and macro level has accelerated the industrial production and it has influenced the general price level in the economy. FDI inflow has helped to raise the output, productivity, domestic consumption, export and employment in respective sectors. In comparison to yester year the judicious policy decisions of present government to liberate FDI inflow at the sectoral level has been appreciated by the global investors. The GOI in order to answer the domestic demand and to cater the unemployment used amendments as a leverage tool and introduced policy initiative to attract more FDI inflows into the country. GOI succeeded in accelerating the pace of industrial production and managed supply side gaps to contain inflationary pressures in the economy and also to accumulate foreign exchange reserves to maintain and enhance the international creditworthiness of the country.[1]

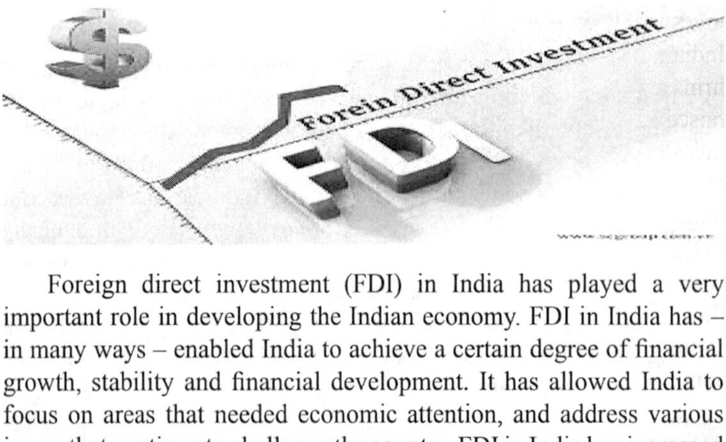

Foreign direct investment (FDI) in India has played a very important role in developing the Indian economy. FDI in India has – in many ways – enabled India to achieve a certain degree of financial growth, stability and financial development. It has allowed India to focus on areas that needed economic attention, and address various issues that continue to challenge the country. FDI in India has increased over a period of time due to the efforts been made by the Indian government. The increased flow of FDI in India has given major boost to the country's economy and hence steps should be taken to make sure that the flow of FDI in India continues to grow. FDI investments are permitted through private equity or preferential allotments, financial collaborations, through capital markets in form of Euro issues, and in

1. Sethi, Narayan, FDI and Economic Growth in India, Rawat Publication, New Delhi, 2019, p. 47.

joint ventures. FDI has an important impact on country's trade balance, increasing labour standards, transfer of technology and innovative ideas, skills and the general business climate. FDI also provides opportunity for technological transfer and upgradation, access to global managerial skills and practices, optimal utilisation of human capabilities and natural resources, making industry internationally competitive, opening up export markets, access to international quality goods and services and augmenting employment opportunities.

Globalisation and liberalisation bring lots of new innovative products to the world, Foreign Direct Investment is the one among this, also there are number of different forms of FDI available currently. Recently, Government of India allowed FDI in different sectors of Indian economy. But several opposition parties are making it a political issue in parliament on these policy decisions and amendments. With a view to infuse globally acceptable best practices, modern management skills and latest technology, it has been decided to allow foreign investment in India. FDIs have created tremendous opportunities for India's development and helped to boost the performance of local firms as well as the globalisation of some of them. This has undeniably raised India's stature among developing countries. India needs massive investments to sustain high-quality economic growth, particularly in the energy and infrastructure sectors, FDIs are favoured, because of their long-term durability and commitment to a host country's economy. FDI's are less susceptible to short-term changes in market conditions, which ensure a certain level of continuity and stability in the money flow. However, many developing economies have tried to restrict, and even resist, foreign investments because of nationalist sentiments and concerns over foreign economic and political influence.[1]

1. Sethi, Narayan, FDI and Economic Growth in India, *op.cit,* p. 48.

Nations desiring for sustainable economic growth has to explore global opportunities and FDI (Foreign Direct Investment) helps in achieving significant development for the economy. FDI is considered to be the most essential medium of development in the emerging sectors of an economy. India is an emerging market globally due to its various prospering aspects like cheap labour, greater market size and abundance of natural resources etc. which attract foreign investors for better prospects in various sectors. India succeeded in attracting foreign investors after the launching of Make in India policy and various other government reforms. In India, various sectors are emerging, for example - tourism, transport, communication, health and education. These sectors desperately require FDI for its prosperity and development.

Inward FDI gives long term benefits to the investing firm by enjoying the surplus profit generation and helps in overcoming the socio-economic problems of hosting nations like unemployment by generating employment opportunities in local economy. It eradicates technological backward problem through technological transfer. It allows to access in the global market platform for the firms and evolve better product through increase in market competition. Thus, it was concluded that FDI contributes in stimulating the economic growth and development of our country. FDI has invested largely to the service sectors of India. There has been a positive impact of Make in India Policy towards FDI in India.[1] It also reduces brain-drain from the host countries and provides to work for better market with upgraded techniques and handsome revenue generation. According to United Nations Conference in Trade and Development (UNCTAD), India managed 10th position across the world to be the largest recipients of FDI with $44 billion foreign investments.

1. Sethi, Narayan, FDI and Economic Growth in India, *op.cit*, p. 48.

Foreign Direct Investment (FDI) is generally referred to as a type of investment that involves inflow or investment of foreign funds by an investor of one country into another economy of the world. FDI is one among the most predominant factor for economic growth as it accelerates increased productivity of the national economy, reducing unemployment, creating job opportunities, increase the use of technology and managerial skills, removing Balance of Payments (BOP) Constraint, promoting Exports, increase in Foreign Exchange, generating a Competitive Environment and many other progressive outputs that differentiate this kind of investment from other funding sources.

FDI are of two types. One is Inward FDI which occurs when investment in local resources is with foreign capital. Major aspects that would boost the inflow of inward FDI include tax breaks, low interest rates and grants. Second is Outward FDI which is also called "Direct Investment Abroad". All risks associated with this type of FDI is backed by the Influx of FDI to India has seen an increase with the initiatives taken by the present ruling government. As per the latest survey and record during the year January 2019 the Foreign Direct Investment in India increased by 3675 USD Million. On an average the Foreign Direct Investment inflow to India was around 1341.88 USD Million from the year 1995 until 2018, which reached an all-time high record of 8579 USD Million in August 2017 and a record low of -1336 USD Million in November of 2017 for which one of the reasons could be Demonetisation by the present ruling government in India. FDI has been one of the factors due to which India has been able to achieve a certain degree of financial stability; growth and development to sustain and compete in the global economy.[1]

1. Pant, Manoj, FDI in India, Orient Blackswan Private Limited, New Delhi, 2019, p. 43.

The problems facing larger FDI in India are in spite of the fact that more than 100 of Fortune 500 companies are already investing in India. These FDI's are already generating employment opportunities, income, technology transfer and economic stability.

3.2 Problems of FDI in India

Right from fhe inception of globalisation and then the establishment of the foreign direct investment, India has seen many ups and downs not only in the FDI growth rate but also political and social instability. This has in turn affected the overall economic development both in a positive and negative way.

This clearly means that there are some problems which India needs to overcome to attain the perfection and deal with the situation tactfully at the time of need.

India is focusing on maximizing political and social stability along with a regulatory environment. In spite of the obvious advantages of FDIs, there are quite a few problems facing larger FDIs in India, such as:

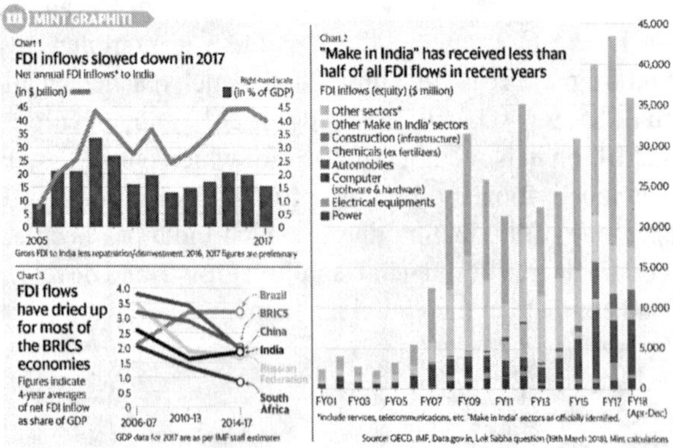

Resource Problems

There is no doubt that India is one of the countries in the world which has cheap as well as skilled labours which is desirable for any foreign investors to put in their resources in.

India also has domestic resources which significantly attracts the investors from outside India. These resources are hugely available in both rural and urban area. But the fact is many of these resources are either unexploited or under-exploited. Hence adequate infrastructure is needed to exploit them. Therefore, increasing the infrastructure in effective and efficient way would be the 1st and foremost challenge.

Equity Problems

Though India has developed in many areas which are considered as the urbanised areas, there still exists a significant portion within the country which is considered as poor and under poverty line. Hence, the economic growth is different in different parts of India as well. It can be concluded that the development has taken place in an uneven manner within the country.[1]

1. Pant, Manoj, FDI in India, *op.cit.*

This is where the social instability comes into picture. No doubt that equalising this instability is a real challenge. Once this is done, the economic growth will be at an equal pace and in a balanced manner.

Political Problems

One of the most challenging areas in India is the sustainability of the political situation. If the political situation gets disturbed, this will have a direct effect on the FDI. Due to the political tension in the past, nation has seen significant decline in the FDI growth rate. It is extremely important that the foreign investors come into the country and invest their resources and time.

In order to do this in an effective way, political situation has to be stable. Next, the overall political structure has to be adequate and well-defined in both the sides- one who invests and one who get invested.

When the foreign investors talk about increasing their scope of work in various sectors like banking, retail, insurance, pharmacy etc, there has to be a governing body which will take care of these demands and handle the situation tactfully.

Federal Problems

The most important challenge is to implement the policies, rules and regulations in order to overcome these challenges.

India has seen many ups and downs in the FDI in the past. Accordingly, the government has taken measures, sometimes modifying the schemes, liberalising and relaxing some of the policies, bringing out new Acts and Regulations, forming different bodies like

Tarapore Committee, FEMA and SEBI. India must also focus on areas of poverty reduction, trade liberalisation, and banking and insurance liberalisation. Challenges facing larger FDI are not just restricted to the ones mentioned above, because trade relations with foreign investors will always bring in new challenges in investments.[1]

However, what is important now is to speed up the implementation procedure so that it is visible within the noted time. Also, this implementation has to be equally fast in all the states of India. All the problems are inter-related if we observe them closely.

Weak Infrastructure

Blame it on the infrastructural bottlenecks and suddenly all the hoopla surrounding FDI inflows goes into a tizzy. Lack of infrastructure remains to be a major cause of worry in India. India is not able to compete with other emerging markets in terms of ports, roads, skills set, etc. Poor transport links, inadequate power supply, poor roads, frequent power cuts, delays in ports, water and sewerage problems etc are the major problems through which India is undergoing even after six decades of planned economic development. Shortage of warehousing and cold storage facilities are the main reasons for 40 percent of the fruits and vegetables to be perished before reaching the markets. In the World Competitiveness Index for 2015-16, India is ranked 55 amongst 140 countries in terms of infrastructure, far behind China which is ranked at 28.

Complicated Tax Structure

Deeply ensconced in the literature and in practice is the fact that to have greater impact on investments in any country, stability and transparency in tax regime along with clarity in tax laws would be

1. Pant, Manoj, FDI in India, *op.cit.*

the main motivational factors. Taking cognizance of the aforesaid, the taxation per se should be simplified. In spite of several steps taken by the government to ease it in India, however presents a picture where the taxation policies remain intrinsically complex. Various tax disputes related to cross border transactions involving big MNC's have been witnessed by India in the recent years. Foreign companies in India are taxed at a rate of 40 percent whereas in most of the nation's corporate tax rates are levied in the range of 15 to 25 percent. A corporate tax rate of 25% along with tax holidays for qualified tax payers is charged in China on foreign companies. India's complicated indirect tax regime enforces number of taxes such as central sales tax, VAT, service tax, central excise duty etc. inflicts lot of inconvenience to the tax payers.[1]

Lack of decision-making authority with the State Governments

The reform process of liberalising the economy is concentrated mainly in the Centre and the State Governments are not given much power. In most key infrastructure areas, the central government remains in control. Brazil, China, and Russia are examples where regional governments take the lead in pushing reforms and prompting further actions by the central government.

Limited scale of Export Processing Zones

India's export processing zones have lacked dynamism because of several reasons, such as their relatively limited scale; the Government's general ambivalence about attracting FDI; the unclear and changing incentive packages attached to the zones; and the power of the central government in the regulation of the zones. India which established its first Export Processing Zone (EPZ) in 1965 has failed to develop the zones when compared to China which took initiative for establishment only in 1980.

Restrictive Labour Laws

Not helping India's cause are the rigorous and inflexible labour laws and over-regulated labour market; the laws for which India is ill famous all over the world. To ensure that the interests of labour covering different aspects namely, fixation and revision of wages, worker's health and safety, mode of payment of wages, payment of

1. https://www.investindia.gov.in/taxation

compensation in the event of industrial accident, provision of social security such as provident fund, gratuity, insurance etc to be protected large number of laws has been formulated by the Indian government. Owing to rigid rules with respect to overtime and financial obligation on the employer upon worker retrenchment, India has evolved as a highly inflexible economy.

Bureaucracy, Regulations and Corruption

A dampener on the spirits is another fact that a major handicap for India is bureaucracy, red tapism and corruption resulting in delays in obtaining licences, approvals and permits. As per the doing business report, India is ranked at 130 out of 189 countries. To drive home the said point, India is plagued by procedural delays that hinder the FDI inflows into the country. Generally, the time taken for registration of a new company is few days in most developed and developing markets which is much longer in India i.e. 4 to 8 weeks. Pendent FDI approvals are prevalent in India that many times impels the investor to withdraw. In comparison to other nations, FDI directives still remain to be restrictive in nature despite being various liberalisation measures undertaken by the government. India becomes a less preferred investment destination due to uncertain and frequently changing government policies, inefficient administrative, overlapping jurisdictions and excessive governance which sometimes lead to inflated transaction costs for companies.[1]

India, for all the talk of doing well in attracting FDI inflows, is still punching below its weight. A resurgent Indian government has wizened to the requirements and has initiated several reforms thus making FDI regulations more lucrative by raising the FDI cap in various sectors, opening many new sectors for FDI and by adopting automatic approval route for some sectors. While the above can be touted as measures in the right direction, the FDI numbers flatter to deceive. In comparison to developing economies like China and Brazil, FDI inflows to India are much lesser. In spite of having an inherent advantage in terms of lower labour cost and huge domestic markets, countries like Indonesia, Vietnam and Philippines emerge as low-cost economies, which would make India lose its advantage. According to Global Competitive Report of 2015-16, India holds 55th position out

1. https://www.theigc.org/blog/bureaucracy-intermediaries-corruption-and-red-tape

of 148 countries, far behind other developing economies like Malaysia (rank 18), China (rank 28), Thailand (rank 32), Indonesia (rank 37), Turkey (rank 51). Hence it is a high time for India to introduce second generation of reforms that could facilitate FDI inflows.

Improvement in labour laws:

- Liberalisation of FDI policies;
- Introduction of Goods & Service Tax (GST) to eliminate multiple taxes;
- Cutting down corporate tax rates;
- Axing down the bureaucratic hindrances;
- Do away with complex regulatory procedures;
- Development of world class infrastructure facilities.

It is expected that India would be able to attract larger FDI inflows in the years to come only by implementing the aforementioned reforms.

3.3 Prospects of FDI in India

Indian economy is one of the top emerging markets of the world. Five years ago, it was considered as part of the fragile five, but no longer. Since 2014, it has emerged as of the one top foreign destination in the world with a significant rise in FDI. The journey of attracting foreign investments started way back in 1991 with New Economic policy and India has unprecedentedly scaled new heights in the level of FDI during 2000's.[1]

The new industrial revolution, driven by frontier technologies, robotisation and digital advancements have made investments and production across the world better, economical and faster than before. This has offered vast opportunities for economic growth and sustainable development. World Economy has seen a rapid rise in foreign direct investment (FDI) for more than three and half decades. One of the significant contributions of globalisation in the past is the growing and spreading FDI amongst the countries, contributing significantly to positive effects on the labour productivity of domestic firms. The FDI and international trade can be substitutes under assumption that labour and capital can move freely between countries and no transportation cost apply. This suggests for an indirect linkage between international

1. http://www.iccrindia.net/economy/

trade and exchange production factors between the two. Most of the emerging economies and those in transition phase view FDI as an important source of financing. FDI finances both ownership change and capital formation. At the same time, it helps in the replacement of the huge volumes of out-dated capital accumulated during years of central planning for transition economies. Attracting FDI inflows with favourable policies has therefore become a key battleground in the transition and emerging markets. The New Growth theory states that in order to have higher economic growth, productivity per person should be higher. This will, in turn raise the real gross domestic product (GDP) and thereby help in satisfying people's pursuit for profits.[1] Therefore, FDI helps the economies by bringing new growth opportunities and massive profits having spillover effect across various sectors of the economies in terms of technical and managerial know how, skill up gradation, better and improved infrastructure, employment opportunities, increased competitiveness and opportunity for local markets to expand globally. This is one facet of FDI other one being negative on the host economies if it leads to repatriation of profits and gives stiff competition to the domestic and local players thereby stealing their markets. Thus, FDI may have both positive and negative effects on the host economies and it is important to look at their Sectoral decomposition and type as that can significantly impact the future growth and performance of the economy.

World Investment Report (2018) stated that there has been a decline in global FDI by 23 percent, i.e. $1.43 trillion. Even with this decline the FDI to developing economies remained stable at $671 billion in 2017. Asia was the largest recipient of FDI in the World with a total of $476 billion inflows in 2017. India has emerged as a major recipient

1. Devajit, M., Impact of foreign direct investment on Indian economy, Research Journal of management Sciences, 2019, 1(2), 29-31.

of FDI in South Asia. It is a resourceful country having an adequate market for both capital and consumer goods. Large number of natural resources in the country as well as excellent market surroundings provide a better platform for investments. FDI has been a major driver of economic growth in India. It is also a major source of non-debt financial resource for the development of the country. Ever since the New Economic Policy of 1991, foreign investments have been flowing into the economy. The liberalisation phase in Indian economy has paid rich dividends to the country. Foreign companies are eager to invest in India in order to take advantage of lower wages, tax exemptions etc. This has generated employment and has helped the economy in upgrading to higher and better technology. A favourable investor friendly policy regime with a robust business environment has ensured regular and smoother flow of foreign capital into the country. Various governments have taken measures to relax FDI norms across a range of sectors like telecommunication, power exchanges, stock market,

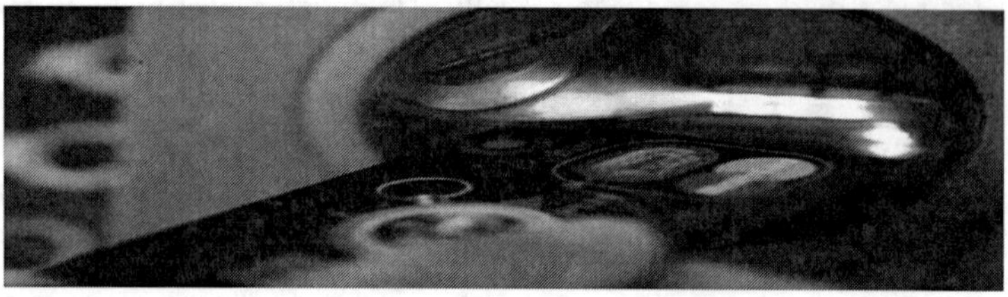

defence, oil refineries in the public sector, etc. As per the Economic Survey (2018-19) reforms in the FDI policy announced in 2018 have brought maximum number of sectors under the automatic approval route, with a few exceptions in the negative list. Thus, in the recent years various governments have been proactive in making profound changes in the investment policies of India and this has helped the country to build and upgrade its industries with more global connect. Government policies since 2014 can be applauded for understanding the global economic landscape well in advance and making deep structural changes in the economy. The investment climate has changed in the country. India's rank has moved by 53 positions in the World Bank's annual 'ease of doing business index'. India currently ranks 77th in the list of 190 countries.[1]

1. Devajit, M., Impact of foreign direct investment on Indian economy, Research Journal of Management Sciences, 2019, 1(2), 29-31.

India has become one of the most attractive emerging markets globally. The gross FDI received from April 2000 to June 2018 is USD 563320 million. This inflow of funds over the years has helped the country in advancement of technology, skill upgradation, employment generation, better infrastructure and management. Foreign corporations have helped the country in transforming its economic structure, bringing additional investors and have attracted investments in innovative sectors. It is observed that in order to have structural transformation there is a proactive policy formulation by Government of India (GOI) especially from 2014 onwards. This has facilitated high number of foreign inflows in different sectors. Thus, adding to higher productivity and promoting sustainable and inclusive development. Service Sector especially banking, financial and non-financial, Insurance, Outsourcing, Research and Development of India has attracted maximum FDI followed by manufacturing sector. Higher volumes of FDI have come in electronics, hardware, automobiles, pharma, etc.

There are various reasons as per industry experts. Manufacturing in India is basically driven by low labour costs and as such only those type of manufacturing are prominent. In the current scenario many countries like Bangladesh, Cambodia, Brazil, Myanmar to name a few have opened their economies as well. Foreign capital is being invested in these countries, for instance European Union and Cambodia free trade agreement. In future, as the labour costs goes up, this type of manufacturing will slowly die down in India and can have serious impacts on the investments. Heavy industries in India could never pick up primarily due to lack of skill. For instance, we learn to make cycles, then motorcycles, then cars and then finally jet engines and aeroplanes, but that is not happening in India, the same has already happened in China. So, unless we develop complex manufacturing the sector will not grow and merely flow of FDI will not be very beneficial. To cite an example here, there is huge demand in aviation but neither is we making planes or any critical part of it and no industry investing in it as well. Low adoption of technology is a primary reason why manufacturing is not looked upon in India. Without technology, scale is not possible and without scale industries cannot compete with global behemoths. So, unless companies look for global scale it's difficult to raise foreign capital. The 'Make in India' programme was launched on 25th September 2014 by GOI with an objective of making India a global hub for manufacturing, research and innovation. The GOI has even identified ten sectors having high potentials. Taking a look at service sector, this sector has emerged as the largest and fastest-growing sector in the global economy. It has contributed to more than 50 percent of global output and has created sufficient employment. In sync with the global trends, service sector in India has also grown rapidly during the last two decades. Its growth has in fact been higher than the growth in agriculture and manufacturing sector.

Looking at Indian service sector, it's definitely globally competitive. The growth pattern of India is interesting to look at. The services led growth that Indian Economy has seen is different from what Clark -Kuznets had envisaged. However, growth is not interesting if it is jobless and spread unevenly in the sector.[1] For instance, some services like software and telecommunications services have grown fast in terms of their share in GDP, Trade and FDI whereas services like health and education have not been able to witness a fast growth. Even though climbed notches in ease of doing business index India

1. Ramachandran, A., Foreign Direct Investment and the Economic Scenario, the Economic Challenger, 2019, 39 (10), 43-49.

still has huge amount of infrastructure bottlenecks along with stringent labour laws. This needs to be looked at in a timely manner by the GOI. Also, the fact that other developing countries are competing with India to attract FDI cannot be ignored. For example, India used to be an attractive business process outsourcing (BPO) destination five years back. Not anymore. Philippines is now a favoured destination for BPO.

The recent changes in FDI policy regime by GOI has helped to remove multiple layers of bottlenecks faced by foreign investors. The investment processes have been rationalised and expedited. The Government has eased 87 FDI rules across 21 sectors in the last 3 years, opening up traditionally conservative sectors like rail infrastructure and defence. India's agriculture sector has also received FDI worth INR 515.49 crore. The changes in the FDI policy regime exhibits the Government will continue to bring about liberalisation of the FDI regime in India in the months to come. All in all, the efforts should be directed to maintain India's trajectory towards remaining the world's most attractive destinations for foreign investment.

The government proposed relaxation in the FDI norms for sectors such as media, aviation, insurance, and single brand retail with a view to attract more overseas investment. India's FDI inflows in 2018-19 grew by 6 percent to $ 64.37 billion.

Govt. propose to further consolidate, the gains in order to make India more attractive FDI destination. The government will examine suggestions of further opening up of FDI in aviation, media, AVGC (Animation, Visual effects, Gaming and Comics) and insurance sector in consultation with stakeholders. Hundred percent Foreign Direct Investment (FDI) will be permitted for insurance intermediaries, and local sourcing norms will be eased for FDI in the single brand retail sector.

Currently, as per the FDI policy, 49 percent foreign investment is allowed in the insurance sector, which includes insurance broking, insurance companies, third party administrators, surveyors and loss assessors.[1]

Representations have been made to the government that insurance brokers should be treated on par with other financial services intermediaries, where 100 percent FDI is permitted.

Insurance penetration in the country was 3.4 percent in 2015 against the world average of 6.2 percent. In 2014, it was 3.3 percent in India.

3.4 Why India

India has emerged as one of the most preferred destinations for foreign investment, just after China and the United States. The government of India has gone a step further and formulated investor-friendly policies to encourage FDI in India. One of the fastest growing economies of the world, India boasts of a stable annual growth rate, booming capital markets, and rising foreign exchange reserves.[2]

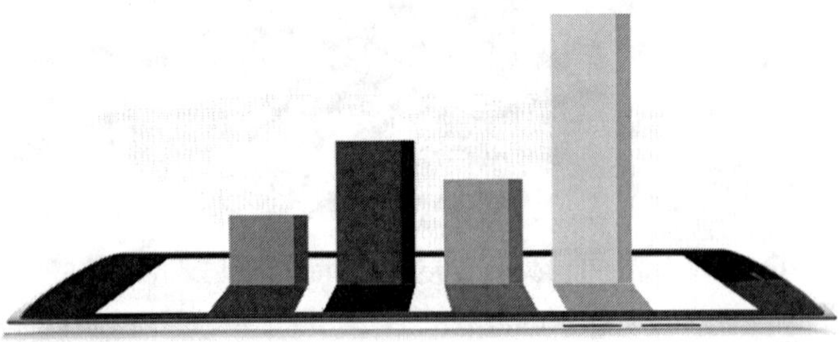

India is a successful economy with abundant natural resources and availability of skilled manpower.

According to the United Nations Population fund, India is to have the world's largest youth population by 2020/2023. This will, therefore, drive innovation, productivity and growth.

1. Mahajan, D., FDI in India not as per her potential, The Economic Challenger, 2019, 41 (11), 59-63.
2. https://www.investindia.gov.in/

- The Indian economy has a lot to offer and exposes investors to a plethora of opportunities from consumer goods and pharmaceuticals to infrastructure, energy and agriculture to automobile and the IT sector.[1]
- India has the third largest group of scientists and technicians in the world.
- India has a booming consumer market with private consumption expecting to be four times by 2025.
- Infrastructure in India has witnessed a growth in spending. Over the next two decades more than USD 1.5 tn investments are planned for infrastructure.
- India is one of the richest tech start-up innovation ecosystems in the world. Now the world's third largest, this start-up ecosystem is maturing rapidly.
- India's strongest exports lie in the services sector, making up over 58 percent of India's economy in 2015, particularly in services like IT, pharmaceuticals, and engineering goods.
- India has one of the oldest stock exchanges in Asia and ranks eighth in terms of "protecting minority investors" according to the World Bank.
- Unlike many other emerging economies, India has a positive macroeconomic environment: inflation is under control, and it has record high foreign exchange reserves and a tamed current account deficit – thus reducing vulnerability to global economic shock.

One of the world's fastest growing Economies

- India represents one sixth of the world and is today the third

1. https://www.investindia.gov.in/

largest economy in terms of purchasing power parity. Even in terms of nominal exchange rate of the dollar, India is the sixth largest economy. It has grown at an average rate of 7% per annum for the past 40 years.

- Since the start of the 21st century, annual average GDP growth has been 6% to 7%, and from 2013 to 2018, India was the world's fastest growing major economy, surpassing China.
- According to IMF projections, India has overtaken the U.K. becoming the world's fifth-largest economy and is now behind only the US, China, Japan and Germany.

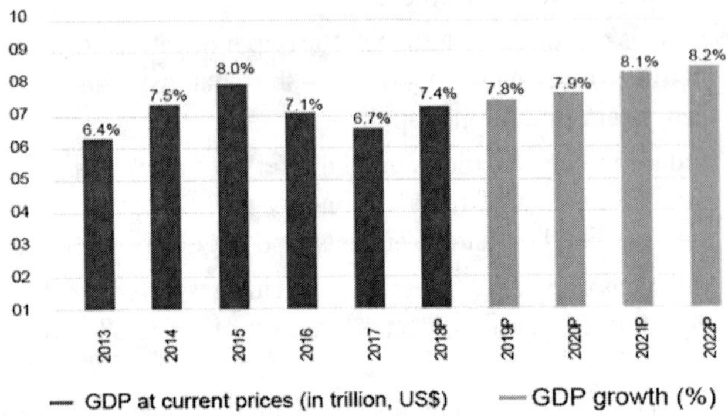

Largest Youth population in the World

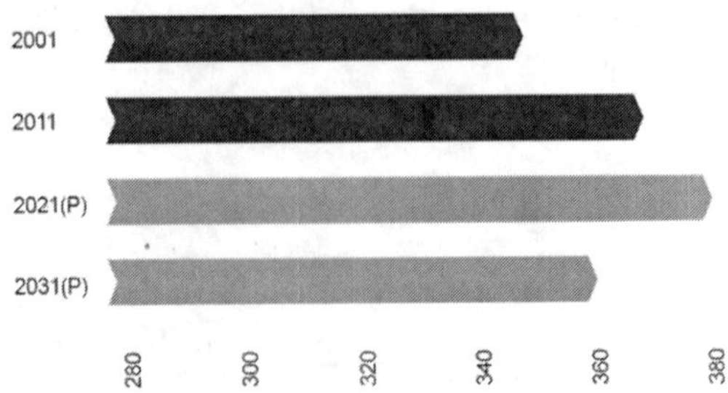

- India has the largest youth population in the world, with more than 808 million people (around 66% of the overall population) under the age of 35.
- India has a booming consumer market with private consumption expected to be four times by 2025.

Global maritime trade to move from the Pacific to the Indian Ocean Region

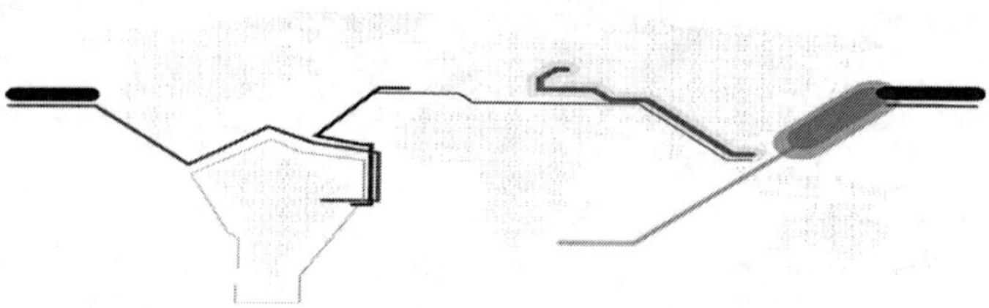

Indian Infrastructure Story

Roads, Renewable Energy and Airports have been the torchbearers, leading the charge when it comes to attracting foreign investment in the infrastructure sector in India.

There are several reasons why these sub-sectors have managed to perform better in attracting private investment compared to other sub-sectors such as railways, ports, and social infrastructure.

The key reason include:

(i) The presence of stable regulatory framework and sovereign rated institutions such as the National Highways Authority of India that has record of delivering on private sector expectations.

(ii) Unambiguous communication by the GOI on targets to be achieved for the sector as whole (for instance GOI's stated goal to generate 175 GW of renewable energy by 2022).

(iii) Robust payment security mechanisms to ensure timely pay-outs to the private investor.

(iv) An overall investor friendly ecosystem, all of which eventually lent to the projects a more 'bankable' status and therefore, provide adequate comfort to foreign investors.

On the contrary, under-performing sub-sectors such as railways, ports and urban social infrastructure are influenced by fiscally strained public sector undertakings which eventually reflects in the poor credit ratings of their projects. It is, however, likely that India's fiscal pressures will eventually force the lackadaisical sub-sectors to reform their positions with GOI's emerging vision of India's infrastructure growth needs.

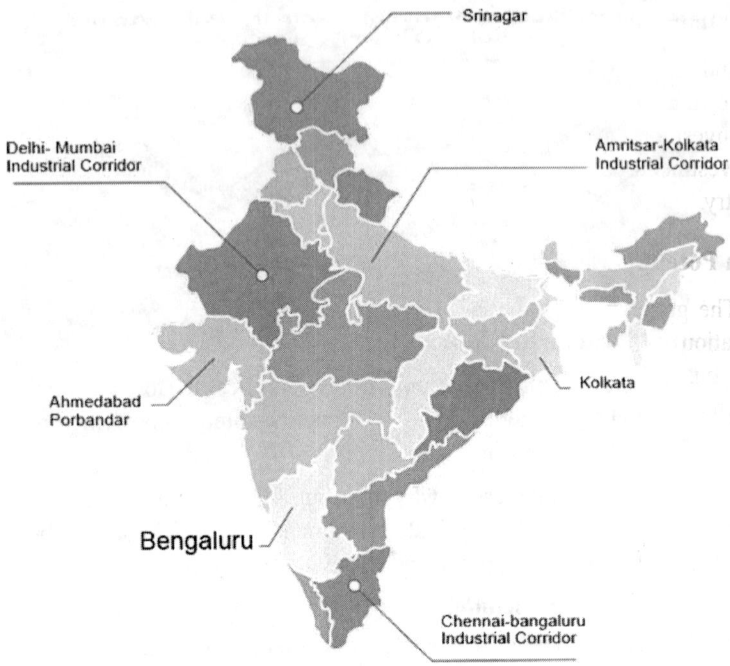

Reforms in FDI policy

- Recently Government of India has taken bold and positive initiatives to promote inbound foreign investment as most sectors have been freed and has been made open for foreign investment in India under the automatic route. The government stance regarding investment is quite investor friendly, which is not only promoting future investments but also facilitating country's economic growth.
- Foreign Investors in India can expect and see a growing India that will certainly grow in the years to come and become an attractive destination for foreign investment. The World Bank prediction of GDP growth in India at 7.6 percent for the year 2016-17, coupled with growing reforms for FDI policy will make it possible.[1]

1. https://www.investindia.gov.in/

Privatisation Programmes

India has been privatising its public sector: like telecommunications, public infrastructure, airways, ports, etc which is proving beneficial for investors looking for investing in India. The department of disinvestments is looking after the privatisation programme in the country.

High Potential Sectors

The government of India is taking various initiatives including relaxation of FDI norms which is making it easier for foreign companies to do business in India. It has taken steps which has made possible implementation of best investment options in India. The sectors of foreign investment are as follows:

- Airport and Ground Handling,
- Computer and Peripherals,
- Education Services,
- Electric Power and Transmission Equipment,
- Food Processing,
- Machine Tools,
- Medical Equipment,
- Mining and Mineral Processing Equipment,
- Oil and Gas Field Machinery,
- Pollution Control Equipment,
- Safety and Security,
- Telecommunications Equipment,
- Textile Machinery,
- Water and Sustainable energies.

In the recent years, India has assumed a notable position on the world canvas as a key international trading partner, primarily because of its investors' friendly FDI policy. At the same time, the global view for India is highly positive. Jack Welch of GE Company says, "India is a developed country as far as intellectual capital is concerned." Similarly, John Chambers of CISCO comments, "We are expanding our presence in India to take advantage of the ample R&D

talent available." Michael Dell quotes, "India can be a major part of Dell's operations and we are looking to capitalise on human capital." This outlook for the country is based on some definite competitive strength which India possesses. India has a vast pool of highly skilled manpower and entrepreneurial expertise.

India has many opportunities for FDI in the development and management of infrastructure. Since infrastructure projects may not be financially viable on their own, public private partnership (PPP) is sought here to bring in private resources and techno managerial capabilities through FDI. The Government is providing 'viability gap funding' in the form of capital grants, operation and management support and interest subsidies etc. for projects related to roads, railways, sea ports, airports, water supply, sewerage and solid waste disposal etc. Moreover, ten years tax holiday is given for road, highways and ports projects. Recent Government initiatives like extending the existing network of roads, developing the highways under National Highway Development Programme (NHDP) through Golden Quadrilateral and North-South East-West (NSEW) Corridor necessitate vast pool of foreign investment.

Power Sector

Power sector promises great potential for foreign investment. With a generation of 1,561 terawatt-hours (TWh), India is the third largest producer and the third largest consumer of electricity in the world. Electricity production reached 360.45 GW as of July 2019. India is ranked 4th in wind power, 5th in solar power and 5th in renewable power installed capacity as of 2018. India ranked sixth in list of countries to make most investment in clean energy at US$ 90 billion.

Renewable energy is fast emerging as a major source of power in India. The Government of India has set a target to achieve 175 GW installed capacity of renewable energy by FY22. As of June 2019, government has launched US$ 5 billion of transmission-line tenders in phases and has set a target of 175 GW by 2022. In FY20 (as of Oct 19), total thermal installed capacity in the country stood at 229.40 GW, while renewable, hydro and nuclear energy installed capacity totalled to 83.37 GW, 45.39 GW and 6.78 GW, respectively. Wind energy is the largest source of renewable energy in India, accounting for 47.44 percent (35.14 GW) (As of Dec 2018) of total installed renewable capacity (81.33 GW) (As of Sep. 19). As of October 31, 2019, India has an installed renewable energy capacity of 83.37 GW. There are plans to double wind power generation capacity to 60 GW by 2022. The government plans to double the share of installed electricity generation capacity of renewable energy to 40 percent till 2030. India has also raised the solar power generation capacity addition target by five times to 100 GW by 2022. The Union Government of India is preparing a 'rent a roof' policy for supporting its target of generating 40 gigawatts (GW) of power through solar rooftop projects by 2022.[1]

All the states and union territories of India are on board to fulfil the Government of India's vision of ensuring 24x7 affordable and quality power for all by March 2019. India is on path to achieve 100 percent household electrification by March 31, 2019, as envisaged under the Saubhagya scheme. More than 26.2 million households have been electrified under Saubhagya scheme. As of September 2018, the Government of India launched a voluntary based programme to promote energy efficient chiller systems in India. It labels the energy performance by providing star ratings and will be effective up to December 31, 2020. Under the Union Budget 2019-20, the Government of India has allocated Rs 5 crore (US$ 0.73 million) to increase capacity of Green Energy Corridor Project along with Rs 920 crore (US$ 130 million) for wind and Rs 3,005 crore (US$ 440 million) for solar power projects. Total FDI inflows in the power sector reached US$ 14.54 billion during April 2000 to June 2019, accounting for 3.48 percent of total FDI inflows in India.[2]

1. https://www.ibef.org/industry/indian-power-industry
2. *ibid.*

Telecommunications Industry

Telecommunications industry in India possesses a vast potential for FDI. India is among the fastest growing telecommunications markets of the world. India is currently the world's second-largest telecommunications market with a subscriber base of 1.20 billion and has registered strong growth in the past decade and half. The Indian mobile economy is growing rapidly and will contribute substantially to India's Gross Domestic Product (GDP), according to report prepared by GSM Association (GSMA) in collaboration with the Boston Consulting Group (BCG). As of January 2019, India has witnessed a 165 percent growth in app downloads in the past two years. 4.8 billion downloads of mobile applications were registered in India in first three months of 2019.

The liberal and reformist policies of the Government of India have been instrumental along with strong consumer demand in the rapid growth in the Indian telecom sector. The government has enabled easy market access to telecom equipment and a fair and proactive regulatory framework that has ensured availability of telecom services to consumer at affordable prices. The deregulation of Foreign Direct Investment (FDI) norms has made the sector one of the fastest growing and a top five employment opportunity generator in the country.

India ranks as the world's second largest market in terms of total internet users. The number of internet subscribers in the country increased at a CAGR of 45.74 percent during FY06-FY19 to reach 636.73 million in 2018-19. Total wireless data usage in India grew 119.00 percent year-on-year to 17,940,576 terabytes between April-June 2019. The internet subscribers reached 665.31 million till June 2019.[1]

1. https://www.ibef.org/industry/telecommunications

Further, India is also the world's second largest telecommunications market, total telephone subscriber base and tele-density reached 1,195.24 million and 90.52 percent, respectively, at the end of September 2019.

Gross revenue of the telecom sector stood at Rs 61,535 crore (US$ 8.93 billion) during April-June 2019.

Over the next five years, rise in mobile-phone penetration and decline in data costs will add 500 million new internet users in India, creating opportunities for new businesses.

With daily increasing subscriber base, there have been a lot of investments and developments in the sector. FDI inflows into the telecom sector during April 2000–June 2019 totalled to US$ 37.05 billion, according to the data released by Department for Promotion of Industry and Internal Trade (DPIIT).[1]

Oil and Natural Gas Industry

Oil and natural gas industry can provide good opportunities for FDI. India is rising as a potential refining hub because the capital costs are lower by 25-20 percent in India in comparison to other Asian countries. In 2017, India retained its spot as the third-largest energy consumer in the world with oil and gas accounting for 37 percent of its total energy consumption. Annual oil consumption stood at 4.69 million barrels per day (MBPD) and 54.20 billion cubic meters (bcm) of gas. By 2035, India's energy demand is expected to double to 1,516 Mtoe by 2035 from 753.7 Mtoe in 2017. According to the International Energy Agency (IEA), India is expected to account for almost one-third of the global growth in energy demand by 2040.

1. https://www.ibef.org/industry/telecommunications

India has proven oil reserves of 600 million metric tonnes (MMT), and gas reserves of 1.2 trillion cubic meters. Production of crude oil reached 0.68 mbpd in 2018-19. Natural gas production during the same period stood at 32.06 bcm.

India has a flourishing crude oil refining industry with an annual capacity of 249.40 MMT, as of Apr 1, 2019.[1]

Several initiatives have been taken by the Government of India including the launch of Open Acreage Licencing Policy (OALP) and Coal Bed Methane (CBM) policy. It has allowed 100 percent foreign direct investment (FDI) in E&P projects/companies and 49 percent in refining under the automatic route.

FDI inflows in India's petroleum and natural gas sector stood at US$ 7,018.78 million during April 2000–March 2019. The government is planning to invest US$ 2.86 billion in the upstream oil and gas production to double the natural gas production to 60 bcm and drill more than 120 exploration wells by 2022. Further, rising demand for oil in India is expected to drive investments in refining capacity expansions and upstream production.[2]

Healthcare Industry

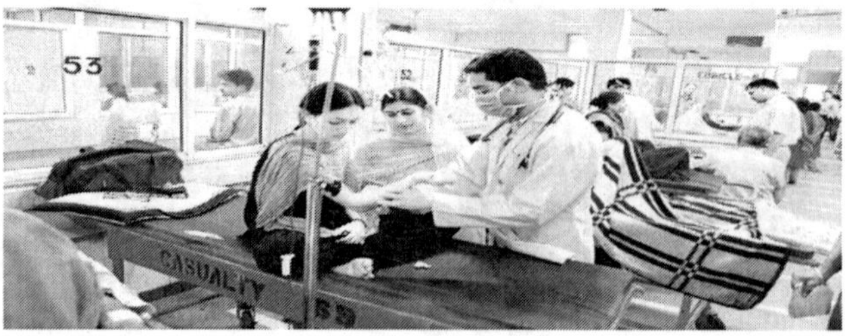

Healthcare industry in India is highly developed and technologically advanced and capable of attracting foreign players. Healthcare has become one of India's largest sectors - both in terms of revenue and employment. Healthcare comprises hospitals, medical devices, clinical trials, outsourcing, telemedicine, medical tourism, health insurance and medical equipment. The Indian healthcare sector is growing at a brisk pace due to its strengthening coverage, services and increasing expenditure by public as well as private players.

1. https://www.ibef.org/archives/industry/indian-oil-and-gas-industry
2. https://www.ibef.org/archives/industry/indian-oil-and-gas-industry

Indian healthcare delivery system is categorised into two major components - public and private. The Government, i.e. public healthcare system comprises limited secondary and tertiary care institutions in key cities and focuses on providing basic healthcare facilities in the form of primary healthcare centres (PHCs) in rural areas. The private sector provides majority of secondary, tertiary and quaternary care institutions with a major concentration in metros, tier I and tier II cities.

India's competitive advantage lies in its large pool of well-trained medical professionals. India is also cost competitive compared to its peers in Asia and Western countries. The cost of surgery in India is about one-tenth of that in the US or Western Europe. The healthcare market can increase three-fold to Rs 8.6 trillion (US$ 133.44 billion) by 2022.

Indian medical tourism market is growing at the rate of 18 percent year on year and is expected to reach US$ 9 billion by 2020. There is a significant scope for enhancing healthcare services considering that healthcare spending as a percentage of Gross Domestic Product (GDP) is rising. The government's expenditure on the health sector has grown to 1.4 percent in FY18E from 1.2 percent in FY14. The Government of India is planning to increase public health spending to 2.5 percent of the country's GDP by 2025.

Health insurance is gaining momentum in India. Gross direct premium income underwritten by health insurance grew 18.2 percent y-o-y to Rs 24,864.01 crore (US$ 3.56 billion) in FY20 (up to September 2019).[1]

The hospital and diagnostic centres attracted Foreign Direct Investment (FDI) worth US$ 6.34 billion between April 2000 and June 2019, according to data released by the Department of Industrial Policy and Promotion (DIPP).[2] Some of the recent investments in the Indian healthcare industry are as follows:

- The value of mergers and acquisitions (M&A) deals in hospital sector jumped by record 155 percent at Rs 7,615 crore (US$ 1.09 billion) in FY19.

1. https://www.ibef.org/industry/healthcare-india.
2. *ibid.*

- In August 2019, Microsoft India and Apollo Hospitals Group entered in agreement to set up a National Clinical Coordination Committee for AI-powered Cardiovascular Disease Risk Score API.
- In January 2019, National Company Law Tribunal (NCLT) approved Tri-Country Premier Hearing Services Inc's plan to acquire Bhilai Scan and Research Pvt Ltd (BSR) Diagnostics Ltd for Rs 67 crore (US$ 9.29 million).
- Healthcare sector in India witnessed 23 deals worth US$ 679 million in H12018.
- India and Cuba have signed a Memorandum of Understanding (MoU) to increase cooperation in the areas of health and medicine, according to Ministry of Health and Family Welfare, Government of India.
- Fortis Healthcare has approved the de-merger of its hospital business with Manipal Hospital Enterprises. TPG and Dr. Ranjan Pal could invest Rs 3,900 crore (US$ 602.41 million) in Manipal Hospital Enterprise.

Automobile Industry

Another high performing sector which can garner a great deal of FDI is the automobile industry which also provides advanced technology, cost-effectiveness and efficient manpower. India became the fourth largest auto market in 2018 with sales increasing 8.3 percent year-on-year to 3.99 million units. It was the seventh largest manufacturer of commercial vehicles in 2018.

The Two Wheelers segment dominates the market in terms of volume owing to a growing middle class and a young population. Moreover, the growing interest of the companies in exploring the rural markets further aided the growth of the sector.

India is also a prominent auto exporter and has strong export growth expectations for the near future. Automobile exports grew 14.50 percent during FY19. It is expected to grow at a CAGR of 3.05 percent during 2016-2026. In addition, several initiatives by the Government of India and the major automobile players in the Indian market are expected to make India a leader in the two-wheeler and four-wheeler market in the world.

Overall domestic automobiles sales increased to 6.71 percent CAGR between FY13-19 with 26.27 million vehicles getting sold in FY19. Domestic automobile production increased at 6.96 percent CAGR between FY13-19 with 30.92 million vehicles manufactured in the country in FY19.[1]

In FY19, year-on-year growth in domestic sales among all the categories was recorded in commercial vehicles at 17.55 percent followed by 10.27 percent year-on-year growth in the sales of three-wheelers.

Premium motorbike sales in India crossed one million units in FY18. During January-September 2018, BMW registered a growth of 11 percent year-on-year in its sales in India at 7,915 units. Mercedes Benz ranked first in sales satisfaction in the luxury vehicles segment according to J D Power 2018 India sales satisfaction index (luxury).

Sales of electric two-wheelers are estimated to have crossed 55,000 vehicles in 2017-18.

In order to keep up with the growing demand, several auto makers have started investing heavily in various segments of the industry during the last few months. The industry has attracted Foreign Direct Investment (FDI) worth US$ 22.35 billion during the period April 2000 to June 2019, according to data released by Department for Promotion of Industry and Internal Trade (DPIIT).[2]

1. https://www.ibef.org/industry/india-automobiles
2. https://www.ibef.org/industry/india-automobiles

Services Sector

The services sector is not only the dominant sector in India's GDP, but has also attracted significant foreign investment flows, contributed significantly to exports as well as provided large-scale employment. India's services sector covers a wide variety of activities such as trade, hotel and restaurants, transport, storage and communication, financing, insurance, real estate, business services, community, social and personal services, and services associated with construction.

As of 2018, 31.45 percent of India's employed population is working in the services sector.

The services sector is the key driver of India's economic growth. The sector has contributed 54.17 percent of India's Gross Value Added at current price in 2018-19. India's services sector GVA grew at a CAGR of 6.96 percent to US$ 1,356.49 billion in FY19 from US$ 846.84 billion in FY12. Net export estimate from April to November 2019 in services is US$ 142.02 billion and import is US$ 89.24 billion.[1]

Nikkei India Services Purchasing Managers' Index (PMI) stood at 52.7 in November 2019. The expansion in services activity was driven by boost in capacity and demand along with favourable public policies.

Some of the developments and major investments by companies in the services sector in the recent past are as follows:

- Services sector is the largest recipient of FDI in India with inflows of US$ 74.94 billion between April 2000 and June 2019.
- Leisure and business travel and tourism spending are expected to increase to US$ 234.4 billion and US$ 12.9 billion in 2018, respectively.

1. https://www.ibef.org/industry/services.

- India's earnings from medical tourism could exceed US$ 9 billion by 2020.

IT-BPM Sector

The global sourcing market in India continues to grow at a higher pace compared to the IT-BPM industry. India is the leading sourcing destination across the world, accounting for approximately 55 percent market share of the US$ 185-190 billion global services sourcing business in 2017-18. Indian IT and ITeS companies have set up over 1,000 global delivery centres in about 80 countries across the world.

India has become the digital capabilities hub of the world with around 75 percent of global digital talent present in the country.

The IT-BPM sector in India stood at US$177 billion in 2019 witnessing a growth of 6.1 percent year-on-year and is estimated that the size of the industry will grow to US$ 350 billion by 2025. India's IT and ITeS industry grew to US$ 181 billion in 2018-19. Exports from the industry increased to US$ 137 billion in FY19 while domestic revenues (including hardware) advanced to US$ 44 billion. IT industry employees 4.1 million people as of FY19.

Spending on information technology in India is expected to reach US$ 90 billion in 2019.

Revenue from digital segment is expected to comprise 38 percent of the forecasted US$ 350 billion industry revenue by 2025.

Indian IT's core competencies and strengths have attracted significant investments from major countries. The computer software and hardware sector in India attracted cumulative Foreign Direct Investment (FDI) inflows worth US$ 39.47 billion between April

2000 and June 2019 and ranks second in inflow of FDI, as per data released by the Department for Promotion of Industry and Internal Trade (DPIIT).

Leading Indian IT firms like Infosys, Wipro, TCS and Tech Mahindra, are diversifying their offerings and showcasing leading ideas in block chain, artificial intelligence to clients using innovation hubs, research and development centres, in order to create differentiated offerings.

Infrastructure Sector

Increased impetus to develop infrastructure in the country is attracting both domestic and international players. Private sector is emerging as a key player across various infrastructure segments, ranging from roads and communications to power and airports. In order to boost the construction of buildings in the country, the Government of India has decided to come up with a single window clearance facility to accord speedy approval of construction projects. In 2018, India was ranked 44th out of 167 countries in World Bank's Logistics Performance Index (LPI) 2018. India was also ranked second in the 2019 Agility Emerging Markets Logistics Index.

During April-September 2019, the cumulative growth of the eight core industries is 1.3 percent. In the road's sector, the government's policy to increase private sector participation has proved to be a boon for the infrastructure industry with many private players entering the business through the public-private partnership (PPP) model. India is expected to become the third largest construction market globally by 2022. India plans to spend US$ 1.4 trillion on infrastructure in the next five years to have sustainable development in the country.

Large investment in infrastructure have provided momentum to overall PE/VC investments into India which touched an all-time high where infrastructure recorded US$ 1.4 billion during October 2019 accounting 43 percent of all the investment of the month. All villages in India will be connected through a road network by 2019 under Pradhan Mantri Gram Sadak Yojana (PMGSY) also to upgrade the 1,25,000 kms of road length over the next five years, the estimated cost of Rs 80,250 crore (US$ 12.03 billion) is envisaged under Pradhan Mantri Gram Sadak Yojana-III (PMGSY). Road building in India has become the second cheapest in Asia. In August 2017, a new Metro Rail Policy was announced to boost private investment in the sector. Metro rail network has touched 657 Km.

The infrastructure sector has become the biggest focus area of the Government of India. Under Union Budget 2019-20, Rs 4,41,704.8 crore (US$ 63.20 billion) was allocated to the sector. As per Union budget 2019-20, investment of Rs 5,000,000 crore (US$ 750 billion) is needed for railways infrastructure between 2018-30. In the Union Budget 2019-20, the Government of India has given a massive push to the infrastructure sector by allocating Rs 24,000 crore (US$ 3.4 billion) for the sector. For 2019-20, budgetary allocation for Ministry of Development of North Eastern Region has been increased to Rs 3,000 crore (US$ 429.25 million) as compared to Rs 2,629 crore (US$ 376.16 million) in 2018-19.

The eight infrastructure sectors that constitute 40.27 percent of the index of industrial production (IIP) almost remaining at 0.2 percent in June 2019.

According to Department for Promotion of Industry and Internal Trade (DPIIT), Construction Development sector and Infrastructure Activities sector received FDI inflows amounting to US$ 15.33 billion and US$ 15.33 billion, respectively from April 2000 to June 2019.[1]

1. https://www.ibef.org/industry/infrastructure

Indian Pharmaceutical Industry

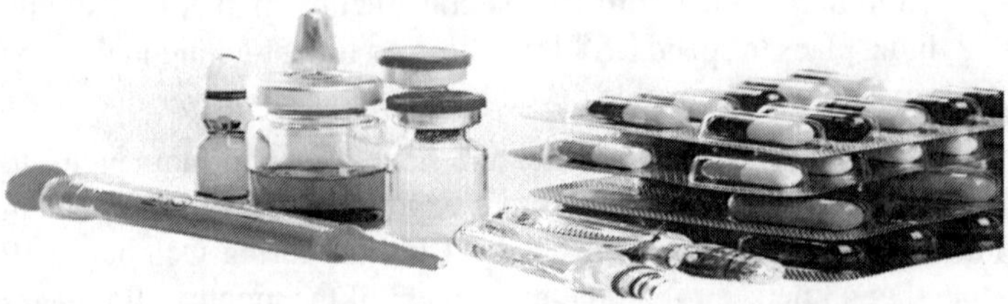

India is the largest provider of generic drugs globally. Indian pharmaceutical sector industry supplies over 50 percent of global demand for various vaccines, 40 percent of generic demand in the US and 25 percent of all medicine in UK.

India enjoys an important position in the global pharmaceuticals sector. The country also has a large pool of scientists and engineers who have the potential to steer the industry ahead to an even higher level. Presently over 80 percent of the antiretroviral drugs used globally to combat AIDS (Acquired Immune Deficiency Syndrome) are supplied by Indian pharmaceutical firms.

The pharmaceutical sector was valued at US$ 33 billion in 2017. The country's pharmaceutical industry is expected to expand at a CAGR of 22.4 percent over 2015–20 to reach US$ 55 billion. India's pharmaceutical exports stood at US$ 17.27 billion in FY18 and have reached US$ 19.14 billion in FY19. Pharmaceutical exports include bulk drugs, intermediates, drug formulations, biological, Ayush & herbal products and surgical.

Indian companies received 304 Abbreviated New Drug Application (ANDA) approvals from the US Food and Drug Administration (USFDA) in 2017. The country accounts for around 30 percent (by volume) and about 10 percent (value) in the US$ 70-80 billion US generics market.

India's biotechnology industry comprising bio-pharmaceuticals, bio-services, bio-agriculture, bio-industry and bioinformatics is expected to grow at an average growth rate of around 30 percent a year and reach US$ 100 billion by 2025.

The Union Cabinet has given its nod for the amendment of the existing Foreign Direct Investment (FDI) policy in the pharmaceutical sector in order to allow FDI up to 100 percent under the automatic route for manufacturing of medical devices subject to certain conditions.

The drugs and pharmaceuticals sector attracted cumulative FDI inflows worth US$ 15.98 billion between April 2000 and March 2019, according to data released by the Department of Industrial Policy and Promotion (DIPP).[1]

Food Processing Industry

Food processing is another sector which has the prospects of FDI. The Indian food industry is poised for huge growth, increasing its contribution to world food trade every year. In India, the food sector has emerged as a high-growth and high-profit sector due to its immense potential for value addition, particularly within the food processing industry. Accounting for about 32 percent of the country's total food market, the Government of India has been instrumental in the growth and development of the food processing industry. The government through the Ministry of Food Processing Industries (MOFPI) is making all efforts to encourage investments in the business. It has approved proposals for joint ventures (JV), foreign collaborations, industrial licences, and 100 percent export-oriented units.

The Indian food and grocery market is the world's sixth largest, with retail contributing 70 percent of the sales. The Indian food processing industry accounts for 32 percent of the country's total food market, one of the largest industries in India and is ranked fifth in terms of production, consumption, export and expected growth. It contributes around 8.80 and 8.39 percent of Gross Value Added (GVA) in Manufacturing and Agriculture respectively, 13 percent of India's

1. https://www.ibef.org/industry/pharmaceutical-india

exports and six percent of total industrial investment. The Indian gourmet food market is currently valued at US$ 1.3 billion and is growing at a Compound Annual Growth Rate (CAGR) of 20 percent. India's organic food market is expected to increase by three times by 2020.

The online food ordering business in India is in its nascent stage, but witnessing exponential growth. With online food delivery players like Food Panda, Zomato, Tiny Owl and Swiggy building scale through partnerships, the organised food business has a huge potential and a promising future.

FDI in the food processing sector was USD 904.9 million in the 2018-19 fiscal, while it stood at USD 727.22 million, USD 505.88 million and USD 515.86 million in 2017-18, 2016-17 and 2015-16 respectively.[1]

1. https://www.ibef.org/industry/indian-food-industry.aspx

CHAPTER – 4

Role of FDI in Development of Indian Economy

4.1 Introduction

FDI in India has a significant role in the economic growth and development of India. FDI in India to various sectors can attain sustained economic growth and development through creation of jobs, expansion of existing manufacturing industries. The inflow of FDI in service sectors and construction and development sector attained substantial sustained economic growth and development through creation of jobs in India. Computer, Software & Hardware and Drugs & Pharmaceuticals sector were the other sectors to which attention was shown by Foreign Direct Investors (FDI). The other sectors in Indian economy the Foreign Direct Investors interest was, in fact has been quite poor.

FDI has helped to raise the output, productivity and employment in some sectors especially in service sector. Indian service sector is generating the proper employment options for skilled worker with high perks. On the other side banking and insurance sector help in providing the strength to the Indian economic condition and develop the foreign exchange system in the country. FDI always helps to create employment in the country and also support the small-scale industries, and helps countries to put an impression on the world wide level through liberalisation and globalisation.

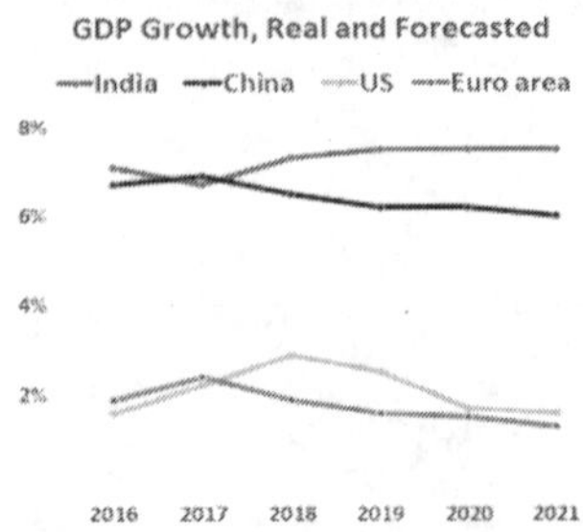

Today the Indian economy is not only one of the largest economies in the world but it is also one of the fastest growing major economies as well. However, to boost the economy, infusion of funds is essential. These funds are like the fuel for the growth engine for any economy. There are many sources through which the funds are infused into an economy – like the Government Funds, Corporate Investments, Debt Funds, FDI's and FII's etc. In this study the specific role of the FDI will be examined with respect to the overall growth dynamics of the Indian Economy.

4.2 Indian Economy: An Overview

The Indian economy is mixed and developing economy. It is the seventh largest economy in the world with respect to the nominal GDP. Also, it is the third largest economy in the world with respect to purchase power parity (PPP).

It is important to know that after the "Globalisation" in the year 1991, the average GDP growth in a fiscal year increased up to 6 percent to

7 percent. It is due to various reasons why Indian economy development is one of the highest in the world among the developing countries.

Few of the reasons are:

- Young and dynamic population
- English proficiency- English being country's official language
- Corresponding low dependency ratio

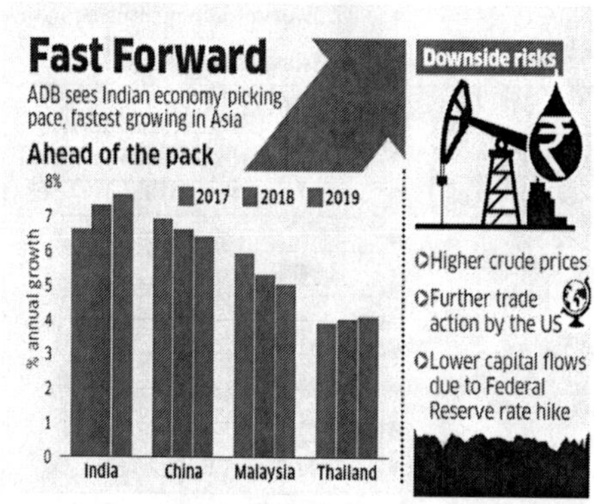

- Healthy savings and investment rates- India being an orthodox believer has always made sure that the savings be its most important component.

With regards to the service sectors, Indian economy has shown its maximum growth in this sector with a growth rate of 9 percent in a year. In the financial year 2017, India became one of the major exporters of IT service, BPOs, and software services. The most significant fact in the India economy growth is that India holds the second position in the start-up business in the world.[1]

In the year 2018-2019, India had a record of 3,100 technology start-ups. Another industry which has shown the higher growth rate and keeps India one of its major is the automobile industry.

1. Economic Survey 2019-20, Press Information Bureau, Government of India.

Economy of India- A Summary	
Broad level Statistics	
Currency	Indian rupee (INR, □)
Fiscal year	1 April – 31 March
Trade organisations	WTO, WCO, WFTU, BRICS, G-20, BIS, AIIB, ADB and others
Country group	• Developing/Emerging • Lower-middle income economy
Statistics	
Population	1.353 billion (2018)
GDP	• $3.202 trillion (nominal; 2020 est.) • $12.36 trillion (PPP; 2020 est.)
GDP rank	• 5th (nominal; 2019) • 3rd (PPP; 2019)
GDP growth	• 4.5% (Q2, FY 2019-20) • 8.2% (16/17) 7.2% (17/18) • 6.8% (18/19e) 5.0% (19/20f)
GDP per capita	• $2,340 (nominal; 2020 est.) • $9,030 (PPP; 2020 est.)
GDP per capita rank	• 139th (nominal; 2019) • 119th (PPP; 2018)
GDP by sector	• Agriculture: 15.4% • Industry: 23% • Services: 61.5% • (2017 est.)
GDP by component	• Household consumption: 59.1% • Government consumption: 11.5% • Investment in fixed capital: 28.5% • Investment in inventories: 3.9% • Exports of goods and services: 19.1% • Imports of goods and services: −22% • (2017 est.)
Inflation (CPI)	• 7.35% (December 2019)
Base borrowing rate	– 6.0% (as on 12 July 2019)
Population below poverty line	• 60.4% on less than $3.20/day (2011) • 3.7% in extreme poverty (December 2018) • (World Poverty Clock estimate)
Gini coefficient	33.9 medium (2013)
Human Development Index	• 0.647 medium (2018) (129th) • 0.477 IHDI (2018)

Labour force	• 519,469,299 (2019) • 45.4% employment rate (2018)
Labour force by occupation	• Agriculture: 44% • Industry: 25% • Services: 31% • (FY 2018)
Unemployment	• 6.1% (FY 2018) • 22.5% youth unemployment (2018)
Main industries	• Textiles • Chemicals • Food processing • Agribusiness • Handicrafts • Petroleum • Petrochemicals • Gems and jewellery • Leather • Iron ore • Steel • Aluminium • Cement • Mining • Metals • Retail • Machinery • Information technology • Construction • Financial services • Electric power • Consumer goods • Pharmaceuticals • Automotive • Telecommunications • Real estate • Paper • Transportation equipment
Ease-of-doing-business rank	63rd (easy, 2020)
External	
Exports	$330 billion (2018–19)
Export goods	• Agricultural products 12.8% • Fuels and mining products 13.8% • Manufacturers 70.5% • Others 2.9%

Main export partners	• Arab League 17.37% • European Union 17.34% • United States 15.88% • ASEAN 11.38% • China 5.08% • Hong Kong 3.94% • Japan 1.47% • South Korea 1.43% • Other 26.11%
Imports	$514 billion (2018–19)
Import goods	• Agricultural products 8.1% • Fuels and mining products 30% • Manufacturers 51.7% • Other 10.2%
Main import partners	• Arab League 19.88% • China 13.68% • ASEAN 11.53% • European Union 11.35% • United States 6.92% • Hong Kong 3.50% • South Korea 3.26% • Japan 2.48% • Other 27.4%
FDI stock	• Inward: $386.35 billion • Outward: $166.19 billion • (2018)
Current account	−$57.2 billion (June 2019)
Gross external debt	$543.0 billion (2019)
Net international investment position	−$436.4 billion (2019)
Public finances	
Public debt	• Rs 146.886 trillion (US$2.1 trillion) • 69.037% of GDP (2019)
Budget balance	−3.4% (of GDP) (2018-19)
Revenues	• Rs 39.29 trillion (US$550 billion) • 20.60% of GDP (2018)
Expenses	• Rs 52.03 trillion (US$730 billion) • 27.28% of GDP (2018)
Economic aid	$3.09 billion (2017)
Foreign reserves	$462.157 billion (17 January 2020) (7th)

Source: https://en.wikipedia.org/wiki/Economy_of_India

Although India is known for its agriculture and it is also the major producer of employer and employee with regards to the agriculture sector, unfortunately since the 2013-2014 India has a major decline in this sector's GDP.

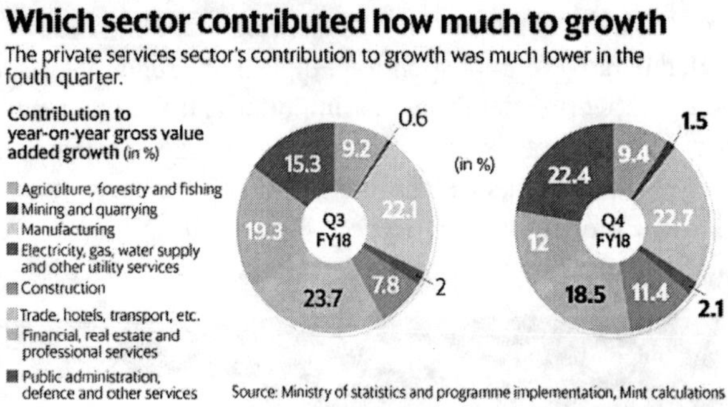

In the year 2019, Indian economy among the global economies surpassed United Kingdom (UK) and became the fifth- largest economy in the world. This is with respect to the annual GDP. In addition to this, India remains to be one of the fastest growing major economies of the world.

The economy of India is characterised as a developing market economy. It is the world's fifth-largest economy by nominal GDP and the third-largest by Purchasing Power Parity (PPP). According to the IMF, on a per capita income basis, India ranked 142nd by GDP (nominal) and 119th by GDP (PPP) per capita in 2018. From independence in 1947 until 1991, successive governments promoted protectionist economic policies with extensive state intervention and regulation; the end of the Cold War and an acute balance of payments crisis in 1991 led to the adoption of a broad programme of economic liberalisation. Since the start of the 21st century, annual average GDP growth has been 6% to 7%, and from 2014 to 2018, India was the world's fastest growing major economy, surpassing China. Historically, India was the largest economy in the world for most of the two millennia from 1st until 19th century.[1]

The long-term growth perspective of the Indian economy remains positive due to its young population and corresponding low dependency

1. https://en.wikipedia.org/wiki/Economy_of_India

ratio, healthy savings and investment rates, and is increasing integration into the global economy. The economy slowed in 2017, due to shocks of "demonetisation" in 2016 and introduction of Goods and Services Tax in 2017. Nearly 60 percent of India's GDP is driven by domestic private consumption and continues to remain the world's sixth-largest consumer market. Apart from private consumption, India's GDP is also fueled by government spending, investment, and exports. In 2018, India was the world's tenth-largest importer and the nineteenth-largest exporter. India has been a member of World Trade Organisation since 1 January 1995. It ranks 63rd on Ease of doing business index and 68th on Global Competitiveness Report. With 520-million-workers, the Indian labour force is the world's second-largest as of 2019. India has

one of the world's highest numbers of billionaires and extreme income inequality. Since India has a vast informal economy, barely 2 percent of Indians pay income taxes. During the 2008 global financial crisis the economy faced mild slowdown, India undertook stimulus measures (both fiscal and monetary) to boost growth and generate demand; in subsequent years economic growth revived. According to 2017 Price water house Coopers (PwC) report, India's GDP at purchasing power parity could overtake that of the United States by 2050. According to World Bank, to achieve sustainable economic development India must focus on public sector reform, infrastructure, agricultural and rural development, removal of land and labour regulations, financial inclusion, spur private investment and exports, education and public health.

India's largest trading partners are China, USA, UAE, Saudi Arabia, Switzerland, Germany, Hong Kong, Indonesia, South Korea, and Malaysia. In 2018-19, the foreign direct investment (FDI) in India was \$64.4 billion with service sector, computer, and telecom industry remains leading sectors for FDI inflows. India has free trade agreements with several nations, including ASEAN, SAFTA, Mercosur, South Korea, Japan and few others which are in effect or under negotiating stage. The service sector makes up 55.6 percent of GDP and remains the fastest growing sector, while the industrial sector and the agricultural sector employs majority of the labour force. The Bombay Stock Exchange and National Stock Exchange are one of the world's largest stock exchanges by market capitalisation. India is the world's sixth-largest manufacturer, representing 3 percent of global manufacturing output and employs over 57 million people. Nearly 70 percent of India's population is rural whose primary source of livelihood is agriculture, and contributes about 50 percent of India's GDP. It has the world's seventh-largest foreign-exchange reserves worth $461 billion. India has a high national debt with 68 percent of GDP, while its fiscal deficit remained at 3.4 percent of GDP. However, as per 2019 CAG report, the actual fiscal deficit is 5.85 percent of GDP. India's government-owned banks faced mounting bad debt, resulting in low credit growth, simultaneously the NBFC sector has been engulfed in a liquidity crisis. India faces high unemployment, rising income inequality, and major slump in aggregate demand. In recent years, independent economists and financial institutions have accused the government of fudging various economic data especially GDP growth.[1]

India ranks second globally in food and agricultural production, while agricultural exports were $38.5 billion. The construction and real estate sector is the second largest employer after agriculture, and a vital sector to gauge economic activity. The Indian textiles industry is estimated at $150 billion and contributes 7 percent of industrial

1. Economic Survey 2019-20, Press Information Bureau, Government of India.

output and 2 percent of India's GDP while employs over 45 million people directly. The Indian IT industry is a major exporter of IT services with $180 billion in revenue and employs over four million people. India's telecommunication industry is the world's second largest by number of mobile phones, smart-phone, and internet users. It is the world's tenth-largest oil producer and the third-largest oil consumer. The Indian automobile industry is the world's fourth largest by production. It has $672 billion worth of retail market which contributes over 10 percent of India's GDP and has one of world's fastest growing e-commerce markets. India has the world's fourth-largest natural resources, with mining sector contributes 11 percent of the country's industrial GDP and 2.5 percent of total GDP. It is also the world's second-largest coal producer, the second-largest cement producer, the second-largest steel producer, and the third-largest electricity producer.[1]

4.2.1 Market Size

India's nominal GDP growth rate is estimated at 12 percent in 2019-20. The estimate for 2018-19 was 11.5 percent. During Q2 of 2019-20, GDP (at constant 2011-12 prices), GDP stood at Rs 33.16 lakh crore (US$ 474.46 billion) showing a growth rate of 4.3 percent over the corresponding quarter of previous year.[2]

India has retained its position as the third largest start-up base in the world with over 8,900-9,300 start-ups, with about 1,300 new start-ups being founded in 2019, according to a report by NASSCOM. India also witnessed the addition of 7 unicorns in 2019 till August, taking the total tally up to 24.

India's labour force is expected to touch 160-170 million by 2020, based on rate of population growth, increased labour force

1. Ministry of Statistics and Programme Implementation
2. https://www.ibef.org/economy/indian-economy-overview

participation, and higher education enrolment, among other factors, according to a study by ASSOCHAM and Thought Arbitrage Research Institute.

India's foreign exchange reserves were US$ 448.59 billion in the week up to November 22, 2019, according to data from the RBI.

4.2.2. Recent Developments

With the improvement in the economic scenario, there have been various investments in various sectors of the economy. The M&A activity in India increased 53.3 percent to US$ 77.6 billion in 2017 while private equity (PE) deals reached US$ 24.4 billion. Some of the important recent developments in Indian economy are as follows:

- Exports from India increased 1.60 percent year-on-year to US$ 356.96 billion in April-November 2019.
- Nikkei India Manufacturing Purchasing Managers' Index (PMI) stood at 52.7 in December 2019, showing expansion in the sector.
- Mergers and Acquisitions (M&A) activity in the country has reached US$ 48 billion during Jan-Sept 2019.
- The gross tax revenue stood at Rs 11.74 lakh crore (US$ 168 billion) out of which Income tax collection contributed Rs 2.67 lakh crore (US$ 38.34 billion) between April-November 2019.[1]
- Companies in India have raised around US$ 114.1 billion through 768 Initial Public Offers (IPO) first nine months of 2019.
- India's Foreign Direct Investment (FDI) equity inflows reached US$ 436.47 billion between April 2000 and June 2019, with maximum contribution from services, computer software and hardware, telecommunications, construction, trading and automobiles.
- India's cumulative growth of Index of Industrial Production (IIP) with base 2011-12 for the period April-September 2019 stands at 1.3 percent, with September 2019 stands at 123.3.

1. https://www.ibef.org/economy/indian-economy-overview

- Consumer Price Index (CPI) – Combined inflation 3.3 percent in April-September 2019.
- Around 12 million jobs in a year were created in India during 2015-19.
- India improved its ranking in the World Bank's Doing Business Report by 14 spots over last year and is ranked 63rd among 190 countries in 2020 edition of the report.
- India is expected to have 100,000 start-ups by 2025, which will create employment for 3.25 million people and US$ 500 billion in value, as per Mr. T V Mohan Das Pai, Chairman, Manipal Global Education.
- The World Bank has stated that private investments in India is expected to grow by 8.8 percent in FY 2018-19 to overtake private consumption growth of 7.4 percent, and thereby drive the growth in India's gross domestic product (GDP) in FY 2018-19.
- India is expected to retain its position as the world's leading recipient of remittances in 2018, with total remittances touching US$ 80 billion, according to World Bank's Migration and Development Brief.

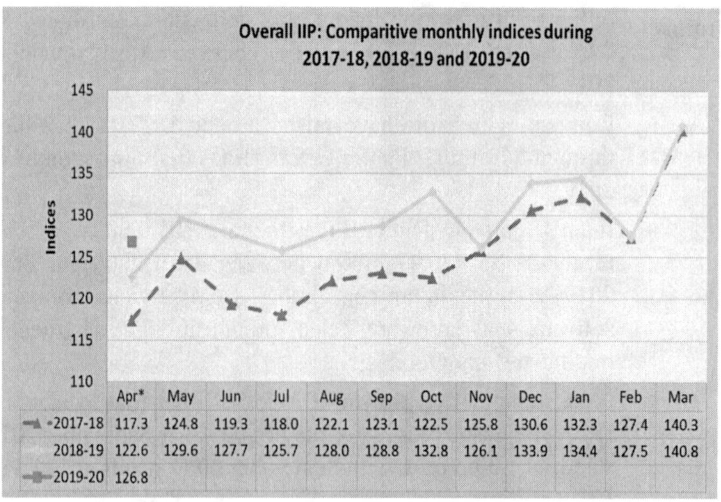

	Apr*	May	Jun	Jul	Aug	Sep	Oct	Nov	Dec	Jan	Feb	Mar
2017-18	117.3	124.8	119.3	118.0	122.1	123.1	122.5	125.8	130.6	132.3	127.4	140.3
2018-19	122.6	129.6	127.7	125.7	128.0	128.8	132.8	126.1	133.9	134.4	127.5	140.8
2019-20	126.8											

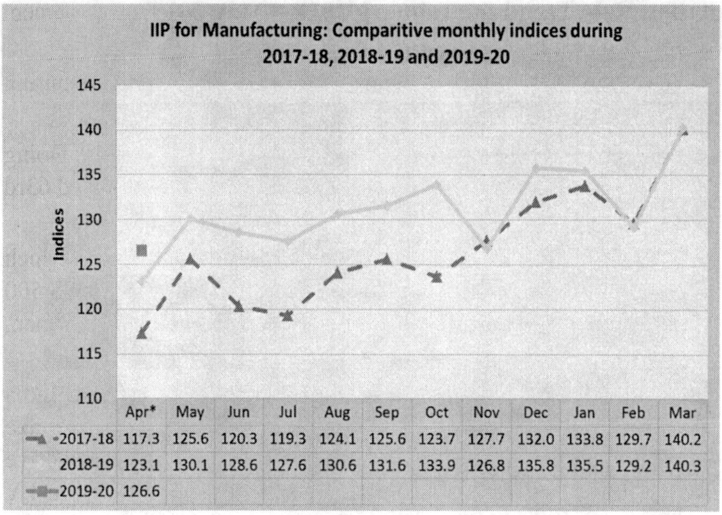

	Apr*	May	Jun	Jul	Aug	Sep	Oct	Nov	Dec	Jan	Feb	Mar
2017-18	117.3	125.6	120.3	119.3	124.1	125.6	123.7	127.7	132.0	133.8	129.7	140.2
2018-19	123.1	130.1	128.6	127.6	130.6	131.6	133.9	126.8	135.8	135.5	129.2	140.3
2019-20	126.6											

- Consumer Price Index (CPI) inflation was recorded at around 3.5 percent for the FY 2018. The inflation has an increasing trend since October 2018; however, it is still lower than the Reserve bank of India's (RBI) medium-term target of 4 percent for 10 consecutive months.[1]

Inflation Rate for last 5 years: 2014 – YTD 2019

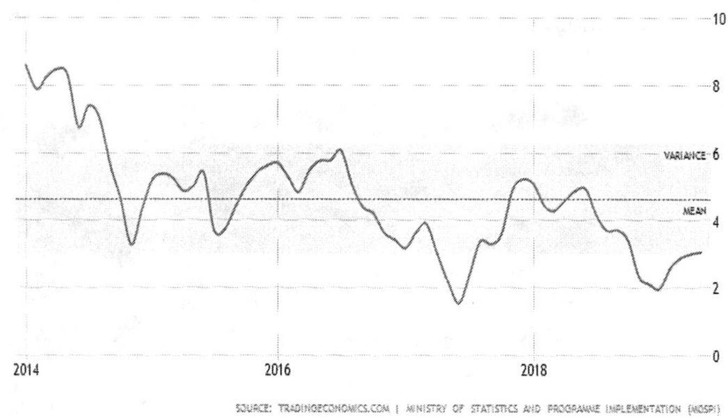

1. https://tradingeconomics.com/india/inflation-cpi

Inflation Rate Trend for January 2018 – May 2019

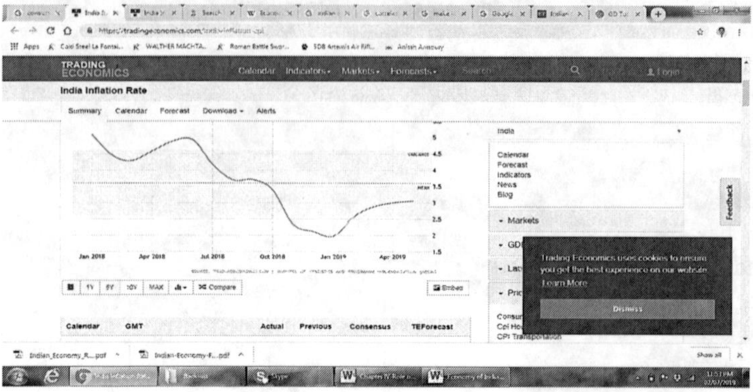

4.2.3 Government Initiatives

The Union Budget for 2019-20 was announced in Parliament on July 05, 2019. India is all set to become US$ 3 trillion economy by the end of FY20. The budget focuses on reducing red tape, making best use of technology, building social infrastructure, digital India, pollution free India, Make in India, job creation in Micro, Small and Medium Enterprises (MSMEs) and investing heavily in infrastructure.

Total expenditure for 2019-20 is budgeted at Rs 2,786,349 crore (US$ 417.95 billion), an increase of 14.09 percent from 2018-19 (budget estimates).[1]

Numerous foreign companies are setting up their facilities in India on account of various government initiatives like Make in

1. https://www.ibef.org/economy/indian-economy-overview

India and Digital India. Mr Narendra Modi, Prime Minister of India, has launched the Make in India initiative with an aim to boost the manufacturing sector of Indian economy, to increase the purchasing power of an average Indian consumer, which would further boost demand, and hence spur development, in addition to benefiting investors. The Government of India, under the Make in India initiative, is trying to give boost to the contribution made by the manufacturing sector and aims to take it up to 25 percent of the GDP from the current 17 percent. Besides, the Government has also come up with Digital India initiative, which focuses on three core components: creation of digital infrastructure, delivering services digitally and to increase the digital literacy.

Some of the recent initiatives and developments undertaken by the government are listed below:

- India is expected to attract investment of around US$ 100 billion in developing the oil and gas infrastructure over the next five years.
- With the help of the new agriculture export policy, the Agri export from India is likely to reach the export target of US$ 60 billion by the year 2022.
- In India, Atal Innovation Mission (AIM), flagship initiative of NITI Aayog, launched the Atal Community Innovation Centre (ACIC) programme in NITI Aayog which aims at spurring community Innovation in underserved and unserved areas of the country.
- National Institute for Transforming India (NITI) Aayog released a strategic document titled 'Strategy for New India @75' to help India become a US$ 4 trillion economy by FY23.
- The Government of India is going to increase public health spending to 2.5 percent of GDP by 2025.
- For implementation of Agriculture Export Policy, government has approved an outlay Rs 206.8 crore (US$ 29.59 million) for 2019, aimed at doubling farmers income by 2022.
- Government is planning to launch Bharat Craft portal, an e-commerce marketing platform to market and sell the products.

- Under the Pradhan Mantri Awas Yojana (Urban), government has sanctioned more than 96.50 Lakh houses under PMAY(U) and approved 606 proposals for the construction of 3,31,075 houses with an overall investment of Rs 15,125 crore (US$ 2.16 billion).
- The Cabinet Committee on Economic Affairs has approved to increase the authorised capital of Food Corporation of India (FCI) from existing Rs 3,500 crore (US$ 500.79 million) to Rs 10,000 crore (US$ 1.43 billion).
- India has registered a 26.9 percent reduction in Maternal Mortality Ratio (MMR) since 2013: Sample Registration System Bulletin-2016.
- Around 26.02 million households have been electrified as on 31st March 2019 under the Pradhan Mantri Sahaj Bijli Har Ghar Yojana (SAUBHAGYA).
- Prime Minister's Employment Generation Programme (PMEGP) will be continued with an outlay of Rs 5,500 crore (US$ 755.36 million) for three years from 2017-18 to 2019-20, according to the Cabinet Committee on Economic Affairs (CCEA).
- As per the Union Budget 2019-20, public sector banks (PSBs) will be provided with a capital infusion of Rs 70,000 crores (US$ 10.02 billion), allowing NBFCs to raise foreign debt.
- The mid-term review of India's Foreign Trade Policy (FTP) 2015-20 has been released by Ministry of Commerce & Industry, Government of India, under which annual incentives for labour intensive MSME sectors have been increased by 2 percent.
- Under the scheme Pradhan Mantri Gram Sadak Yojana (PMGSY-III), government plans to spend Rs 50,250 crores (US$ 7.19 billion) to build roads to boost rural connectivity.

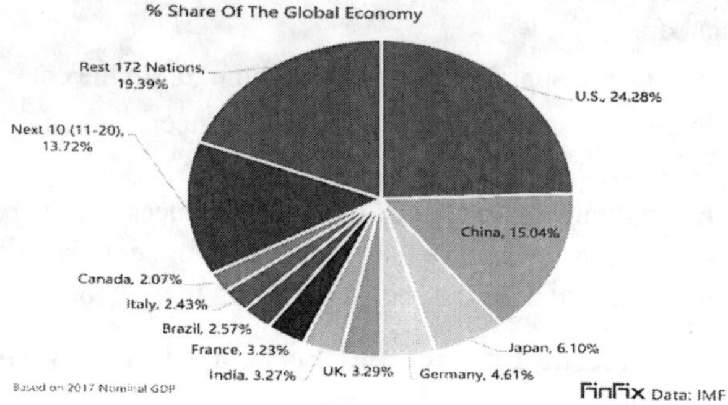

Figure I: Share of the country's economy among the global economy.[1]

4.3 Gross Domestic Product (GDP)

Before we move onto the Foreign Direct Investment, it is extremely important to understand the concept of Gross Domestic Product (GDP).

According to the Organisation for Economic Co-operation and Development (OECD)-

"An aggregate measure of production which equals the sum of the gross value of the residential and institutional units engaged in the production is known as the Gross Domestic Product (GDP)".

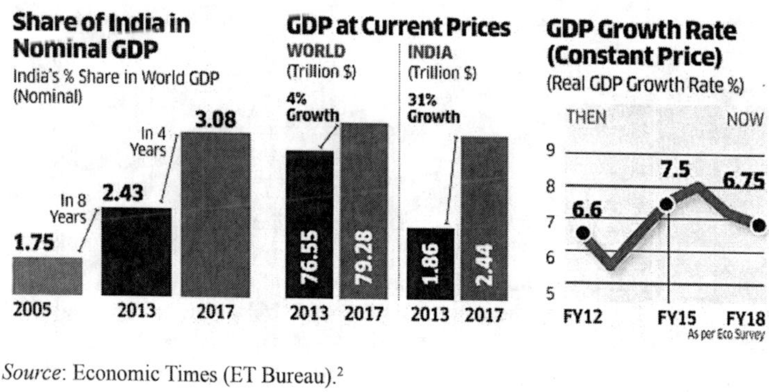

Source: Economic Times (ET Bureau).[2]

1. IMF's World Economic Outlook Database, April 2018.
2. https://economictimes.indiatimes.com/news/economy/policy/putting-india-on-the-road-to-faster-growth/articleshow/63052068.cms

There are three ways with which the gross domestic product can be calculated:

- Production approach: Sum of the output of all the enterprise.
- Income approach: Income of the producers is equal to the value of the product.
- Expenditure approach: All the good produces will be bought by someone and hence the production will be nearly equal to the expenditure of the people in buying those goods.

4.4 Gross Domestic Product and Foreign Direct Investment (FDI) in India

Now that the definition and details of both the Gross Domestic Product (GDP) and the Foreign Direct Investment (FDI) are covered, it is significant to understand how these two are related and together build the Indian economy.

The Foreign Direct Investment is directly proportional to the Gross Domestic Product. If the FDI trend is on a higher side then, the GDP trend is also on positive growth path.

To understand the relationship between FDI and GDP, let us look into the below chart where X- Axis is the Year; Y- Axis: FDI as percent of GDP:

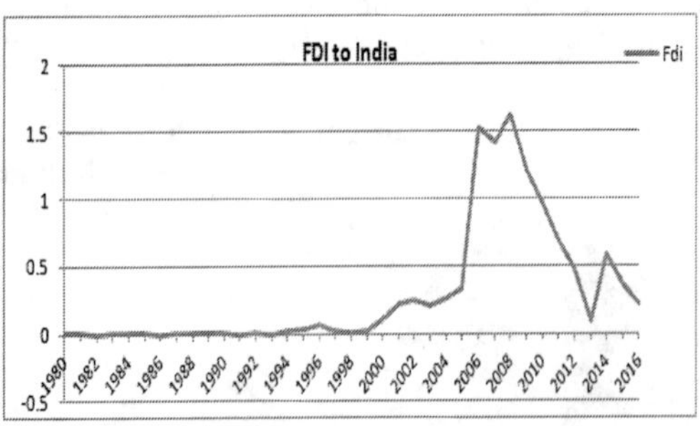

Figure II: Distribution of FDI as a percent of GDP in India from the year 1980 till Year 2016.[1]

The above analysis is from 1980 until 2016. The source of the time-series is the World Bank Report.

1. World Bank Report https://data.worldbank.org/indicator/bx.klt.dinv.wd.gd.zs

The impact of the FDI over the GDP is clearly evident from the above time-series before (until 1991) and after (from 1991) liberalisation. This also shows that the FDI inflows started increasing from the year 2000 and reached its peak during 2008-2009.

Let us look closely the period between 2006 and 2009. Here it is clearly evident that FDI as percent of GDP is maximum during the year 2008.

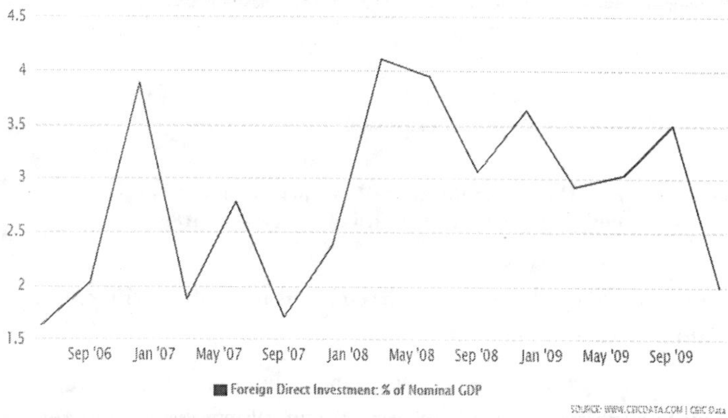

Figure III: Distribution of FDI as a percent of GDP in India from the June 2006 till December 2009.[1]

Next, is more recent data to understand the relationship between GDP and FDI from Year 2010 until 2018.

The relation between FDI and GDP has been long since pre-liberalisation period and the increase in FDI inflow being directly proportional to the GDP growth made its relation even more strong.

This directly signifies how FDI is responsible for Indian economic growth post globalisation.

Increase in GDP increases FDI because the buying and selling of good also increases the inflow of monetary resource increases and helps in overall development of the country's economy.

1. www.ceicdata.com

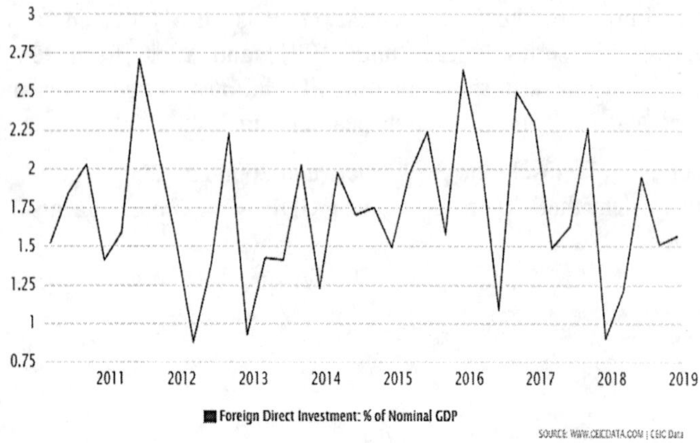

Figure IV: Distribution of FDI as a percent of GDP in India from the January 2010 till December 2018.[1]

4.5 Foreign Direct Investment (FDI) and its Role in the Indian Economic Revolution

After India gained independence, the policy-makers realised that the FDI is an important medium for gaining knowledge with regards to the latest and greatest technology which would in turn help in mobilising the foreign exchange resources.

Therefore, the 1st Prime Minister of India took an initiative to build the policies with the help of the policy-makers in order to implement the FDI so as to secure the technical, industrial, and scientific knowledge and the resources.

India very well knew that it has skilled workforce and reserves to work-on; the only thing that was needed is the capital which was what FDI provided. Hence, the FDI was permitted and the policy-makers created strict rules and regulations for its implementation. Gradually, there were changes made in the policies in accordance to the economic and political situation prevailing in India. The country allowed various multi-national organisations to trade in India through the technical collaboration.

1. www.ceicdata.com

But India faced a major economic crisis during its second five-year plan and hence the government created more liberal policies so that frequent foreign investment occurs in India.

They did this by allowing frequent equity participation to foreign entities and by accepting their equity through technical collaborations. In order to boost the inflow of the FDI, India made itself more liberal thereby started giving out tax incentives, removed reservations over the industries like pharmaceuticals, fertilisers, and heavy electrical equipment. Also, it simplified the licencing procedures.

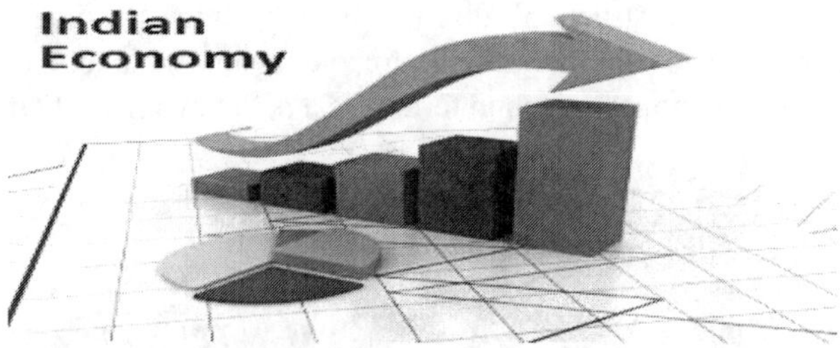

But this did not continue long as it was observed that too much of the capital was being out-flown from the country in the form of royalties, profits, etc. Hence, the government again had to create some stringent foreign policies in the year 1970. "Foreign Investment Board" was setup by the Government of India and "Foreign Exchange Regulation Act" was passed in order to efficiently regulate the inflow and outflow of the capital through the Foreign Direct Investment.

The Government of India again had to make modifications in the foreign policy due to a significant rise in oil prices during 1980s which lowered down the export and deteriorate the Balance of Payment.

During this period of time, the Foreign Direct Investment came into picture which was encouraged by the then government. This again brought the MNCs to India whose increased operation brought liberalisation to the country's economy.

The policy-makers created stable and non-discriminatory policy for FDI in order to reform the industrial sector so as to create a competitive and efficient environment. But in 1990s India again saw a severe degradation in balance of payment due to increase in petroleum prices because of the Gulf War. There was major downfall in the export business.

In addition to this, the money kept in India by the NRIs was taken by them which in turn gave a serious blow to the Indian economy. Inflation increased to its record height of 13 percent during this period of time. On top of this, the continuous uncertainty of the political situation in the country further deteriorated the situation. This resulted in downfall of India's credit rating in the international market.

During this critical situation, the then Finance Minister of India, took help from the World Bank and introduced the macro-economic stabilisation and structural adjustment programme. In order to gain the confidence of the foreign investors yet again, India took out some liberal foreign policy which in turn gave a pathway for the FDI inflow.

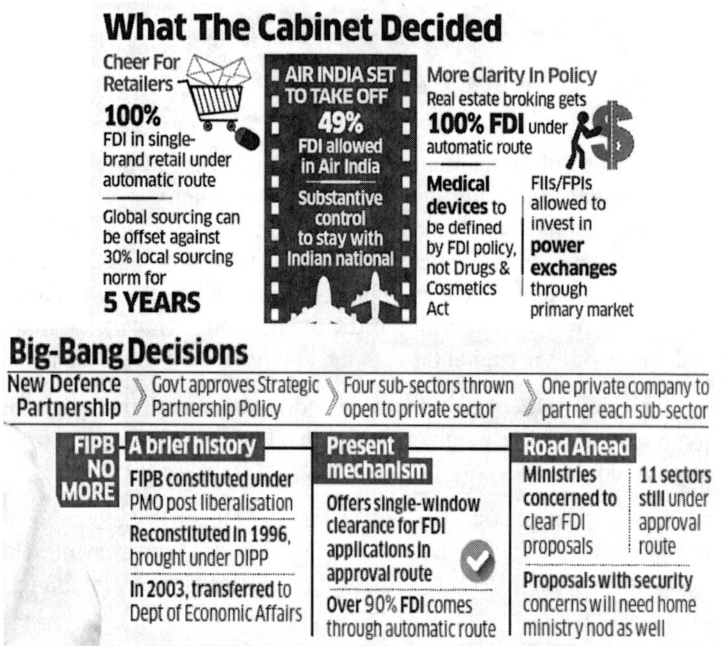

It became extremely important to discuss the policy, rules and regulations with the foreign investors in an effective and efficient manner. Keeping this in mind, the Government of India established the Foreign Investment Promotion Board (FIPB) whose main function was to communicate, invite and facilitate with the foreign investors from the Prime Minister's Office. However, during the FY 2016, the FIPB has been dissolved and the norms for FDI were eased.[1]

Under this policy, the government allowed the foreign investors to put in their name as the brand name over the domestic products produced in India. Further, in order to secure and protect the foreign investments, India became part of Multilateral Investment Guarantee Agency (MIGA).

MIGA is an International financial institution which provides insurance against political risks. These insurance helps the investors from the foreign countries to protect their investment; especially in the developing countries from any kind of political or non-commercial risks.

There are five types of insurance that MIGA provides to cover the non-commercial risks:

- Currency inconvertibility and transfer restriction
- Government expropriation

1. https://www.business-standard.com/budget/article/foreign-direct-investment-rules-eased-for-insurance-pension-securities-and-nbfcs-116030100037_1.html

- War, terrorism, and civil disturbance
- Breaches of contract
- Non-honoring of financial obligations

MIGA
Multilateral Investment
Guarantee Agency
WORLD BANK GROUP

MIGA is a member of the World Bank Group and India is one of the members of MIGA. The FERA Act which came in the year 1973 had stringent rules for the Multi-National Companies to continue their operations. This Act was revised and the restrictions were removed from the operations done by these MNCs. India indulged itself to different sectors and made them open to the foreign investors like mining, telecommunication, banking, construction. With this, the Foreign Direct Investment policy too became liberal so that the market becomes more and more investor friendly.

All these changes and the macro-economic stabilisation technique uplifted the overall Indian economy to greater heights. In fact, India started to be on the top three among the list of global investment destination and the achievement was that this entire thing was recognised by the World Bank and in accordance to the United Nations Organisation report.[1]

What was really important among all these processes was that the Foreign Direct Investment became an integral part of the growth of India the energy required for an Economy.

FDI not only helped in sustaining the skills, technologies of the existing companies but it also supplemented the domestic capital which helped the Indian Economy being more liberalised and globalised. This created a number of companies and hence new jobs in the market.

The new insurance underpins of the FDI showed are cord high business of $3.2 billion. This would in turn catalyse another $2.6 billion and this was enough to create huge number of jobs, energy of the power, technology which in turn helped the countrymen to get more jobs and settle and thus generate revenue to which will ultimately increase the growth of the Indian Economy.

---

1. Economic Survey 2019-20, Press Information Bureau, Government of India.

The security measures that were taken by the MIGA could cater to different regions across the continent and in different sectors like mining, telecommunication, agricultural business, transportation and financial services.

In the year 2018, the World Bank Group endorsed a new Country Partnership Framework (CPF) for India. According to the World Bank South Asia Vice President, Hartwig Schafer, "With a fast growing economy, global stature, and its unique experience of lifting the highest number of poor out of poverty in the past decades, India is well-positioned to become a high middle-income country by 2030". Thus, the CPF's main goal is to support India to convert it into the higher middle income country.[1]

Few of the key components, the CPF are planning to address is:

- Resource efficient and inclusive growth,
- Job creation,
- Building its human capital.

One of the largest country programmes of the World Bank Group is represented by the Country Partnership Framework. It is trying to collaborate between India and some of the World Bank Group's institutions like:

- The International Bank for Reconstruction and Development (IBRD),
- International Finance Corporation (IFC),
- Multilateral Investment Guarantee Agency (MIGA).

1. Economic Survey 2019-20, Press Information Bureau, Government of India.

Thus, MIGA is an integral part of the Indian economy's revolutionary growth wherein the foreign investors will invest more and more due to the protected law.

Another extremely important step towards the Indian economic revolution is the campaign introduced by the Honorable Prime Minister of India– "**Make in India**" in the year 2014.

"Make in India" is an international market strategy introduced by the Honorable Prime Minister of India to attract foreign investors and build the country's economy with the country's resources thereby building India's manufacturing sector stronger.

This campaign came into being on September 25, 2014. With this concept of Make in India, Mr Modi wanted to make India, the manufacture hub. In order to do this the then Cabinet Ministry allowed nearly 100 percent FDI for the defence sector followed by 24 other sectors including electronics, telecommunication, power, energy, automobile, etc.[1]

With regards to this, the nation has to strengthen itself in the field of innovation, skill development, and infrastructural development. This campaign ultimately resulted in increase in development, FDI and in turn increases the GDP of the country.

The main focus of this campaign is to make sure that the foreign and domestic investors are manufacturing their product in India.

Significant advantages of Make in India are as follows:

- Increase in job opportunities and in turn increase in employment.
- Make in India is mainly related to the manufacturing sector. This sector progresses and made the GDP increase to a reasonable amount.

1. Economic Survey 2019-20, Press Information Bureau, Government of India.

- Though India has skilled labours, skill development is a continuous process. The foreign investments helped in developing these skills.
- Due to incoming of foreign investors, FDI inflow increases.
- Investing in Indian market has its own advantage like huge market size, skilled labour, fast developing economy, diversified people.

Few of the advantages of FDI due to the Make in India campaign are:

- Due to inflow of money from the foreign resources, the domestic capital of the country increases,
- There is significant increase in tax revenue,
- Considerable improvement of GDP,
- Forex reserve increase to a significant level,
- International trade increase to a reasonable level.

This campaign has received recognition and response from countries across the globe. Due to this campaign, government introduced and modified few reforms and policies to attract more and more foreign investors which will in turn increase the FDI inflow.

Most importantly the "Make in India" campaign led to an increase of the FDI inflow to a substantial level by 32 percent (US$64.8 bn). This was only 16 percent in the last 15 month before the inception of this campaign.

In the year 2015-2016, India witnessed a commendable growth rate of 7.6 percent whereas, the world economy expanded by 3.1 percent. Such a growth rate placed India as the fastest growing major economy in the world.

With this campaign, the manufacturing sector contributes to 17.4 percent of the overall value added to the Indian economy.

This clearly shows the importance of the Make in India campaign and its effect on the Gross Domestic Product and the Foreign Direct Investment.

4.6 Role of FDI in the Indian Economic Reform Programme

Tarapore Committee

Before Liberalisation, the two major components of the Capital Account of India's Balance of Payment (BOP) were "External Aid" and "Debt". Reliance Industries in India started economic reform programme which helped in reducing the external aids to a large extent.[1]

With the help of these economic reforms programme, India started emphasizing on creating long term non-debt capital such as Foreign Direct Investment (FDI). Also, on the other hand, it started ignoring the short-term inflows into the country's economy.

Like it is said in the earlier part of this study that Globalisation was nothing new in India and it existed since around 1800s; but the term globalisation was a new concept.

With regard to this, FDI played a major role in uplifting the country's economy. India has seen both uplifts and downfalls during the years post-independence.

It was extremely important to make the policies, rules and regulations transparent and stable. In order to do this, the committee on the Capital Account Convertibility (CAC) which is also known as the Tarapore Committee was established by the Reserve Bank of India (RBI) under the guidance of Dr. C. Rangarajan and Dr. S.S. Tarapore. This committee helped in relieving the restrictions on the capital outflows but in a non-disruptive manner. As there were no standards of the convertibility of the Rupee into foreign transactions, CAC gave the freedom to convert the local financial assets into the foreign financial assets and vice-versa but at the market defined rates.

1. https://www. tarapore-committee-on-capital-account-convertibility/

Though the recommendations of this committee were not fully implemented, few of the measures were taken as below:

- The corporate organisations in India were allowed a full convertibility of the capital into overseas ventures but to a limit of $500 million which means that limited companies were allowed to invest in overseas ventures.
- The corporate has to pre-pay the external borrowings if the loan amount exceeds $500 million.
- As in individual, a person can invest up to $2,00,000 per year into a foreign undertakings.[1]
- One of the major schemes was that unlimited amount of Gold was allowed to be imported.

There was a "Second Tarapore Committee" setup by the Reserve Bank of India which was established to set up a framework for a full account convertibility.

Few highlighted points under this committee are:

- NRIs should be allowed to invest in India
- NRIs should be given tax exemptions against their investments
- Bank regulations improvement schemes
- Foreign Institutional Investments were restricted to invest fresh money raised to participatory notes.

This was considered as a bold step towards the liberalisation. With the help of these reforms, the foreign investors became more confident in investing their resources into the Indian economy.

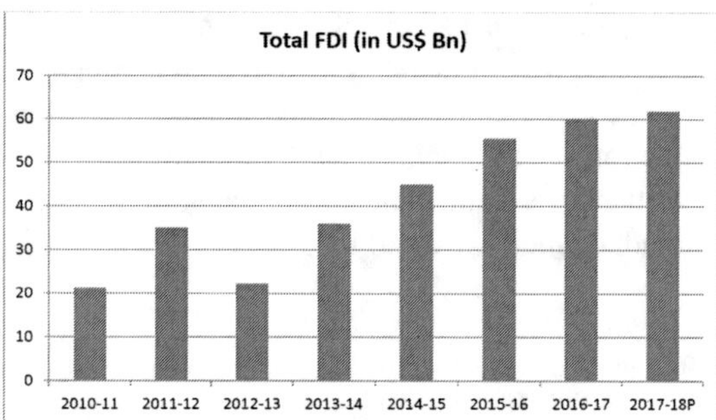

1. https://www. tarapore-committee-on-capital-account-convertibility/

With due course of time, numerous amendments were proposed with regards to the FDI policy 2014 which in turn increased the inflows and opportunities for the growth and development of the Indian economy through FDI post globalisation. After the research and surveys about the pros and cons of these proposals, final amendment of the Consolidated FDI policy came into effect on December 3, 2014.

4.7 Foreign Exchange Management Act (FEMA)

Figure: Total FDI over the years (2010-2011 to 2017-18).[1]

The year 1991 is seen as the initiation of the globalisation in India. Also, during this period, Foreign Exchange Management Act (FEMA) came into picture. Before the liberalisation or globalisation came into existence, Foreign Exchange Regulation Act (FERA) was in place. In order to cope-up with the policies introduced during the liberalisation, Foreign Exchange Management Act (FEMA) was established.

This act came into existence on 1st June 2000. Post liberalisation, foreign investors came in with huge expectation in India during the FDI process. Hence, it became extremely important to maintain the foreign exchange adequately and efficiently. This became one of the primary objectives of FEMA. Keeping in mind to promote an efficient and effective way of developing and maintaining the foreign exchange market, FEMA consolidated and amended the law which was related to the foreign exchange. One of the significant information about FEMA is that it is applicable in all states of India and to all offices outside India which is owned by any person who is resident of India.[2]

1. https://data.gov.in/resources/year-wise-increase-total-foreign-direct-investment-fdi-inflows-2013-14-2017-18-ministry
2. https://www.incometaxindia.gov.in/

4.8 Securities and Exchange Board of India (SEBI)

The Securities and Exchange Board of India (SEBI) is a government authority 'regulator' who is responsible for the securities market in India came into existence in the year 1988. Initially, this was a non-statutory body but it became an autonomous body after the Government of India gave the authority/ statutory powers to control the securities market under the SEBI Act in the year 1992.

In order to protect the interest of the investors in the securities and to work on the development of the securities market, SEBI was established.

The SEBI has to be on its toes to be responsive enough towards:

- Investors who are investing from the foreign countries into the Indian market through FDI
- Organisation who issue the securities
- Market intermediaries

These above mentioned three groups constitute the overall market.

The main functions of the SEBI are categorised into 3 parts:

- Quasi-legislative: Through the legislative capacity of SEBI, it basically drafts the rules and regulations.
- Quasi-judicial: Though the judicial power of the SEBI, it passes these rules, orders and regulations.
- Quasi-executive: Through the executive power of the SEBI, it organises the investigations and imparts the action items to the various teams. Though this is a very powerful tool, yet people can appeal for the further justice (if required) at 2 levels:
  - 1st appeal to the Securities Appellate Tribunal
  - 2nd appeal to the Supreme Court

4.9 SEBI and Foreign Direct Investment (FDI)

The SEBI and FDI are very well inter-related. If the foreign investor has to invest in Indian market, it has to go through the SEBI registration process and get a certificate.

An investor cannot buy or sell their goods and also cannot deal with the securities until and unless, it holds the certificate from SEBI which the investor has to buy before investing in the securities market.

Due to ups and downs of the market, the foreign direct investment act has been modified and revamped quite a few times. This is to increase either the inflow or outflow of the FDI. This has also led to the modification in the SEBI regulations as well; main modification was done in the year 1996-97.

These modifications were done in order to facilitate the debt securities market in India through the FDI route.

Few important modifications/changes are as follows:

- The categories of the FDI expanded to the university grants, loans, foundations, charitable trusts (which had a significantly good track record in the last 5 years in the countries from where the investors belong to), endowments.

- Each of the FDI account holders were permitted to invest up to 10 percent of the equity of any one company. This also increased the overall percentage to 24 percent through the various FDI accounts like FII, NRI, OCB.
- As a result of this the companies which had the shareholder approval, the overall limit increased from 24 percent to 30 percent.
- The Foreign Institutional Investments (FII) is allowed to invest from their proprietary funds.
- The FII also allowed the investment into the unlisted securities.
- The FIIs which has the approval from SEBI is allowed to invest 100 percent of their portfolios into the debt securities.

In the Indian securities, the FDI is possible by purchasing:

- Global Depository Receipts
- Foreign Currency Convertible Bonds
- Foreign Currency Bonds issued by Indian issuers

Through the SEBI Regulation Act, the foreign direct investment is made easy for the securities market, be it equity or debt. This undoubtedly increased the inflow of FDI thereby helping in the growth of the overall India in economy.

4.10 Foreign Direct Investment Inflows to India

June 2013 saw a continuous de-evaluation of Indian rupee as a result of which the central government relieved many norms related to FDI and also permitted FDI in different operations like defence, insurance, public sector, stock exchange, telecommunication, oil refineries, power sector etc.

The telecommunication sector saw a 100 percent rise in the Foreign Direct Investment which was initially 74 percent. Similarly, the infrastructure sector saw a 100 percent rise in FDI which itself marked the importance of FDI in the economic development of India after globalisation. Moving on, next is the insurance sector which moved from 26 percent to 49 percent and a similar rise is reflect on the most secured and protected sectors of the country, which is the defence sector.

It is truly a matter of pride that since 2000 which is almost the inception of the globalisation in India, the country has received a total foreign investment of USD 306.88 billion. For the years between 1999-2014, India received foreign investment of USD 19.52 billion and from 2004-09, the total collective investment from the FDI in the country was USD 14.55 billion which gain rose to 172.82 billion US dollar in between 2009-2013.[1]

Like in every other process there are ups and downs here as well. Hence, during this period, FDI also saw some fall and this is well documented in the Department of Industrial Policy (DIPP), Government of India.

The amount by which FDI declined during this period of time are US$ 2.94 billion (2009-10); US$ 1.23 billion (2010-11); US$ 0.73 billion and US$ 0.13 billion in the year 2011-12 and 2013-14 respectively.

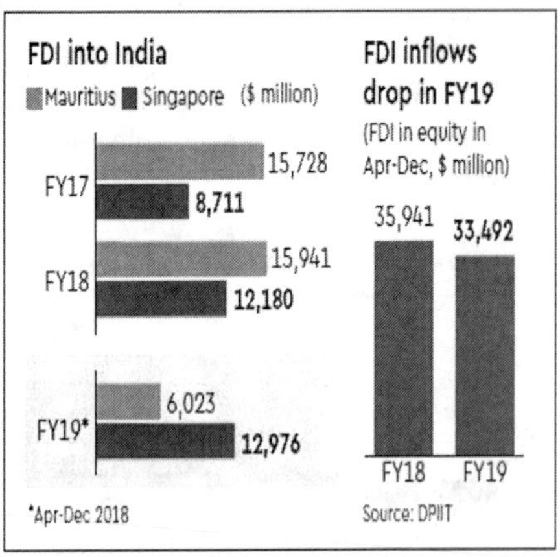

1. https://www.incometaxindia.gov.in/

It is also important to understand the leading nations who invested in the Indian economy. These nations are Mauritius, Singapore, US, and UK. With regards to the sectors, few of the biggest beneficiaries sectors are chemicals, services, construction, tourism, and pharmaceuticals.

During the year 2013, India also witnessed few significant merges and deals which sums up to around US$ 26.76 billion.

In order to facilitate the FDI transactions in a smooth and effective manner, the government of India started the share purchase which ideally allowed the authorised dealers to open a bearing escrow accounts in Indian rupee without any payment of interest. This also depicted the importance of the foreign exchange and gave the permission to the authorised dealers to keep their securities in possession. This entire development was made in order to give enough flexibility to the operational activities and ease the steps to perform such work. In addition to this, even the banks played a major role by pledging these shares which were acquired under the FDI for taking loans within India or outside India.

The Government of India gave permissions to the Indian corporate to perform their transaction without any prior approval from the Reserve Bank of India. But in order to do this, the corporate has to meet certain guidelines of the "Securities and the Exchange Board of India (SEBI)" and then only they can transfer their shares under the different schemes of FDI in the financial sector. It was also decided that if some global level investment is done through transfer of shares specially in the oil sector by any Indian organisation to Non-resident Indian, this entire procedure will be a part of the Foreign Direct Investment.[1]

1. Economic Survey 2019-20, Press Information Bureau, Government of India

Below is the FDI Inflows to India:

4.11 Foreign Direct Investment (FDI) Inflows to India: Country-wise (in US$ million)[1]

Source/ Industry	2013-14	2014-15	2015-16	2016-17	2017-18
Total FDI	16,054	24,748	36,068	36,317	37,366
Country-Wise Inflows					
Mauritius	3,695	5,878	7,452	13,383	13,415
Singapore	4,415	5,137	12,479	6,529	9,273
Netherlands	1,157	2,154	2,330	3,234	2,677
USA	617	1,981	4,124	2,138	1,973
Japan	1,795	2,019	1,818	4,237	1,313
Cayman Islands	25	72	440	49	1,140
Germany	650	942	927	845	1,095
Hong Kong	85	325	344	134	1,044
United Kingdom	111	1,891	842	1,301	716
Switzerland	356	292	195	502	506
UAE	239	327	961	645	408
France	229	347	392	487	403
China	121	505	461	198	350
Italy	185	167	279	364	308
South Korea	189	138	241	466	293
Cyprus	546	737	488	282	290
Canada	11	153	52	32	274
Others	1,626	1,682	2,243	1,490	1,889

1. Reserve Bank of India Annual report 2017-18. https://rbi.org.in/Scripts/AnnualReportPublications.aspx?Id=1249

4.12 Total Foreign Direct Investment (FDI) Inflows to India: Country-wise (in US$ million and in Indian Rupees) from April 2000- December 2018[1]

Sl. No	Name of the Country	Amount of Foreign Direct Investment Inflows		%age with Inflows
		(In Rs crore)	(In US$ million)	
1.	Mauritius	723,654.96	132,408.32	32.36
2.	Singapore	483,061.68	79,746.67	19.49
3.	Japan	168,016.41	29,519.14	7.21
4.	United Kingdom	138,276.90	26,494.00	6.48
5.	Netherlands	155,762.55	26,432.77	6.46
6.	USA	140,765.01	24,759.41	6.05
7.	Germany	63,446.24	11,419.91	2.79
8.	Cyprus	51,489.05	9,861.07	2.41
9.	France	36,466.18	6,592.53	1.61
10.	UAE	35,054.45	6,053.83	1.48
11.	Switzerland	24,701.94	4,482.61	1.10
12.	Hong Kong	21,962.72	3,667.41	0.90
13.	South Korea	21,306.37	3,557.34	0.87
14.	Cayman Islands	20,715.63	3,443.95	0.84
15.	Spain	15,480.98	2,801.75	0.68
16.	Luxembourg	16,871.18	2,747.80	0.67
17.	Italy	15,344.41	2,724.92	0.67
18.	China	13,627.57	2,168.15	0.53
19.	Canada	10,754.74	1,762.29	0.43
20.	Sweden	8,110.66	1,522.00	0.37
21.	British Virginia	7,860.55	1,437.32	0.35
22.	Belgium	7,778.31	1,349.49	0.33
23.	Russia	6,989.51	1,238.25	0.30
24.	Australia	5,012.76	928.23	0.23
25.	Malaysia	5,088.88	923.14	0.23
26.	Poland	3,648.02	671.51	0.16
27.	Indonesia	2,941.61	629.11	0.15

1. RBI's Quarterly Fact Sheet: https://rbi.org.in/Scripts/QuarterlyPublications.aspx?head=Quarterly%20Statistics%20on%20Deposits%20and%20Credit%20of%20Scheduled%20Commercial%20Banks

28.	Denmark	3,054.02	560.72	0.14
29.	Ireland	3,249.57	556.44	0.14
30.	The Bermudas	2,252.20	502.07	0.12
31.	Oman	2,542.32	491.92	0.12
32.	Thailand	2,788.04	456.54	0.11
33.	South Africa	2,585.46	446.33	0.11
34.	Finland	2,356.72	438.17	0.11
35.	Austria	2,255.07	397.02	0.10
36.	Bermuda	2,516.35	376.16	0.09
37.	Virgin Islands (US)	2,057.70	311.48	0.08
38.	Taiwan	1,876.20	308.88	0.08
39.	Norway	1,372.13	244.05	0.06
40.	Philippines	1,518.37	241.86	0.06
41.	Saudi Arabia	1,297.03	210.58	0.05
42.	Seychelles	1,257.52	206.35	0.05
43.	Turkey	1,090.42	186.00	0.05
44.	Bahrain	1,056.08	169.49	0.04
45.	Israel	938.23	160.75	0.04
46.	Chile	721.98	151.93	0.04
47.	Morocco	660.72	138.66	0.03
48.	Mexico	789.95	132.88	0.03
49.	British Isles	465.78	100.93	0.02
50.	Portugal	594.41	96.89	0.02
51.	Sri Lanka	506.45	86.12	0.02
52.	West Indies	353.89	79.17	0.02
53.	Kuwait	427.59	70.90	0.02
54.	New Zealand	346.57	64.11	0.02
55.	St. Vincent	293.57	55.84	0.01
56.	Channel Islands	277.38	47.77	0.01
57.	Panama	218.10	45.74	0.01
58.	Liechtenstein	278.39	43.46	0.01
59.	Korea (North)	218.08	41.62	0.01
60.	Bahamas	203.34	40.66	0.01
61.	Cambodia	255.68	36.36	0.01
62.	SAMOA ISLANDS	219.79	33.60	0.01
63.	Saint Kitts & Nevis	147.88	33.53	0.01

64.	Isle of Man	180.12	30.69	0.01
65.	Jordan	168.41	30.61	0.01
66.	Brazil	159.79	30.02	0.01
67.	Qatar	182.84	27.93	0.01
68.	Kazakhstan	135.78	26.36	0.01
69.	Czech Republic	129.71	25.80	0.01
70.	Kenya	109.72	22.82	0.01
71.	Iceland	102.43	22.50	0.01
72.	Scotland	139.25	21.98	0.01
73.	Gibraltar	92.60	20.90	0.01
74.	Hungary	101.00	18.77	0.00
75.	Slovakia	97.69	16.67	0.00
76.	Malta	79.63	16.24	0.00
77.	Liberia	65.51	14.70	0.00
78.	MOZAMBIQUE	105.09	14.63	0.00
79.	Nigeria	74.58	14.44	0.00
80.	BELORUSSIA	89.91	13.80	0.00
81.	Guernsey	82.74	13.21	0.00
82.	Belarus	56.68	13.18	0.00
83.	Romania	75.05	12.62	0.00
84.	Argentina	47.17	10.29	0.00
85.	Maldives	48.60	9.19	0.00
86.	Greece	52.20	9.00	0.00
87.	Myanmar	35.78	8.97	0.00
88.	Slovenia	42.33	8.75	0.00
89.	Egypt	52.19	8.46	0.00
90.	Ghana	40.56	7.69	0.00
91.	Belize	36.14	7.16	0.00
92.	Uganda	45.47	7.13	0.00
93.	Ukraine	43.12	7.07	0.00
94.	East Africa	41.12	6.29	0.00
95.	Uruguay	26.99	5.33	0.00
96.	Colombia	30.97	5.12	0.00
97.	Rep. of Fiji Islands	22.30	5.07	0.00
98.	Tunisia	23.98	4.96	0.00
99.	Vietnam	32.90	4.95	0.00

100.	Tanzania	19.98	3.45	0.00
101.	Vanuatu	18.94	3.20	0.00
102.	West Africa	15.89	3.03	0.00
103.	AZERBAIJAN	20.90	2.91	0.00
104.	Bulgaria	17.93	2.88	0.00
105.	Lebanon	17.57	2.88	0.00
106.	Trinidad & Tobago	15.34	2.74	0.00
107.	Nepal	12.98	2.52	0.00
108.	Monaco	14.00	2.51	0.00
109.	SAINT LOUSIA	16.94	2.47	0.00
110.	Estonia	15.06	2.43	0.00
111.	Botswana	14.74	2.29	0.00
112.	Afghanistan	13.74	2.05	0.00
113.	Yemen	8.20	1.95	0.00
114.	SAN MARINO	9.41	1.52	0.00
115.	TAJIKISTAN	8.98	1.37	0.00
116.	Cuba	4.73	1.04	0.00
117.	Iran	6.18	1.00	0.00
118.	Guyana	4.60	1.00	0.00
119.	Togolese Republic	5.07	0.92	0.00
120.	MARSHALL ISLANDS	6.21	0.92	0.00
121.	Congo (DR)	2.66	0.57	0.00
122.	Croatia	2.47	0.54	0.00
123.	Peru	3.53	0.52	0.00
124.	Jamaica	2.80	0.51	0.00
125.	Latvia	3.08	0.49	0.00
126.	Brunei Darussalam	2.85	0.43	0.00
127.	Aruba	1.96	0.43	0.00
128.	Lithuania	2.31	0.36	0.00
129.	Anguilla	1.47	0.29	0.00
130.	Iraq	1.18	0.24	0.00
131.	Yugoslavia	1.13	0.24	0.00
132.	Zambia	1.14	0.22	0.00
133.	SURINAME	1.28	0.21	0.00
134.	Georgia	1.33	0.21	0.00
135.	St. Lucia	0.62	0.10	0.00

136.	Swaziland	0.49	0.07	0.00
137.	Bangladesh	0.41	0.07	0.00
138.	Libya	0.28	0.07	0.00
139.	Mongolia	0.27	0.06	0.00
140.	Sudan	0.24	0.05	0.00
141.	Costa Rica	0.29	0.05	0.00
142.	Ivory Coast	0.30	0.05	0.00
143.	Fiji Island	0.29	0.04	0.00
144.	Serbia	0.10	0.02	0.00
145.	Cape Verde	0.10	0.01	0.00
146.	Muscat	0.06	0.01	0.00
147.	Algeria	0.06	0.01	0.00
148.	Moldova	0.05	0.01	0.00
149.	Venezuela	0.03	0.01	0.00
150.	Djibouti	0.02	0.00	0.00
151.	Cameroon	0.01	0.00	0.00
152.	TURKMENISTAN	0.02	0.00	0.00
153.	Bolivia	0.01	0.00	0.00
154.	Barbados	0.01	0.00	0.00
155.	Kyrgyzstan	0.01	0.00	0.00
156.	Syria	0.01	0.00	0.00
157.	Paraguay	0.00	0.00	0.00
158.	SENEGAL	0.00	0.00	0.00
159.	Rwanda	0.00	0.00	0.00
160.	Mali Republic	0.00	0.00	0.00
161.	FII's	0.25	0.06	0.00
162.	NRI ***	20,383.66	4,684.25	1.14
163.	Country Details Awaited	30,982.65	6,980.16	1.71
	Sub Total	**2,301,749.40**	**409,146.63**	
164.	**RBI's- NRI Schemes**	**533.06**	**121.33**	
	GRAND TOTAL	**2,302,282.46**	**409,267.96**	

Source: https://dipp.gov.in/

The table illustrate about the total FDI inflows to India from different countries. In order to understand the numbers better, the values are given in both US dollars and Indian Rupees.

The table shows the distribution of the FDI inflows from countries across the globe from the April 2000 to December 2018 which presents a very clear idea about the current situation as well. Financial year-wise analysis is presented later in this report.

With regards to the Foreign Direct Investment Inflows, the total countries contributing towards the FDI is more than 160. Among them, Mauritius tops the list with an inflow of Rs 723,654 CR /US$132,408 million followed by Singapore, Japan, United Kingdom, Netherlands, USA, Germany and so on. Singapore seconds the list with 483,061 CR and Japan takes the 3rd position with an inflow of Rs 168,016 CR.[1]

One of the important inflows is from the Non-Resident Indians with the inflow value of Rs 20,383 CR, though not among the highest but definitely significant in terms of the total contribution.

The percentage distribution of the FDI inflow varies from 32 percent to 1.71 percent. The total FDI inflow from all the countries in between the year 2000-2018 is 2,302,282 CR which is reasonably a good amount and thus contributing significantly in the growth of the Indian Economy.

4.13 Graphical Distribution of the Country-wise FDI Flows[2]

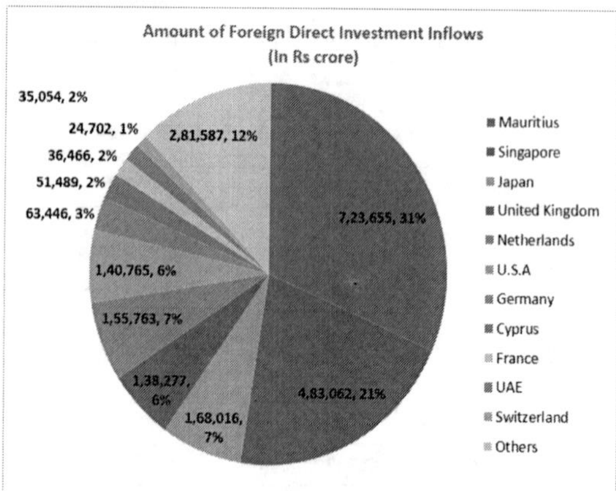

1. https://dipp.gov.in/
2. RBI's Quarterly Fact Sheet: https://rbi.org.in/Scripts/QuarterlyPublications.aspx?head=Quarterly%20Statistics%20on%20Deposits%20and%20Credit%20of%20Scheduled%20Commercial%20Banks

4.14 Foreign Direct Investment (FDI) Inflows to India: Sector-wise (in US$ million)[1]

Sector-wise Inflows

Sectors	2013-14	2014-15	2015-16	2016-17	2017-18
Communication Services	1,256	1,075	2,638	5,876	8,809
Manufacturing	6,381	9,613	8,439	11,972	7,066
Retail & Wholesale Trade	1,139	2,551	3,998	2,771	4,478
Financial Services	1,026	3,075	3,547	3,732	4,070
Computer Services	934	2,154	4,319	1,937	3,173
Business services	521	680	3,031	2,684	3,005
Electricity and other energy Generation, Distribution & Transmission	1,284	1,284	1,364	1,722	1,870
Construction	1,276	1,640	4,141	1,564	1,281
Transport	311	482	1,363	891	1,267
Miscellaneous Services	941	586	1,022	1,816	835
Restaurants and Hotels	361	686	889	430	452
Real Estate Activities	201	202	112	105	405
Education, Research & Development	107	131	394	205	347
Mining	24	129	596	141	82
Trading	0	228	0	0	0
Others	293	232	215	470	226

In order to increase the FDI inflows in the sectors like insurance, aviation, retail and infrastructure, the Government of India relaxed the FDI norms especially in the retail sector and thereby forwarded a 51 percent of FDI in the multi-brand retail.

This was mainly done due to the much highly prevailing difference of opinions among the various stakeholders mainly due to the under-pricing of the brands. This was thought –of fact that if the pricing of the retail goes down below a datum level, then small scale sectors would face a significant low in business and on the other hand, the large-scale retail sector would create a monopoly in the market.

1. Reserve Bank of India Annual report 2017-18. https://rbi.org.in/Scripts/AnnualReportPublications.aspx?Id=1249

This kind of mentality and apprehensions in FDI was very different when compared to the international market. This actually created a competitive market with regards to the retail business and this was lowering down the prices which in turn were improving the consumer welfare.

This also helped the supply chain management sector which was supporting the infrastructure which includes cold storage. Outside India, countries like China also the retailing sector emerged as one of the major ones in FDI. The Government of India raised the FDI in single branding from 51 percent to 100 percent in the year 2012.

By observing the above table, it is very well evident that not only retail but many other sectors have also outgrown FDI significantly. With the effective competitive market that is created by FDI, has made it a significant player in terms of the outflow and inflow of the monetary sources.

In order to sustain the impact of the FDI outflow from India, it is extremely important to balance the domestic investment in the FDI policy. Also, the significant rise in the insurance sector where the Indian corporate take the insurance either to fund the joint venture or to own a self-subsidiary in abroad has actually made the bank to think twice as in how to capture the market when taking loans and shares are in place.

The physical filing of three FDI related returns was discontinued by the Government of India to maintain a transparency towards the rational and liberal procedures.

The three FDI related returns were named as –

- Advance Remittance Form (ARF),
- Foreign Currency Gross Provisional Return (FCGPR), and
- Foreign Currency Transfer of Share (FC-TRS).

Also, the government introduced "Government-E-Biz portal where returns can be filed online. The new guidelines and norms were much more liberal and the Authorised Dealers under the Diamond Dollar Account Scheme was handed out to the Reserve Bank of India.

On a similar note, the return filing of any trade related matters, loans and advances to the overseas was also handed out from the EEFC account. Also, the submission of the documents by Full-Fledged Money Changers (FFMC) became more transparent and opens to all with this new initiative taken by the Government of India.

For the software exporters, the government made some norms liberal than before and the procedures of opening branches while single filing of the SOFTEX forms were facilitated as well.

In the Insurance sector, the FDI limit was increased from 26 percent to 49 percent. The entities which had a significant experience and positive output results of running a credit information bureau in a well-defined environment, the government provided a FDI up to 100% in CICs[1].

Though government took an initiative in restricting FDI to the products like tobacco and its substitutes, cigars, cigarettes but the wholesale cash and retail trading was still permissible.

With the inception of the liberalisation and pro-investor policy and its effective implementation, India became one of the most favoured destinations with regards to the foreign direct investment (FDI) in the year 2015-2016. This year also marked the achievement of receiving the highest net-flow within a year. Though the level of positive energy was on its highest peak during this period of time due to capital inflows and the liberalisation policies, few things were managed carefully too; for example, the repayment of FCNR (B) deposits under the swap scheme. With regards to this, the amount of reserves which were covered by the forward assets delivered huge amount of resources.

Though the situation was highly challenging because new things were coming up and the competition was also at its highest level, the astute management which has an increasing liberal and transparent FDI policy and also its approach is futuristic; made sure that the improvement in the external sector sustains equally and the reserved went up to US$ 17.9 billion on the Balance of Payment.

Next, let's talk about the most secured and protected sector of the country- the defence sector. In order to increase the inflow of FDI, the government of India puts in its best possible effort and thereby touching the important sectors like the broadcasting and defence.

1. https://dipp.gov.in/

An extremely important initiative taken by the Government of India in order to cash the inflow of the FDI is the "Make in India" initiative. With this initiative, India could increase the gross inflow of FDI in the year 2015-2016 to 36 billion USD. In total, the FDI inflow for the financial year was 55.6 billion USD which was supposed to be the highest till date. The financial year 2015-2016 saw some significant mergers and acquisitions which was as well part of the FDI growth in India.

The green field investment was always dominated by China until 2015 which is when India took over due to huge FDI inflow almost three times than the previous year. The non-resident Indian and their deposits too played a major role in uplift the FDI growth rate thereby uplifting the overall Indian economy- this increased up to 16 billion USD during one financial year. This was about the inflows which were going high. But on the other hand, the net outflows from India went to negative (3.5 billion USD from equity market and 0.5 billion USD from the debt market).

This slowness was mainly due to the increasing geo-political tensions across the nation. The overall financial market was into stake due to the higher increase rates in the US market and this resulted in selling-off the EMEs and ECBs like debt flows. This in turn made the trade credit negative which became a matter of concern.

As a result of this, government revamped the FDI policy during 2015-2016 and numerous policy initiatives were taken by the then government. Several studies and research were done to understand the root cause, to evaluate the overall amendments and what could be the impact on the economy as a whole.

4.15 Total Foreign Direct Investment (FDI) Inflows to India: Sector-wise (in Indian Rupees and US$ million) from April 2000 to December 2018[1]

Sl. No.	Sector	Amount of FDI Inflows		%age of Total Inflows
		(In Rs crore)	(In US$ million)	
1.	SERVICES SECTOR	398,161.37	71,579.14	17.49
2.	COMPUTER SOFTWARE & HARDWARE	211,768.10	35,819.13	8.75
3.	TELECOMMUNI-CATIONS	185,638.87	32,450.33	7.93
4.	CONSTRUCTION DEVELOP-MENT: Townships, housing, built-up infrastructure and construction-development projects	118,653.85	24,910.06	6.09
5.	TRADING	133,580.37	21,594.26	5.28
6.	AUTOMOBILE INDUSTRY	120,183.55	20,846.12	5.10
7.	CHEMICALS (OTHER THAN FERTILIZERS)	89,904.97	16,417.76	4.01
8.	DRUGS & PHARMACEUTI-CALS	83,824.27	15,934.42	3.89
9.	CONSTRUCTION (INFRA-STRUCTURE) ACTIVITIES	90,808.16	14,372.70	3.51
10.	POWER	77,206.73	14,218.04	3.48
11.	HOTEL & TOURISM	68,219.78	11,997.47	2.93
12.	METALLURGICAL INDUSTRIES	58,786.87	11,181.95	2.73
13.	MISCELLANEOUS INDUSTRIES	54,276.25	10,761.44	2.63
14.	FOOD PROCESSING INDUSTRIES	54,448.97	8,942.20	2.19
15.	ELECTRICAL EQUIPMENTS	45,342.83	7,841.59	1.92

(Contd...)

1. RBI's Quarterly Fact Sheet: https://rbi.org.in/Scripts/QuarterlyPublications.aspx?head=Quarterly%20Statistics%20on%20Deposits%20and%20Credit%20of%20Scheduled%20Commercial%20Banks

16.	NON-CONVENTIONAL ENERGY	45,731.26	7,602.07	1.86
17.	INFORMATION & BROADCASTING (INCLUDING PRINT MEDIA)	43,303.07	7,503.93	1.83
18.	PETROLEUM & NATURAL GAS	34,847.65	7,003.67	1.71
19.	HOSPITAL & DIAGNOSTIC CENTRES	35,992.48	5,995.14	1.47
20.	CEMENT AND GYPSUM PRODUCTS	29,287.96	5,275.87	1.29
21.	INDUSTRIAL MACHINERY	29,315.79	5,155.19	1.26
22.	CONSULTANCY SERVICES	25,888.94	4,602.90	1.13
23.	SEA TRANSPORT	23,367.02	3,940.06	0.96
24.	MISCELLANEOUS MECHANICAL & ENGINEERING INDUSTRIES	18,534.19	3,566.58	0.87
25.	TEXTILES (INCLUDING DYED, PRINTED)	17,843.52	3,092.32	0.76
26.	RUBBER GOODS	16,603.92	2,819.29	0.69
27.	FERMENTATION INDUSTRIES	14,741.25	2,649.69	0.65
28.	MINING	14,174.84	2,526.34	0.62
29.	ELECTRONICS	12,497.37	2,268.86	0.55
30.	EDUCATION	13,388.63	2,213.49	0.54
31.	AGRICULTURE SERVICES	10,995.73	2,100.56	0.51
32.	PRIME MOVER (OTHER THAN ELECTRICAL GENERATORS)	12,176.76	2,091.92	0.51
33.	AIR TRANSPORT (INCLUDING AIR FREIGHT)	11,063.55	1,820.62	0.44
34.	MEDICAL AND SURGICAL APPLIANCES	10,181.03	1,725.86	0.42
35.	PORTS	6,730.91	1,637.30	0.40
36.	RETAIL TRADING	10,380.40	1,590.00	0.39
37.	SOAPS, COSMETICS & TOILET PREPARATIONS	8,431.45	1,456.65	0.36
38.	PAPER AND PULP (INCLUDING PAPER PRODUCTS)	7,507.05	1,394.71	0.34

(Contd...)

39.	PRINTING OF BOOKS (INCLUDING LITHO PRINTING INDUSTRY)	7,290.03	1,183.08	0.29
40.	DIAMOND, GOLD ORNAMENTS	6,666.38	1,151.48	0.28
41.	MACHINE TOOLS	5,105.84	951.00	0.23
42.	RAILWAY RELATED COMPONENTS	5,451.79	940.92	0.23
43.	VEGETABLE OILS AND VANASPATI	5,207.22	892.30	0.22
44.	CERAMICS	4,143.95	824.77	0.20
45.	FERTILIZERS	3,834.09	677.22	0.17
46.	GLASS	3,667.38	657.62	0.16
47.	AGRICULTURAL MACHINERY	2,512.48	472.14	0.12
48.	EARTH-MOVING MACHINERY	2,494.44	440.58	0.11
49.	COMMERCIAL, OFFICE & HOUSEHOLD EQUIPMENTS	1,994.89	381.18	0.09
50.	BOILERS AND STEAM GENERATING PLANTS	1,623.70	263.29	0.06
51.	SCIENTIFIC INSTRUMENTS	1,560.99	261.54	0.06
52.	SUGAR	1,276.72	213.44	0.05
53.	LEATHER, LEATHER GOODS AND PICKERS	1,069.31	193.41	0.05
54.	TIMBER PRODUCTS	1,011.55	173.46	0.04
55.	GLUE AND GELATIN	929.98	145.44	0.04
56.	TEA AND COFFEE (PROCESSING & WAREHOUSING COFFEE & RUBBER)	708.99	140.28	0.03
57.	DYE-STUFFS	521.64	89.93	0.02
58.	INDUSTRIAL INSTRUMENTS	392.31	79.61	0.02
59.	PHOTOGRAPHIC RAW FILM AND PAPER	273.76	67.29	0.02
60.	COAL PRODUCTION	119.19	27.73	0.01
61.	MATHEMATICAL, SURVEYING AND DRAWING INSTRUMENTS	39.80	7.98	0.00

(*Contd*...)

62.	DEFENCE INDUSTRIES	41.19	7.26	0.00
63.	COIR	22.05	4.07	0.00
	Sub Total	**2,301,749.40**	**409,146.63**	
64.	**RBI's- NRI Schemes (2000-2002)**	**533.06**	**121.33**	
	GRAND TOTAL	**2,302,282.46**	**409,267.96**	

The table in Figure 4.15 illustrate about the total FDI inflows to India from different sectors. In order to understand the numbers better, the values are given in both US dollars and Indian Rupees.

The table shows the distribution of the FDI inflows from sectors across the globe from April 2000 to December 2018 which gives a very clear-cut idea about the current situation as well. With regards to the sector-wise FDI inflow, the service sector tops the list with inflow rate of 17 percent (value of Rs 398,161 CR).

Service sector comprises of Finance, Banking, Insurance, R&D, Outsourcing, Technical Analysis, etc. Computer hardware and technology and Telecommunication sits on the 2nd and the 3rd position with FDI inflow rate of 8.7 percent and 7.93 percent respectively.

Other sectors which contribute are Power, Automobile Industry, Construction development like housing, built-up infrastructure, townships, etc, Drugs and Pharmaceuticals, Trading, Hotel and Tourism and so on.

It is very much evident that in order to increase the FDI inflow rate, FDI policies have been relaxed in sectors like insurance, banking, retail.

India has always been conservative in implementing policies and rules. But in case of FDI, India has shown quite different attitude, it has taken some significant step when the Indian economy was at stake. These bold steps taken the then Government has made the country rise to its heights yet again.

Chart Distribution of Sector-wise FDI Inflow in India[1]

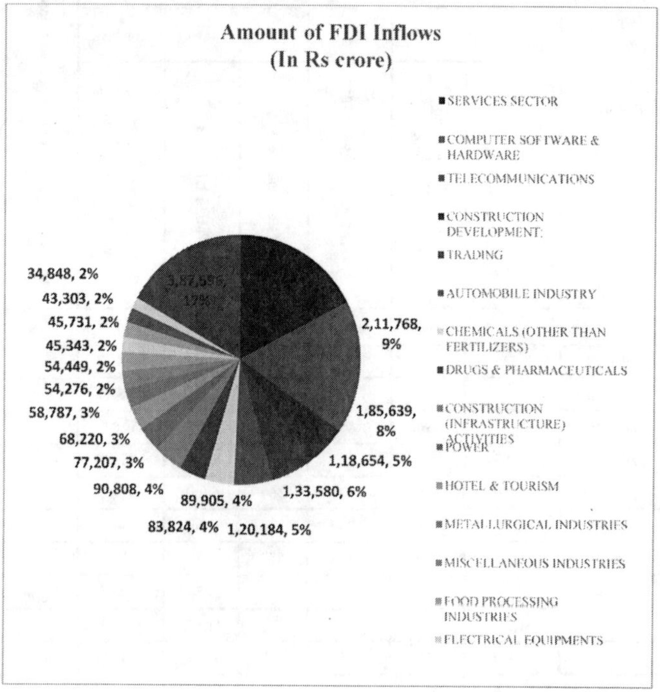

4.16 Foreign Direct Investment (FDI) Inflows to India: Financial Year-wise (in US$ million)[2]

1. RBI's Quarterly Fact Sheet: https://rbi.org.in/Scripts/QuarterlyPublications.aspx?head=Quarterly%20Statistics%20on%20Deposits%20and%20Credit%20of%20Scheduled%20Commercial%20Banks
2. RBI's Quarterly Fact Sheet: https://rbi.org.in/Scripts/QuarterlyPublications.aspx?head=Quarterly%20Statistics%20on%20Deposits%20and%20Credit%20of%20Scheduled%20Commercial%20Banks

Sl. No.	Financial Year (April-March)	FOREIGN DIRECT INVESTMENT (FDI)						Investment by FII's Foreign Institutional Investors Fund (net)
		Equity		Re-invested earnings +	FDI Flows in India			
		FIPB Route/ RBI's Automatic Route/ Acquisition Route	Equity capital of unincorpo-rated bodies #		Other capital +	Total FDI Flows	%age growth over previous year (in US$ terms)	
FINANCIAL YEARS 2000-01 TO 2018-19								
1.	2000-01	2,339	61	1,350	279	4,029	-	1,847
2.	2001-02	3,904	191	1,645	390	6,130	(+) 52 %	1,505
3.	2002-03	2,574	190	1,833	438	5,035	(-) 18 %	377
4.	2003-04	2,197	32	1,460	633	4,322	(-) 14 %	10,918
5.	2004-05	3,250	528	1,904	369	6,051	(+) 40 %	8,686
6.	2005-06	5,540	435	2,760	226	8,961	(+) 48 %	9,926
7.	2006-07	15,585	896	5,828	517	22,826	(+) 155 %	3,225
8.	2007-08	24,573	2,291	7,679	300	34,843	(+) 53 %	20,328
9.	2008-09	31,364	702	9,030	777	41,873	(+) 20 %	(-) 15,017
10.	2009-10	25,606	1,540	8,668	1,931	37,745	(-) 10 %	29,048
11.	2010-11	21,376	874	11,939	658	34,847	(-) 08 %	29,422
12.	2011-12	34,833	1,022	8,206	2,495	46,556	(+) 34 %	16,812
13.	2012-13	21,825	1,059	9,880	1,534	34,298	(-) 26%	27,582
14	2013-14	24,299	975	8,978	1,794	36,046	(+) 5%	5,009
15.	2014-15	30,933	978	9,988	3,249	45,148	(+) 25%	40,923
16.	2015-16	40,001	1,111	10,413	4,034	55,559	(+) 23%	(-) 4,016
17.	2016-17	43,478	1,223	12,343	3,176	60,220	(+) 8%	7,735
18.	2017-18	44,857	664	12,542	2,911	60,974	(+) 1%	22,165
19.	2018-19 (P) (up to Dec.-18)	33,493	495	9,973	2,663	46,624	-	(-) 13,694
CUMULATIVE TOTAL (from April, 2000 to Dec, 2018)		**412,027**	**15,267**	**136,419**	**28,374**	**592,087**	-	**202,781**

With regards to the data from the Reserve Bank of India about the Financial year-wise FDI investment, it is clearly observed that the FDI inflow in India has always been on an increasing side with few declines. In the initial year (2011-12), the FDI rise was up to around 23,000 crore rupees whereas next year saw a decline down to around 18,000 crore and further there was a decline seen due to increase in the political tensions globally.

Until 2014, India saw declining rate in FDI but 2015-16 showed an increasing trend yet again. This was possible because of many initiatives taken by the government and changes and modifications in the foreign exchange policies and FDI policy as well. This had a significant implication on the overall economic growth in India.

4.17 Foreign Direct Investment (FDI) Inflows to India (Month-wise): Financial Year 2018-19 (in Indian Rupees and US$ million)[1]

Financial Year 2018-19 (April-March)		Amount of FDI Inflows	
		(In Rs Crore)	(In US$ mn)
1.	April 2018	35,104	5,348
2.	May 2018	30,479	4,513
3.	June 2018	19,597	2,891
4	July2018	19,025	2,770
5.	August 2018	17,441	2,508
6.	September 2018	33,472	4,653
7.	October 2018	34,595	4,698
8.	November 2018	12,495	1,739
9.	December 2018	31,056	4,391
2018-19 (form April, 2018 to December, 2018)		**233,263**	**33,492**
2017-18 (form April, 2017 to December, 2017)		**231,457**	**35,947**
%age growth over last year		**(+) 1%**	**(-) 7%**

The table in Figure 4.17 illustrate about the total FDI inflows to India for the financial year 2018-2019. In order to understand the numbers better, the values are given in both US dollars and Indian Rupees.

1. RBI's Quarterly Fact Sheet: https://rbi.org.in/Scripts/QuarterlyPublications.aspx?head=Quarterly%20Statistics%20on%20Deposits%20and%20Credit%20of%20Scheduled%20Commercial%20Banks

This analysis gives the current situation of the foreign direct investment inflows and its trend across a single financial year.

April 2018 shows the inflow value of Rs 35,104 CR. From May 2018 until August 2018, there was a downturn where the FDI inflow decreased from Rs 30,479 CR (May 2018) to Rs 17,441 CR (August 2018). This downturn was due to increase in oil prices and some amount of recession that was observed. September and October 2018 again show an increase in the inflow up to Rs 34,595 CR. Again, a significant drop is observed during the month of November 2018 and then a sudden jump in the month of December 2018. Hence, overall the analysis shows that the FDI inflow in the fiscal year 2018-19 is not a smooth one but significant ups and downs are observed.

The happy part is that even the inflow is not very smooth this year, yet there is 1 percent increment in the overall FDI inflow rate when compared to the last year.

4.18 Foreign Direct Investment (FDI) Inflows to India and its corresponding GDP: Financial Year 2003 to 2018 (in Rs Lakhs)[1]

Year	Inflow of FDI	GDP	Imports	Exports
2003-04	104,411	22223150.0	21523.7	15956.1
2004-05	160,711	23190630.0	23087.3	20357.1
2005-06	161,344	24537870.0	24520.0	20901.8
2006-07	95,639	25479280.0	29720.6	25513.7
2007-08	147,814	27649590.0	35910.8	29336.7
2008-09	192,707	29714640.0	50106.5	37534.0
2009-10	503,573	32542160.0	66040.9	45641.8
2010-11	654,950	35660110.0	84050.6	57177.9
2011-12	1397,255	38989580.0	101231.2	65586.4
2012-13	1,309,799	41625090.0	137443.6	84075.5
2013-14	960,149	44937430.0	136373.6	84553.4
2014-15	1,283,877	45463699.1	140942.5	88505.7
2015-16	1,411,669	47790231.8	153675.2	95883.4
2016-17	1,674,733	50116764.5	172238.2	105573
2017-18	1,832,619	52443297.3	185557.8	113081

1. RBI, Database on Indian Economy, Reserve Bank of India.

The above table shows the FDI inflows along with its corresponding GDP for the fiscal years. It is clearly evident that with the increase of FDI inflow, both GDP and Export increases. This means that if the FDI inflow increases, this indicates more and more investors investing the Indian market and hence more import of goods takes place. Thus, it implies that FDI and GDP is inter-related.

After the liberalisation, FDI inflow has increased to a significant amount. From time to time, different challenges in terms of resources, money, branding, etc came in and hence the FDI policy was modified and revamped accordingly by the policy makers. It is also very evident that due to more and more investment from the foreign companies into India, the Gross Domestics Product value increased as well.

Initially India was very conservative in its approach onwards establishment of the Foreign Direct Investment technique. It took considerable time for India to understand the end-results of FDI. Due to initial stringent policies for MIGA and other tough rules for other segments, India went under huge loss in terms of the overall economic growth. Gradually, the then Prime Minister took some serious steps, took some calculated risks to bring back the economy on a competitive level. Also, after this India's economy has significantly paced up and eventually reached its highest peak.

The capital inflow from the foreign investors results in transfer of technology, economical management strategies, job-opportunities and in turn enhance the domestic capital of the country thereby increasing the economic growth of the country.

The FDI inflow has been seen in both micro and macro levels which has paced up the industrial production and hence lifted up the overall price level of the economy. In order to cater the unemployment in the country, the Government of India has liberalised the policies many a times to attract the investors from the foreign nations. With filling in gaps of the supply and demand, the government along with its policies attracted the investors thereby increasing the FDI flow and improves the global credit-worthiness of the India.

Looking at the challenges, it is evident that the Government of India has to be on its foot always to take and overview of the resources, man-power, technology, and outsourcing which can affect the FDI inflows and outflows; hence the policy-makers need to be flexible enough to modify the existing rules and make it more stringent if required or more flexible depending on the situation.

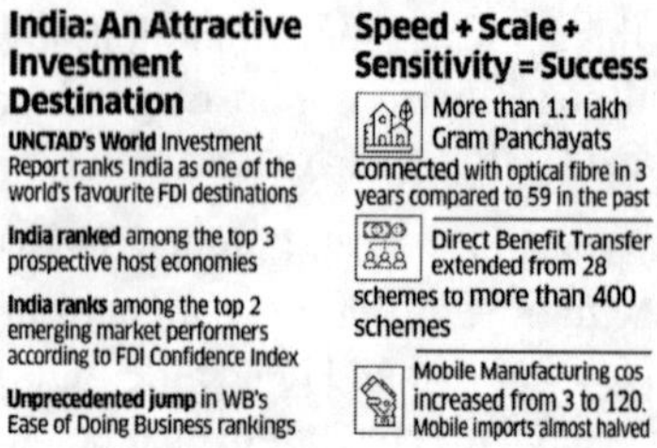

FDI is important to create a 'lasting interest' in a market or an economy. According to OECD (Organisation for Economic Co-operation and Development), lasting interest is determined when the organisation acquires a minimum of 10 percent of voting power in another organisation. When a company invests the profits from its overseas operations, or grants an intra - organisational loan or borrowings to overseas subsidiaries then these are also categorised as FDI.

It is important to note here that the meaning of FDI is not restricted to overseas movement of capital only, rather it encapsulates the international movement of other complementary elements of the capital like skills, processes, procedures, knowledge, management, technology etc. as well.

FDI can be Greenfield or Brownfield depending on the available opportunities in the market, vision of the investing organisation, Govt. policies of the country accepting the FDI and availability of the supporting macro market environment.

The following benefits can be safely concluded from this study that the Indian economy has witnessed due to the Foreign Direct Investment (FDI):

1. Increased Employment

For a developing nation like India, one of the most lucrative advantages of FDI is creation of new jobs in the economy. Increase in FDI boosts both the manufacturing and the services sectors, which in turn creates more jobs. Thus, FDI is an extremely effective instrument to counter unemployment. Increase in employment opportunities has improved the income level of the population which in turn has resulted in better buying/spending capacity of people. Increased buying power encourages consumerism and boosted the economy of the country.

India is teeming with a wide work force but not enough jobs. When multinational businesses are established, it leads to job creation which the indigenous industries are not able to provide on such a wide scale. According to a report in the Business Today magazine, between 2000 and 2016, British FDI created 371,000 jobs, 10 percent of all jobs created by FDI. The total number of people employed by British companies in India currently stands at 788,000-representing 5.3 percent, or one in twenty, of private sector jobs.

Revenue Generation

Sometimes, when a giant venture is to be started, capital is hard to come by. At such times, FDI comes in handy as a saviour and provides with necessary revenue to meet the initial infrastructural demands required for a project. For example, in May 2018, Walmart acquired a 77 percent stake in Flipkart for a consideration of USD 16 billion while in February 2018, Ikea announced its plans to invest up to Rs 4,000 crore (USD 612 million) in the state of Maharashtra to set up multi-format stores and experience centres.

2. Human Resource Development and Human Capital of the Country

This is one of the underrated and less obvious impacts of FDI. However, as a matter of fact, when the overseas organisations invest in a country, they not only create job opportunities but also invest in training the man-power that they hire on their processes and technologies to create a sustainable base for their operations. Such practices and investments on training has definitely benefited the organisation, but it has also improved the overall quality of the Human Capital of the country, which is a huge competitive advantage for any country for future growth.

3. Socio-economic Growth of Rural, Remote and Backward Areas

One of the most crucial advantages of FDI for a developing economy like India is that it has enabled the transformation of rural, remote and the backward areas in industrial hubs. This has a major impact on the socio-economic growth of these regions and thus, supports a more homogeneous growth platform for the Economy of India.

4. Access to Global Financial Tools and Technology Best Practices

The FDI brings with them the global best practices and tools to the countries they are investing. India has gained a lot in terms of knowledge of the best of the financial tools and technologies of the international standards. It has improved the overall knowledge and skill bases of India's working population and also helped the local and indigenous companies as well. This has helped the local companies to improve their productivity and efficiency by adopting such best practices, processes and tools.

5. Increase in Exports

The output produced by the FDI is not only for the domestic consumption. Many of such companies are utilising India as their production hub for this region and a significant amount of output are produced for global/ overseas consumption. This has in turn, increased the exports of India and creation of 100 percent Export Oriented Units and Economic Zones have further helped these companies (FDI units) in increasing their exports from India.

6. Steadiness of the Exchange Rate

A steady flow of FDI means a continuous flow of, for example, in the economy. This has helped the RBI to create and maintain reserves of the foreign exchange which has in turn resulted in stability in the exchange rates.

7. Better Capital Flow

The FDI has also resulted in inflow of capital in the economy. This has helped India to optimize its external debts and borrowing from other countries and external financial institutions.

8. Developing a Competitive Market

FDI has resulted in breaking the monopolies of the local player. It has brought in better products at competitive rates through implementing latest technologies, global best practices and processes. This has given the customers more choices and forced the local companies to upgrade and improve their processes, practices and products to survive in the market. This has brought in a healthy competition in the market and the power has shifted to the consumers from the producers.

In order to expand the market influence and business operations, the multinational corporate uses FDI as a medium to get hold of new production and consumption markets. Along with this, it also gets hold on the limited resources such as fossil fuels and precious metals, unskilled labours, technologies and management expertise. One of the ways to lower down the production cost is to use FDI as a method to access less expensive resources by approaching the raw material markets directly instead of buying them from third parties at a greater cost. The companies also accrue different tax advantages through FDI by allowing tax deductions on foreign income and on the other hand, the recipient country which incurs FDI allows tax deductions and organisational benefits.

9. Encouragement to the Overall Economic Development

FDI is a way to bring in foreign currency or external capital to India. This automatically makes FDI a reason for the overall economic development of India. In this method, the local and cheap labours, raw materials, equipment are utilised while constructing a new company. Once the construction work is done, few of these labours are hired by the company itself along with the raw materials and services thereby helping the workforce earn more than what they used to earn. This in turn helps them to stabilise their socio-economic development which creates more and more jobs for India. Also, the physical and financial infrastructure of the country is improved because these factories ultimately create the additional tax revenue for the Government of India.

10. Cultural Exchange

Working shoulder-to-shoulder with people from different cultural backgrounds helps everyone evolve and develop a sense of comfort in any atmosphere if they have to live in it. Multinational businesses offer an opportunity of a multilevel cultural exchange which cannot be seen otherwise. It leads to a certain level of acceptability for the different cultures all over the world.

11. Infrastructure Development

With International brands pouring in to the domestic country, there is scope for better infrastructure, be it in the field of education, health-care, information technology, constitutional bodies, construction of rail, road, vehicles among others. FDI also helps to make the Indian infrastructure at par with the facilities available in foreign countries.

In June 2018, Idea's appeal for 100 percent FDI was approved by Department of Telecommunication (DoT) followed by its Indian merger with Vodafone. This merger made Vodafone Idea the third largest telecom operator in India resulting in better overall reach of the company.

Hence it can be safely concluded that the foreign direct investment has proven itself to be the major factor for the growth of the Indian economy post globalisation.

CHAPTER – 5

Conclusion

FDI is the process by which the residents of one country (the source country) acquires the ownership of assets for the purpose of controlling the production, distribution and other productive activities of a firm in another country (the host country). Developing economies attract and promote foreign direct investment in order to supplement domestic capital, technology and skill, for accelerated economic growth. Foreign direct investment, has the 'lasting interest' in the host country in which the capital inflows take place as against the Portfolio investment whose stay is short term in nature and often described as Hot Money. The FDI flows comprise equity and non-equity forms of investment. The equity capital flows comprise the foreign direct investor purchase of shares of an enterprise and also includes the foreign direct investors share in reinvested earnings. The other two types of FDI include Market oriented foreign direct investment and export directed investment based on their motives for entering host economy.

On the basis of production function activities, foreign direct investment is divided into two types, horizontal and the other is vertical. Horizontal FDI arises when a firm duplicates its home country-based activities at the same value chain stage in a host country through FDI. Vertical FDI takes place when a firm through FDI moves upstream or downstream in different value chains i.e., when firms perform value- adding activities stage by stage in a vertical fashion in a host country. Besides, FDI can also take the form of Greenfield investment, Brownfield investment, Mergers and Acquisitions and Joint venture.

A Greenfield investment is the investment in a manufacturing, office, or other physical company-related structure or group of structures in an area where no previous facilities exist. Greenfield investment is the primary objective of the host nations as it creates new production capacity and jobs, transfer technology and knowhow and can lead to linkage to the global market place. Brownfield investment is formally on acquisition but acquiring firms completely, also replacing the plant and equipment, labour and product line. A merger is a combination of two companies to form a new company, while an acquisition is the purchase of one company by another in which no new company is formed. In joint venture, two or more parties agree to pool their resources for the purpose of accomplishing a specific task and each of the participants is responsible for profits, losses and costs associated with it.

FDI's utility lies in the fact that investing country usually transfers some of its financial, technical, managerial, trademark and other resources to the recipient country. FDI has a role in Capital Formation. FDI is an important source of financing for transition economies as it helps to cover the current account deficit, fiscal deficit (in case of privatisation related FDI), and supplements inadequate domestic resources to finance both ownership change and capital formation. There are two sources of Capital Formation which include Domestic and Foreign/External. The domestic sources of capital formation consist of taxation, profits from the public sector undertakings, deficit financing, and curbing of international demonstration effect, utilisation of disguised unemployment, voluntary and forced savings. Foreign / External sources consist of foreign aid, restriction of imports, and improvement in terms of trade for exports, encouraging exports and external borrowings in the form of loans and advances and lastly foreign investment in domestic market. FDI investors are cautious regarding the rate of interest/ foreign exchange rate i.e. most important factor to foreign capital movements is the difference in the rate of interest prevailing at different places. Conditions influencing private foreign investment include market potential and infrastructural facilities. The size of the population and the income level of a country have an important bearing on the market opportunities.

The government policies, particularly towards foreign investment, foreign collaboration, remittances, profits, taxation, foreign exchange control, tariffs and monetary, fiscal and other incentives, also influence the foreign investment in a country. On the other hand, political influence on the business practices like change in taxes, industrial policies adversely effect the movement of foreign investment in the country. With regard to India, FDI inflows can be seen from the point of view of two demarcated time periods after independence. Firstly, since independence, the domestic resources were not sufficient to support the higher growth requirement, hence the government announced in the industrial policy resolution of 1949 that foreign investment is invited. Prior to 1991, all FDI proposals were approved on a case-by-case basis with a 40 percent total foreign equity participation cap. Secondly, after 1991 India has significantly liberalised its foreign investment policy. As per the rules, policies and procedures of liberalisation, FDI comes through four routes i.e. (i) automatic route, (ii) Government (SIA/FIPB), (iii) NRI's Investments and (iv) Acquisition of Share. Since Globalisation, the regulatory environment in terms of foreign investment has been consistently eased to make it investor-friendly. The automatic route was introduced to facilitate FDI inflows. The companies proposing foreign investment under this route can issue shares up to the limit of foreign equity capital prescribed for the foreign investors. The government route is non-automatic route. In this route, FIPB gives clearance after consulting the concerned ministries and considering the size of investment. Normal processing time is four to six weeks. FIPB adopts liberal approach for all sectors and all types of proposals. On the other hand, NRIs investment belongs to a Non-Resident individual who is either a citizen of India or a person of Indian origin but also who is not 'resident' in India. NRI's also include companies, partnership firms, trusts, societies and corporate bodies where 60 percent of the equity is owned by the NRIs.

Indian government offers various opportunities to attract surplus funds of NRI's. They can deposit in India through banks accounts like Non-Resident External Rupee (NRE) account, Foreign Currency Non-Resident Bank Account (FCNR) and Non-Resident Ordinary Rupee (NRO) account. However, the Acquisition of shares route has been introduced since January, 1996. According to new provisions of FEMA, the proposals for FDI involving acquisition of share in already existing companies are considered only if, application made by Indian company or related proposal is supported by board resolution of Indian company.

In India, FDI Policy is being facilitated /regulated by Secretariat for Industrial Assistance (SIA), Foreign Investment Promotion Board (FIPB), Foreign Investment Implementation Authority (FIIA), Foreign Investment Promotion Council (FIPC), Investment Commission (IC) and India Brand Equity Foundation (IBEF).

FDI has become the buzz word across the globe, every country wants to optimize its resources and would like to increase its share in the world trade and would want to farewell on account of the indices which would ensure that its economy's trajectory is on the right track, in order to attract foreign investment and expertise to meet its target. Every country should try to eliminate the uncertain environment which would negatively affect FDI. Investment Treaty Arbitration has important implications for investment and rule of law in FDI decision making. If the purpose of foreign investor is long term investment, then it will significantly contribute to host country's economy because wider the gap between host and source countries' technology greater will be the productivity spillover effect. Always, local linkage investment begins with lower risk profile project. Every host country which seeks FDI must remove bottlenecks with regard to poor infrastructure, low labour efficiency, red tapism, corruption, indifferent attitude and availability of investment information, political stability, at the same time it should put in place the institutional mechanisms to make environment favourable for FDI; apart from strengthening the skills of the populace to attract FDI. Market size, export incentives, trade pattern, flexible labour laws, scope for cross border Mergers and Acquisitions, free competitive environment, higher productivity level, managerial skills, good infrastructure, advanced technology, higher patents, transparent corporate governance models, trend to adopt ISO benchmarks, are the universal factors which attract FDI, it can be easily verified by the ability of developed economies to attract higher FDI in comparison to developing economies. Whether economic development is happening in a country or not can well be judged by its ability to attract foreign capital.

LPG reforms done in true spirit are the only mantra to attract FDI and thus promote economic development. FDI is complementary in nature and it results into increasing technological capabilities; its diffusion the financial resources for development of the host country. Democracy is one of the attractive forces for FDI across the globe due to the principles of rule of law, independent judiciary and active civil society. FDI plays positive role for developing countries terms of trade. Higher contribution of FDI in GCF has positive effect on the level of GDP and hence on growth. Both international trade and FDI are explanatory variables for predicting variations in exports. Generally, FDI creates investment environment favourable by technology transfer and managerial techniques but sometimes it crowds out domestic investment, strategic equity holding by foreign investor results into outward FDI. Historical ties between host and source countries make FDI decision simpler and easier. As far as international established brands are concerned, they easily make their space in any country they chose, as they have ready market in form of higher income segment population even in developing countries. FDI seeker takes into account both financial risk and unexplained country risk which the host country try to replace with higher Return on Assets on offer.

There is strong relationship between privatisation and FDI, although this relationship is unequal. Privatisation dominates FDI whereas FDI is not the dominant form of privatisation. There is complementary and substitution relationship between vertically and horizontally integrated industries respectively. There is strong paired relationship between FDI and Economic growth in both developed and developing countries. There is stronger invented U-shaped relationship between MNCs of developed and developing countries. There is curvilinear relationship with FDI of MNCs and their effect on productivity. Domestic producer lose market share due to significant and positive relationship between FDI and economic growth. There is negative relationship between variable and dependent variables, where FDI is variable and GDP, debt, inflation and trade are dependent variables. Except Debt, all dependent variable showed significant influence on FDI. There is long term relationship among FDI, international trade and economic growth, also there is long term relationship between total factor productivity and FDI. There is long run equilibrium and causal relationship between dependent and independent variable which are FDI and GDP, GNI respectively. There is bidirectional causality between economic growth and FDI. There is unidirectional causality from exports to economic growth both in long and short run.

The concept of Globalisation has brought in the Foreign Direct Investment (FDI) in India. The foreign investors when merged with the skilled labours and resources from India gave rise to good and valuable products.

As stated in these studies that Government of India has been stringent in earlier years of FDI ingress in the country, with its conservative approach but with the trend of Globalisation in the world, and all countries opening up their market and inviting foreign investment, Government of India too had to adapt with global ongoing reforms of Foreign Direct Investment to catch up with the world market in financial and economic terms and trade.

After the liberalisation, FDI inflow has increased to a significant amount. From time to time, different challenges in terms of resources, money, branding, etc came in and hence the FDI policy was modified and revamped accordingly by the policy makers. It is also very evident that due to more and more investment from the foreign companies into India, the Gross Domestic Product value increased as well.

The capital inflow from the foreign investors results in transfer of technology, economical management strategies, job-opportunities and in turn enhance the domestic capital of the country thereby increasing the economic growth of the country.

According to Department for Promotion of Industry and Internal Trade (DPIIT), FDI equity inflows in India in 2018-19 stood at US$ 44.37 billion, indicating that government's effort to improve ease of doing business and relaxation in FDI norms is yielding results.

The net foreign direct investment stood US$ 3.034 billion in May 2019 and US$ 7 billion in June 2019. India invited US$ 7.8 billion of foreign investment in month of June 2019 as compared to US$ 1.6 billion in previous year.

Data for 2018-19 indicates that the services sector attracted the highest FDI equity inflow of US$ 9.16 billion, followed by computer software and hardware – US$ 6.42 billion, trading – US$ 4.46 billion and telecommunications – US$ 2.67 billion. Most recently, the total FDI equity inflows for the month of March 2019 touched US$ 3.60 billion.

During 2018-19, India received the maximum FDI equity inflows from Singapore (US$ 16.23 billion), followed by Mauritius (US$ 8.08 billion), Netherlands (US$ 3.87 billion), USA (US$ 3.14 billion), and Japan (US$ 2.97 billion).

Problems and Prospects of FDI

Right from the inception of globalisation and then the establishment of the foreign direct investment, India has seen many ups and downs not only in the FDI growth rate but also political and social instability. This has in turn affected the overall economic development both in a positive and negative way.

This clearly means that there are some problems which India needs to overcome to attain the perfection and deal with the situation tactfully at the time of need.

India is focusing on maximizing political and social stability along with a regulatory environment. In spite of the obvious advantages of FDI's, there are quite a few problems facing larger FDI's in India, such as:

1. Though India has developed in many areas which are considered as the urbanised areas, there still exists a significant portion within the country which is considered as poor and under poverty line. Hence, the economic growth is different in different parts of India as well. It can be concluded that the development has taken place in an uneven manner within the country. This is where the social instability comes into picture. Equalising this instability is a real challenge. Once this is done, the economic growth will be at an equal pace and in a balanced manner.
2. One of the most challenging areas in India is the sustainability of the political situation. If the political situation gets disturbed, this will have a direct effect on the FDI. Due to the political tension in the past, nation has seen significant decline in the FDI growth rate. It is extremely important that the foreign investors come into the country and invest their resources and time. In order to do this in an effective way, political situation has to be stable. Next, the overall political structure has to be adequate and well-defined in both the sides- one who invests and one who get invested. When the foreign investors talk about increasing their scope of work in various sectors like banking, retail, insurance, pharmacy etc, there has to be a governing body which will take care of these demands and handle the situation tactfully.

3. The most important challenge is to implement the policies, rules and regulations in order to overcome these challenges. India has seen many ups and downs in the FDI in the past. Accordingly, the government has taken measures, sometimes modifying the schemes, liberalising and relaxing some of the policies, bringing out new Acts and Regulations, forming different bodies like Tarapore Committee, FEMA and SEBI. India must also focus on areas of poverty reduction, trade liberalisation, and banking and insurance liberalisation. Challenges facing larger FDI are not just restricted to the ones mentioned above, because trade relations with foreign investors will always bring in new challenges in investments. However, what is important now is to speed up the implementation procedure so that it is visible within the noted time. Also, this implementation has to be equally fast in all the states of India. All the problems are inter-related if we observe them closely.
4. Blame it on the infrastructural bottlenecks and suddenly all the hoopla surrounding FDI inflows goes into a tizzy. Lack of infrastructure remains to be a major cause of worry in India. India is not able to compete with other emerging markets in terms of ports, roads, skills set, etc. Poor transport links, inadequate power supply, poor roads, frequent power cuts, delays in ports, water and sewerage problems etc are the major problems through which India is undergoing even after six decades of planned economic development. Shortage of warehousing and cold storage facilities are the main reasons for 40 percent of the fruits and vegetables to be perished before reaching the markets. In the World Competitiveness Index for 2015-16, India is ranked 55 amongst 140 countries in terms of infrastructure, far behind China which is ranked at 28.
5. Deeply ensconced in the literature and in practice is the fact that to have greater impact on investments in any country stability and transparency in tax regime along with clarity in tax laws would be the main motivational factors. Taking cognizance of the aforesaid, the taxation per se should be simplified. In spite of several steps taken by the government to ease it in India, however presents a picture where the taxation policies remain intrinsically complex. Various tax disputes related to cross

border transactions involving big MNCs have been witnessed by India in the recent years. Foreign companies in India are taxed at a rate of 40 percent whereas in most of the nation's corporate tax rates are levied in the range of 15 to 25 percent. A corporate tax rate of 25 percent along with tax holidays for qualified tax payers is charged in China on foreign companies. India's complicated indirect tax regime enforces number of taxes such as central sales tax, VAT, service tax, central excise duty etc. inflicts lot of inconvenience to the tax payers.

6. Red Tapism and corruption is a major handicap for Indian bureaucracy, resulting in delays in obtaining licences, approvals, permits and interrupted procedural. As per the doing business report, India is ranked at 130 out of 189 countries. To drive home the said point, India is plagued by procedural delays that hinder the FDI inflows into the country. Generally, the time taken for registration of a new company is few days in most developed and developing markets which is much longer in India i.e. 4 to 8 weeks. Pendent FDI approvals are prevalent in India that many times impels the investor to withdraw. In comparison to other nations, FDI directives still remain to be restrictive in nature despite being various liberalisation measures undertaken by the government. India becomes a less preferred investment destination due to uncertain and frequently changing government policies, inefficient administrative, overlapping jurisdictions and excessive governance which sometimes lead to inflated transaction costs for companies.

7. India, for all the talk of doing well in attracting FDI inflows, is still punching below its weight. A resurgent Indian government has wizened to the requirements and has initiated several reforms thus making FDI regulations more lucrative by raising the FDI cap in various sectors, opening many new sectors for FDI and by adopting automatic approval route for some sectors. While the above can be touted as measures in the right direction, the FDI numbers flatter to deceive. In comparison to developing economies like China and Brazil, FDI inflows to India are much lesser. In spite of having an inherent advantage in terms of lower labour cost and huge domestic markets, countries like Indonesia, Vietnam

and Philippines emerge as low-cost economies, which would make India lose its advantage. According to Global Competitive Report of 2015-16, India holds 55th position out of 148 countries, far behind other developing economies like Malaysia (rank 18), China (rank 28), Thailand (rank 32), Indonesia (rank 37), Turkey (rank 51). Hence it is a high time for India to introduce second generation of reforms that could facilitate FDI inflows. It is expected that India would be able to attract larger FDI inflows in the years to come only by implementing the aforementioned reforms.

FDI contributes in stimulating the economic growth and development of our country. FDI has invested largely to the service sectors of India. There has been a positive impact of Make in India Policy towards FDI in India. It also reduces brain-drain from the host countries and provides to work for better market with upgraded techniques and handsome revenue generation. According to United Nations Conference in Trade and Development (UNCTAD), India managed 10th position across the world to be the largest recipients of FDI with $44 billion foreign investments. In the recent years, India has assumed a notable position on the world canvas as a key international trading partner, primarily because of its investors' friendly FDI policy. At the same time, the global view for India is elevating.

India has many opportunities for FDI in the development and management of infrastructure. Since infrastructure projects may not be financially viable on their own, public private partnership (PPP) is sought here to bring in private resources and techno managerial capabilities through FDI. The Government is providing 'viability gap funding' in the form of capital grants, operation and management support and interest subsidies etc. for projects related to roads, railways, sea ports, airports, water supply, sewerage and solid waste disposal etc. Furthermore, ten years tax holiday is given for road, highways and ports projects. Government of India recent initiatives like extending the existing network of roads, developing the highways under National Highway Development Programme (NHDP) through Golden Quadrilateral and North- South East-West (NSEW) Corridor entailed vast pool of foreign investment.

freedom to states, so that they can attract FDI inflows at their own level. The government should also provide additional incentives to foreign investors to invest in states where the level of FDI inflows is quite low.

13. Government should open doors to foreign companies in the export – oriented services which could increase the demand of unskilled workers and low skilled services and also increases the wage level in these services.
14. Government must target at attracting specific types of FDI that are able to generate spillover effects in the overall economy. This could be achieved by investing in human capital, R&D activities, environmental issues, dynamic products, productive capacity, infrastructure and sectors with high income elasticity of demand.
15. The Government must promote policies which allow development process starts from within (i.e. through productive capacity and by absorptive capacity).
16. It is suggested that the government endeavour should be on the type and volume of FDI that will significantly boost domestic competitiveness, enhance skills, technological learning and invariably leading to both social and economic gains.
17. It is also suggested that the government must promote sustainable development through FDI by further strengthening of education, health and R&D system, political involvement of people and by ensuring personal security of the citizens.
18. Government must pay attention to the emerging Asian continent as the new economic power – house of business transaction and try to boost the trade within this region through bilateral, multilateral agreements and also concludes FTAs with the emerging economic Asian giants.
19. FDI should be guided so as to establish deeper linkages with the economy, which would stabilise the economy (e.g. improves the financial position, facilitates exports, stabilise the exchange rates, supplement domestic savings and foreign reserves, stimulates R&D activities and decrease interest rates and inflation etc.) and providing to investors a sound and reliable macroeconomic environment.

20. As the appreciation of Indian rupee in the international market is providing golden opportunity to the policy-makers to attract more FDI in Greenfield projects as compared to Brownfield investment. So, the government must invite Greenfield investments.
21. It is suggested that the policy-makers should ensure optimum utilisation of funds and timely implementation of projects. It is also observed that the realisation of approved.
22. China gets maximum FDI in the manufacturing sector, which has helped the country become the manufacturing hub of the world. In India the manufacturing sector can grow if infrastructure facilities are improved and labour reforms take place. The country should take initiatives to adopt more flexible labour laws.
23. Though the Government has hiked the sectoral cap for FDI over the years, it is time to revisit issues pertaining to limits in such sectors as coal mining, insurance, real estate, and retail trade, apart from the small-scale sector. Government should allow more investment into the country under automatic route. Reforms like bringing more sectors under the automatic route, increasing the FDI cap and simplifying the procedural delays has to be initiated. There is need to improve SEZs in terms of their size, road and port connectivity, assured power supply and decentralised decision-making.
24. The issues of geographical disparities of FDI in India need to address on priority. Many states are making serious efforts to simplify regulations for setting up and operating the industrial units. However, efforts by many state governments are still not encouraging. Even the state like West Bengal which was once called Manchester of India attracts only 1 percent of FDI inflow in the country. West Bengal, Bihar, Jharkhand, Chhattisgarh are endowed with rich minerals but due to lack of proper initiatives by governments of these states, they fail to attract FDI.
25. India's volume of FDI has increased largely due to Mergers and Acquisitions (M&A) rather than large Greenfields projects. M&A's not necessarily imply infusion of new capital into a country if it is through reinvested earnings and intra-company loans. Business friendly environment must

be created on priority to attract large Greenfields projects. Regulations should be simplified so that realisation ratio is improved (Percentage of FDI approvals to actual flows). To maximize the benefits of FDI persistently, India should also focus on developing human capital and technology.

26. India has a well developed equity market but does not have a well developed debt market. Steps should be taken to improve the depth and liquidity of debt market as many companies may prefer leveraged investment rather than investing their own cash. Therefore, it is said that countries with well-developed financial markets tend to benefit significantly from FDI inflows.
27. India has a huge pool of working population. However, due to poor quality primary education and higher education, there is still an acute shortage of talent. FDI in Education Sector is lesser than one percent. By giving the status of primary and higher education in the country, FDI in this sector must be encouraged. However, appropriate measure must be taken to ensure quality education. The issues of commercialisation of education, regional gap and structural gap have to be addressed on priority.
28. India should consciously work towards attracting greater FDI into R&D as a means of strengthening the country's technological prowess and competitiveness.
29. A contingency framework which outlines conditions under which FDI flow related to national trade surplus and /or deficit based in the dominant strategic motives of investing firms should be put in place.
30. Minimum threshold of human capital stock for higher productivity through FDI is required, without which the entire Demographic Dividend would go waste.
31. Important is the need for adequate and standard vocational skills imparting programmes which would act as the pool from which efficient manpower requirement can be fulfilled.
32. Economy should be made to reach the level where it would be in our interest to allow Capital Account Convertibility which would further instil confidence in the foreign investors to invest with ease in India.

33. That efforts should be immediately made not only in removing the imperfection and making the policy framework more consistent, transparent and rule based but also in creating an investor friendly environment by eliminating different obstacles to proper implementation of these measures, as well as providing necessary infrastructure facilities.
34. Non-implementation of approved projects, infrastructure backwardness, low labour efficiency as well as procedural delays because of red tapism and corruption should be eliminated and rather scrapped if not viable from the financial and operational perspective.
35. Regulation relaxation alone would not enhance the FDI into India, besides more sectors need to be opened up and FDI policy should be given the strategic tag in order to break the hesitation of the foreign investors. Here, the Government also needs to provide level playing field to domestic sector and sub-sectors in terms of cheap finance, quality infrastructure, access to modern technology among other factors which will be in the larger interest of India.
36. Regular publication of documents needs to be done like newsletter that would highlight opportunities in India and a detailed focus on India's area of strength and opportunities, so that foreign firms could come forward and discuss their areas of expertise and would show their interest in investing permanent capital i.e. FDI.
37. Indian states have their own area of strength and specialisation and there is an urgent need to utilise their specialisation and strength to the advantage of the country, by allotting the countries across the world to them, to find market for them, and central government's key ministries viz. external affairs, commerce and industry, and key departments of finance, culture and tourism, human resource development should make special desks within Indian Government's relevant ministries and Embassies across the world. This would not only bind the foreign policy but also improve the financial condition of the masses across the country. The government has to institute some safeguards in its national interest while welcoming foreign investment at the same time.

38. A Central Commission having representatives from the states must be established to study the problems of the retail sector and to evolve policies that will enable them to cope with FDI and when it comes along the lines of the Empowered group of ministers which paved the way for VAT (earlier) and GST recently.
39. India would do better by focusing on improving infrastructure, human resources, developing local entrepreneurship, creating a stable macroeconomic framework and conditions favourable for productive investments to augment the process of development.
40. The Indian government has not focused adequately on the Agriculture Sector and its negative impact is clearly visible on the farming communities and the associated groups. Adequate research is available at national and international level but the Indian farmers and farms have been left untouched by these researches. An active mass farmers' movement needs to be built up and then strengthened for the benefit of the farmers. Agriculture lacks in irrigation, improved seeds quality, adequate use of fertilisers and pesticides. A comprehensive policy needs to be built to address the problems by strengthening the ICAR and its centers and branches.
41. More needs to be done in order to strengthen 'Make in India' campaign for filling up the gap left by the occupational lacuna of transformation of Indian Economy from Primary to Tertiary sector, thereby bypassing the Secondary sector which has not been adequately attended by the Policymakers. More focus should be on R&D and patenting for strengthening Innovation and inventions.
42. Efforts should be made to reform and improve institutional quality, macroeconomic policies, and domestic financial markets to further the cause of FDI inflows into the country. The government should provide an enabling environment in the area of security so that foreign investors would be encouraged to invest more and local investors will not relocate to neighbouring countries. Easy accessibility to export market, government incentives, developed infrastructure,

cost-effectiveness, and macro-economic climate should be ensured.

43. Intensive financial assistance and higher enrolments in technical studies such as engineering, medicine, architecture etc., are essential ingredients for FDI to enhance growth. Therefore, the policymakers should focus to strengthen such infrastructure and manpower which could impart the required skills to the willing.

Bibliography

Books

Murthy, Gopala Krishna, Foreign Institutional Investors – Indian and Global Scenario, ICFAI University Press, Hyderabad, 2017.

Khan, A.Q., Strategy for Foreign Investment Management in 21st century, Kitab Mahal Publication, New Delhi, 2018.

Baskaran, A, The Impact of Foreign Direct Investment on Indian Economy, Excel Books, New Delhi, 2016.

Kehal, H. S., Foreign Investments in Developing Countries, Palgrave Macmillan, New York, 2015.

Garg, Kamal, Foreign Direct Investments in India, Bharat Law House Private Limited, New Delhi, 2014.

Seethapathi, K., FDI: Issues in Emerging Economies, ICFAI University Press, Hyderabad, 2012.

Chakravarthy, Lata M., Foreign Direct Investment in India, ICFAI University Press, Hyderabad, 2016.

Pant, Manoj, Foreign Direct Investment in India, Lancer Books, New Delhi, 2015.

Sen, Raj Kumar, Pan, Suvranshu, Foreign Direct Investment and Trade in India, Deep & Deep Publications Pvt. Ltd., New Delhi, 2009.

Shandilya, T.K., Thakur, A.K., Foreign Direct Investment in India: Problems and Prospects, Deep and Deep Publications, New Delhi, 2018

Kumar, Nagesh, Globalisation and the Quality of FDI, Oxford University Press, New Delhi, 2019.

Pant, Manoj Kumar, FDI in India: History, Policy and the Asian Perspective, Orient Blackswan Private Limited, New Delhi, 2019.

Tiwari, Ram Kumar, Foreign Direct Investment in India: Problems and Prospects, Lancer Books, New Delhi, 2017.

Bhasin, Niti, Foreign Direct Investment (FDI) in India, New Century Publications, New Delhi, 2018.

Thakur, Anil Kumar and Shandilya, T.K., Foreign Direct Investment in India: Problems and Prospects, Deep and Deep Publications Pvt. Ltd, New Delhi, 2016.

Ahmad, Rais, Foreign Direct Investment (FDI) and Global Financial Crisis, New Century Publications, New Delhi, 2017.

Bhati, Usha, Foreign Direct Investment: Contemporary Issue, Deep and Deep Publications Pvt. Ltd, 2016.

Chary, S. Narasimha, Industrial Development in India, Anmol Publications Pvt. Ltd., 2017.

Chaturvedi, Sharad Kumar, Foreign Investment Law and Its Impact on Labour, Deep and Deep Publications Pvt. Ltd., New Delhi, 2018.

Chopra, Chanchal, Foreign Investment in India: Liberalisation and WTO- The Emerging Scenario, Deep and Deep Publications Pvt. Ltd, New Delhi, 2016.

Sornarajah, M, The International Law on Foreign Investment, Cambridge University Press, 2012.

Wallace, D. C, Foreign Investment: A New Climate in the Third World, Amsterdam: Martinus Nijhoff Publishers, 2005.

Morrison, Janet, International Business, Macmillan, St. Martins Press, New York, 2008.

Moosa, Imad. A, Foreign Direct Investment-Theory, Evidence and Practice, Palgrave Publishers Ltd, New York, USA, 2002.

Articles

Grubaugh, S.J., Determinants of Direct Foreign Investment, Review of Economics & Statistics, November, 2018, p. 147.

DIPP, Consolidated FDI Policy, Ministry of Commerce and Industry, Government of India, April 2014, p. 39.

Narayanana, M. R., Inflow of Foreign Direct Investment in India- Patterns, Performance, Implications, Foreign Trade Review, Vol. XXXIV, 2019.

Sornarajah, M (2008), The International Law on Foreign Investment, Cambridge University Press, p. 4.

Wallace, D. C, Foreign Investment: A New Climate in the Third World, Amsterdam: Martinus Nijhoff Publishers, 1990.

Morrison, Janet (2009), International Business, Macmillan, St. Martins Press, New York.

Moosa, Imad. A (2002), Foreign Direct Investment-Theory, Evidence and Practice, Palgrave Publishers Ltd, New York, USA.

Frankel, J.A and Romer, D, Does trade cause growth? American Economic Review, Issue 89, 2018.

Faeth, I, Determinants of Foreign Direct Investment - A Tale of Nine Theoretical Models, Journal of Economic Survey, Volume 23, 2009.

Sornarajah, M, The International Law on Foreign Investment, Cambridge University Press, 2012.

Wallace, D. C, Foreign Investment: A New Climate in the Third World, Amsterdam: Martinus Nijhoff Publishers, 2005.

Morrison, Janet, International Business, Macmillan, St. Martins Press, New York, 2008.

Moosa, Imad. A, Foreign Direct Investment-Theory, Evidence and Practice, Palgrave Publishers Ltd, New York, USA, 2002.

Grubaugh, S.J., Determinants of Direct Foreign Investment, Review of Economics & Statistics, November, 2015, pp. 149-152.

Srivastava, Sadhana (2003), What Is the True Level of FDI Flows to India?, Economic and Political Weekly, February 15, 2003.

Kumar, Nagesh (2005), Liberalisation, Foreign Direct Investment Flows and Development Indian Experience in the 1990s, Economic and Political Weekly, April 2, 2005.

Kathuria, V. (2002), Liberalisation, FDI and Productivity Spillovers: An Analysis of Indian Manufacturing Firms, Oxford Economic Papers, Vol. 54, pp. 688-718.

Chandrasekhar, C.P. and Ghosh, Jayati (2002), The Market that Failed: A Decade of Neoliberal Economic Reforms in India (Delhi), p. 133.

Acharyya, Rajat (2002), Globalisation, Rigged Rules and Double Standards - A Review of Oxfam International 2002, Rigged Rules and Double Standards: Trade, Globalisation and the Fight against Poverty, Washington Oxfam International Advocacy Office, Decision, Indian Institute of Management, Kolkata, Vol. 29, July-December.

Kisore, Naval (2003), FDI in post globalize era; India's strategy and prospects, Business Perspectives, Vol. 5, No. 1, pp. 59-72.

Mohd. Firoz Alam (2005), Impact of FDI on Indian Economy since Economic Liberalisation, Public Opinion - Monthly Survey, Vol. 1, No. 8, pp. 11-17.

Kathuria, V. (2002), Liberalisation, FDI and Productivity Spillovers: An Analysis of Indian Manufacturing Firms, Oxford Economic Papers, Vol. 54, pp. 688-718.

Chandrasekhar, C.P. and Ghosh Jayati (2002), The Market that Failed: A Decade of Neoliberal Economic Reforms in India (Delhi), p. 133.

Acharyya, Rajat (2002), Globalisation, Rigged Rules and Double Standards - A Review of Oxfam International 2002, Rigged Rules and Double Standards: Trade, Globalisation and the Fight against Poverty, Washington Oxfam International Advocacy Office, Decision, Indian Institute of Management, Kolkata, Vol. 29, July-December.

Kisore, Naval (2003), FDI in post globalize era; India's strategy and prospects, Business Perspectives, Vol. 5, No. 1, pp. 59-72.

Srivastava, Sadhana (2003), What Is the True Level of FDI Flows to India?, Economic and Political Weekly, February 15, 2003.

Sharma, Shalini and Sharma, Ruchi (2003), Globalisation, FDI and Development, Business Perspective, Vol. 5, No. 1, pp. 27-35.

Narayana, M.R. (2004), Inflow of Foreign Direct Investment in Karnataka: Patterns, Performance, Implications, Foreign Trade Review, Vol. XXXIV, pp. 3-27.

Kumar, Nagesh (2005), Liberalisation, Foreign Direct Investment Flows and Development Indian Experience in the 1990s, Economic and Political Weekly, April 2, 2005.

Mohd. Firoz Alam (2005), Impact of FDI on Indian Economy since Economic Liberalisation, Public Opinion - Monthly Survey, Vol. 1, No. 8, pp. 11-17.

Sharma, Shalini and Sharma, Ruchi (2003), Globalisation, FDI and Development, Business Perspective, Vol. 5, No. 1, pp. 27-35.

Pradhan, J. Prakash (2003), Foreign Direct Investment and Economic Growth in Developing Countries: further evidence from panel data, Foreign Trade Review, Vol. XXXII, pp. 32-38.

Reports

Government of India, Annual Report (2019-20), Ministry of Finance

Government of India, Annual Report (2018-19), Ministry of Finance

Government of India, Annual Report (2017-18), Ministry of Finance

Government of India, Annual Report (2016-17), Ministry of Finance

Government of India, Annual Report (2015-16), Ministry of Finance

Government of India, Annual Report (2014-2015), Ministry of Finance

UNCTAD, WIR (2019) World Investment Report

UNCTAD, WIR (2018) World Investment Report

UNCTAD, WIR (2017) World Investment Report

Websites

http://articles.economictimes.indiatimes.com

http://dipp.nic.in

http://ficci.in

http://finmin.nic.in/bipa

http://indiainbusiness.nic

http://unctad.org

http://www.advocatekhoj.com

http://www.business-standard.com

http://www.incometaxindia.gov.in

http://www.indembassy-tokyo.gov.in
http://www.investindia.gov.in
http://www.mea.gov.in
http://www.nishithdesai.com
http://www.sezindia.nic.
http://www.trai.gov.in
http://www.worldbank.org
https://en.portal.santandertrade.com
https://www.pwc.in

Index

D

E

J

K

L

M